Paradise of Cities

Paradise of Cities

Nineteenth-century Venice
Seen through Foreign Eyes

JOHN JULIUS NORWICH

VIKING
an imprint of
PENGUIN BOOKS

VIKING

Published by the Penguin Group
Penguin Books Ltd, 80 Strand, London WC2R 0RL, England
Penguin Putnam Inc., 375 Hudson Street, New York, New York 10014, USA
Penguin Books Australia Ltd, 250 Camberwell Road,
Camberwell, Victoria 3124, Australia
Penguin Books Canada Ltd, 10 Alcorn Avenue, Toronto, Ontario, Canada M4V 3B2
Penguin Books India (P) Ltd, 11 Community Centre,
Panchsheel Park, New Delhi – 110 017, India
Penguin Books (NZ) Ltd, Cnr Rosedale and Airborne Roads,
Albany, Auckland, New Zealand
Penguin Books (South Africa) (Pty) Ltd, 24 Sturdee Avenue,
Rosebank 2196, South Africa

Penguin Books Ltd, Registered Offices: 80 Strand, London WC2R 0RL, England

www.penguin.com

First published 2003
1

Copyright © John Julius Norwich, 2003

The moral right of the author has been asserted

Set in 12/14.75pt Monotype Bembo
Typeset by Rowland Phototypesetting Ltd, Bury St Edmunds, Suffolk
Printed in Great Britain by Clays Ltd, St Ives plc

A CIP catalogue record for this book is available from the British Library

ISBN 0-670-89401-X

ENDPAPER: Nocturne, 1879–80 (etching and drypoint) by James Abbott McNeill Whistler
Private Collection/Fine Art Society, London, UK/Bridgeman Art Library

For my grandchildren

If I were to assign a particular quality which conduces to that dreamy and voluptuous existence which men of high imagination experience in Venice, I should describe it as the feeling of abstraction which is remarkable in that city and peculiar to it. Venice is the only city which can yield the magical delights of solitude. All is still and silent. No rude sound disturbs your reveries; fancy, therefore, is not put to flight. No rude sound distracts your self-consciousness. This renders existence intense. We feel everything. And we feel thus keenly in a city not only eminently beautiful, not only abounding in wonderful creations of art, but each step of which is hallowed ground, quick with associations that, in their more various nature, their nearer relation to ourselves, and perhaps their more picturesque character, exercise a greater influence over the imagination than the more antique story of Greece and Rome.

Benjamin Disraeli, *Contarini Fleming*

It is a fact that almost everyone interesting, appealing, melancholy, memorable, odd, seems at one time or another, after many days and much life, to have gravitated to Venice by a happy instinct, settling in it and treating it, cherishing it, as a sort of repository of consolations; all of which today, for the conscious mind, is mixed with its air and constitutes its unwritten history. The deposed, the defeated, the disenchanted, the wounded, or even only the bored, have seemed to find there something that no other place could give.

Henry James

Only in Venice, why? What reason for Mark's Square
Rather than Timbuctoo?

Robert Browning, *Fifine at the Fair*, civ

Contents

Acknowledgements

I should like particularly to thank Professor John Law of the University of Swansea for his help and encouragement, particularly with relation to Rawdon Brown; Mr Michael Severne, for having allowed me to publish the letter from his uncle, Rowland Burden-Muller, describing his life with Lady Layard in the early years of the last century; and Mr Michael Meredith, for his close reading of the chapter on Browning.

For the illustrations, I have to thank the owner of the Millais portrait of Ruskin for letting me reproduce it here and my friend Dr Marino Zorzi, Director of the Biblioteca Marciana, in respect of the portrait of Rawdon Brown. The colour portraits of Byron, Henry James and Layard are in the collection of the National Portrait Gallery, London. Mr Adam Grummitt, of the Gallery's staff, has been unfailingly helpful with my inquiries.

As always, too, I must express my warmest thanks to the staff of the London Library, where virtually every word of this book has been written. Indeed, I could not possibly have done it anywhere else.

Illustrations

BLACK AND WHITE

1. The Four Horses of St Mark carried off by the French army (artist unknown) (Timepix)
2. The Ruskin party in Venice, June/July 1872
3. The Market in Campo S. Giacomo di Rialto (Osvaldo Böhm, Venice)
4. The Piazzetta (Bridgeman)
5. *Rose la Touche*: portrait by Ruskin
6. Portrait of Rawdon Brown (artist unknown)
7. Horatio Brown
8. John Addington Symonds in 1864, soon after his marriage
9. Daniele Manin (Civico Archivio Fotografico, Milan)
10. Field Marshal Radetzky (Civico Archivio Fotografico, Milan)
11. Palazzo Vendramin (Roger Viollet/Getty Images)
12. *Katharine de Kay Bronson*: watercolour by Ellen Montalba, c. 1892
13. Mr and Mrs Curtis in the Palazzo Barbaro
14. Constance Fenimore Woolson
15. Robert Browning in 1889
16. James Abbott McNeill Whistler: *Self-portrait* (Chelsea Arts Club, London, UK/Bridgeman Art Library)
17. J. A. M. Whistler. *Nocturne Palaces* (Private collection/Bridgeman Art Library)
18. J. A. M. Whistler. *The Doorway* (Christie's Images Ltd)
19. Frederick Rolfe
20. After the fall of the Campanile, 14 July 1902 (Osvaldo Böhm, Venice)
21. The Riva degli Schiavoni, western end (Osvaldo Böhm, Venice)
22. The Basin of St Mark (Culver Pictures)
23. A canal
24. The Zattere (Osvaldo Böhm, Venice)
25. Castello: Canale di S. Pietro (Osvaldo Böhm, Venice)
26. Doge's Palace – Scala dei Giganti (Osvaldo Böhm, Venice)

Introduction

It may well be considered that I have written enough about Venice. After two volumes of history, one anthology and heaven knows how many articles, the appearance of yet another work on the subject will quite possibly be received with something like dismay. My excuse is, first, that I love the place so much that I can't really resist writing about it; second, to advance the story. Everyone knows that the life of the Most Serene Republic, having endured over a thousand years, was in 1797 brought to a sudden and all too humiliating end by the army of the young Napoleon. But what, people wonder, happened next?

The short answer is that after a few miserable years of being tossed like a shuttlecock backwards and forwards between France and Austria, Venice was placed by the Congress of Vienna firmly in Habsburg hands, in which – with one short, glorious but quixotic interruption – she remained for another half-century. Finally in 1866 she was absorbed into a united Italy. Her independence was gone, never to return; gone, too, were the Doge and the Golden Book, the courtesans and the Carnival, the 'balls and masques begun at midnight, burning ever till mid-day' and – not least of her regrets – the young English *milords* on their Grand Tour, stopping off for a few weeks of mild debauchery before returning home, cheerfully enough, with a couple of Canalettos and a mild dose of the clap. Venice in the nineteenth century was a poor, sad shadow of what she had been in the eighteenth; how, then, could the story of that century best be told?

Not, certainly, by a straightforward recital of political events; such a treatment would have been depressing (which is bad enough) or boring (which is far, far worse). And so the idea came to me of looking at Venice through the eyes of others – those of famous visitors or residents who, even if they did not make the city their home, were involved with it closely enough not simply for their views of it to be of value but for their names to be permanently associated with it in the minds of future generations. Obviously, Napoleon himself – though he paid only one brief visit lasting less than a fortnight – had to be the first subject of study. I thought long and hard about whether or not to include the puzzling story of Nahir de Lusignan, eventually deciding on a compromise by relegating her to a parenthetic postscript. I hardly dare hope that some reader will be able to cast light on the mystery – though how wonderful it would be if one did.

Byron, equally obviously, had to be the second. I have never liked him, and after completing Chapter 3 felt even less sympathetic towards him than before. (Is it not mildly astonishing, incidentally, that he should have spent some three years in Ravenna without giving a single indication that he even knew that the city possessed by far the greatest early Byzantine mosaics anywhere in the world, far less that he ever bothered to visit them?) I am conscious, too, that after the countless books about him – more, I suspect, with the possible exception of Shakespeare, than about any other English writer – the story of his life in Venice is already almost too well known. On the other hand, that story is undeniably a good one; and in any case, to leave him out of a book of this kind would be almost as reprehensible as his own attitude to those mosaics – to say nothing of his rather different attitude to the ladies of Venice, over whom he seemed to cast so magical a spell.

Then of course comes Ruskin – who cast no spell at all on ladies, but whose prose, when he pulls out all the stops, I unashamedly prefer to most of Byron's poetry. He was, I suppose, a sort of genius, though certainly a deeply flawed one: however much the city fascinated him and however many benefits he conferred upon it, he never really understood what it was all about. The late Sir Kenneth Clark used to maintain that the reason why most English nineteenth-century travellers preferred Florence to Venice was that Ruskin's *Mornings in Florence* was a single volume slim enough to fit comfortably into the pocket of one's Norfolk jacket, while for *The Stones of Venice* one needed a wheelbarrow; he might well have added that of all the great works of English literature, Ruskin's majestic work is surely the most unreadable from end to end. I usually disapprove of abridgements, but in the case of *The Stones* I am prepared to make an exception. (Of *St Mark's Rest*, the less said the better.)

After Ruskin the choice was not quite so easy. Few but true Venice aficionados nowadays have ever heard of Rawdon or Horatio Brown, but the two seemed to me to deserve inclusion simply because together they represented the British colony in Venice for very nearly a hundred years – years in which no English visitor to the city would have omitted to call on one or the other. To the indefatigable researches of Rawdon Brown, moreover, historians – and particularly those of the Tudor period – owe an immeasurable debt. Horatio, too, did much to put Venice once again on the map; and his association with John Addington Symonds alone makes a few pages on him more than worth while.

I could not possibly leave out Henry James, whose formidable intelligence was able to penetrate far deeper into the Venetian soul than any of his companions in this book (though Browning was to run him close). For years he was a regular visitor to Daniel and Ariana Curtis in Palazzo Barbaro, who might well have had a chapter to themselves; he knew Venice like the back of his hand; and *The Aspern Papers*, short as it is, is for me the greatest novel ever set in the city. There is the tragic story, too, of Constance Fenimore Woolson, and the curious relationship that existed between the two cousins. (To this day I never pass Palazzo Semitecolo without thinking of the dreadful night of her suicide, a blow from which, I suspect, the guilt-ridden James was never altogether to recover.)

And so we come to the Layards. Sir Henry, admittedly, was better known for his record in Mesopotamia than for anything he did in Venice – though his revival of the mosaic industry was no small achievement; but his wife reigned (I believe this is the right word) from her magnificent Palazzo Cappello for nearly forty years – much, one suspects, to the discomfiture of poor Horatio Brown, who must have found himself hopelessly outshone. (I still like to think, though, that there may have been a good many Monday evenings when a guest at 'the refrigerator' slipped quietly away to the less daunting atmosphere of Ca' Torresella.) Another reason for giving the Layards a chapter of their own is that doing so enables me to include the hilarious letter by their nephew – surely the best ever written from Venice – which I should otherwise have had to omit.

James McNeill Whistler and John Singer Sargent were both displaced American painters, but there the resemblance ends. Their characters could scarcely have been more different; and the same is true of the conditions under which they worked in Venice. Whistler, for all his panache, was obliged to live in comparative poverty after his recent bankruptcy; Sargent by contrast was affluent, sought after by every Venetian hostess, frequenting all the best palaces and *salons* and enjoying the degree of luxury that was to be found only with the Curtises at the Barbaro. He too was a regular Venetian visitor; Whistler went only once to the city, though he stayed much longer. The two of them qualify above all because Venice meant so much to them – stimulating both, with its beauty, its light and its ever-changing colour, to some of their most brilliant work.

The same, I think, could be said of Richard Wagner. He may not have lived in the city for very much of his life, and indeed on his first visit he was initially unimpressed; yet it is clear that even had Venice not inspired the second act of *Tristan und Isolde* it would always have been important to him. We shall never know whether or not he made a conscious decision to die there. Certainly, when he took Palazzo Vendramin-Calergi for his last visit he had no delusions as to how ill he was; he must have known, too, that Venice could provide him with a more dramatically sumptuous funeral than any other city in Europe – which she duly did. (Venetian virtuosity in this respect was to be proved by the astonishing obsequies which took place eighty-eight years later in honour of that almost equally great composer, Igor Stravinsky. He had actually died in New York, but had asked to be buried near his friend and patron Serge Diaghilev in the Orthodox section of the cemetery on the island of S. Michele. No one, I think, who attended the funeral service in April 1971 at SS Giovanni e Paolo will ever forget it.)

The story of Robert Browning and Venice hinges above all on two people: his son Pen and Mrs Katharine de Kay Bronson. Pen remains a shadowy figure, perhaps because of his extraordinary lack of personality – a characteristic which emerges from every description I have ever read of him. His father loved him dearly, and tried hard to admire him; but Pen's paintings varied between the deeply uninspired and the quite embarrassingly bad, and his only true achievement seems to have been – owing to an unhappy marriage with an American heiress – his restoration, regardless of expense, of the Ca' Rezzonico, perhaps the grandest of all the palaces on the Grand Canal. Mrs Bronson, on the other hand, revealed herself to the Brownings – as she did to so many other English and American visitors to Venice – as a source of boundless hospitality and generosity. In Chapter 8 Henry James describes her (it need hardly be said) a thousand times better than I could; I shall only add that without her and her daughter at Ca' Alvisi – and the Curtises at the Barbaro – this book would be a good deal slimmer than it is. Thanks to Pen and Mrs Bronson – and of course to Venice itself – Robert Browning was probably happier during his later visits to the city than at any time since his wife's death. He did not, I think, foresee that one day it would be the scene of his own; but the idea of dying there would certainly not have dismayed him. Venice in midwinter – he took his last breath a fortnight before Christmas – has a funereal air about it; and there are surely worse fates than to die, if die one must, in a glorious Venetian palazzo, looking out on to the Grand Canal.

The last of our deaths in Venice is that in 1913 of the insufferable Frederick Rolfe, 'Baron Corvo'. My original plan for this book was that it should be confined to the nineteenth century; but if I had stuck to that I should have been compelled to omit that monstrous figure, who cast his baleful shadow over the city only during the first decade of the twentieth. Such an omission, I felt, would not only have been sad; it would also have been unforgivably pedantic. So Corvo slips into the book by the skin of his teeth, and

I welcome him – which is more than anyone in Venice would have done, at least for long. Another reason for his inclusion (apart from the fun of writing about him) is the fact that on both sides of the Atlantic I have been struck by the number of people – those who have never read A. J. A. Symons's *The Quest for Corvo* or are too young to have seen Alec McCowen's dazzling performance in the dramatized *Hadrian the Seventh* – to whom his very name is unknown. A pity: he writes like no one else and gives us, in *The Desire and Pursuit of the Whole*, a picture of turn-of-the-century Venice that has never been surpassed.

There is one short chapter that I have not mentioned. I am aware that it does not lie down quite happily with the rest, since it deals with nobody in particular; at the same time, how can one possibly write about nineteenth-century Venice without discussing, however briefly, the Revolution of 1848? Fortunately it makes a fascinating story; and its central figure, Daniele Manin, though far from being a romantic swashbuckler, seems somehow to have been possessed of an element of true heroism. From the beginning he must have known that Venice had no real hope of keeping the entire Habsburg Empire at bay; yet he fought to the last, and his final surrender was prompted less by the Austrian bombardment than by an epidemic of cholera, which threatened to wipe out virtually the whole population of the city. Even when I had written this chapter, a problem remained: where was I to put it? Its present position is therefore largely arbitrary: the reader is welcome to read it at whatever point in the book seems most desirable. But then the same applies, come to think of it, to most of the chapters; after Napoleon and Byron, there is too much overlap to allow of any strict chronological order.

No matter. The purpose of this book is to paint a picture of the century, not to record its chronological progress. Then, even more than today, Venice offered respite from the outside world. It was a city in which the pace of life was slower, geared either to the amble of the pedestrian or to the glide of a gondola; in which the sun shone, if not all the time, at least far more often than in more northern latitudes; and in which beauty was to be found on every side. True, Napoleon hated it; but Napoleon was an exception to every rule. For the rest of us – and I include not only the subjects of the following chapters but the Bronsons and the Curtises, W. D. Howells and James Fenimore Cooper, Bernard Berenson and Isabella Stewart Gardner and countless others – Venice has been a tonic and an inspiration, an indispensable element in our lives. Hence this book.

John Julius Norwich
London, May 2002

1. After the Fall
(1797–9)

What will happen now to the city of Venice? This city could exist in all its wealth, splendour and beauty only when a capital, inhabited by the aristocracy who governed the Republic. When you are all gone, you patricians, to live on the mainland, Venice will waste away. And is it not true that you are leaving? What would you do in Venice, when you have nothing to do?

Giacomo Casanova to Pietro Zaguri,
4 December 1797

Some time in November 1798 Lorenzo da Ponte, Mozart's greatest librettist and a former Jesuit priest, arrived in Venice for the first time since he had been expelled from the city for gross immorality nineteen years before. He tells in his memoirs of how he entered St Mark's Square under the clock tower, and of his horror at what he saw. 'My reader will judge,' he wrote, 'my surprise and grief, when in all that vast space, where in happy times nothing is to be seen but a great concourse of gay and contented people, I myself saw on every side only melancholy, silence, solitude and desolation . . . There were only seven people when I entered the Piazza . . . Even the cafés were empty.'

It was no wonder. Just eighteen months before, threatened by the young Napoleon Bonaparte at the culmination of his triumphant campaign across Italy, the Venetian Republic had come to an end. It had lasted, by the most conservative reckoning, for 1,070 years – a period of time comfortably longer than that which separates Queen Elizabeth II from William the Conqueror – and the Venetians were still in a state of shock. Many of them also felt no small degree of shame; for they themselves, as they were well aware, had been largely responsible for the speed and suddenness of their collapse. Venice had long since lost the last vestiges of her former greatness, and even of the respect which, in former days, she had enjoyed throughout Europe and beyond. Her commercial supremacy – the source of all her wealth – had failed to survive the discovery of the Cape route to the Indies, which had gradually reduced the Middle Sea to a backwater; moreover the relentless advance of the Ottoman Turks, both before and after the capture of Constantinople by Sultan Mehmet II in 1453, had led to the annihilation, one by one, of her trading colonies in the Near East. Cyprus had fallen in August 1571; nine weeks later Venice, Spain and the Papacy had admittedly scored a spectacular victory over the Turks at Lepanto – the last sea battle in history to be fought by oared galleys – but even this engagement, though it provided a temporary boost to flagging western morale, had had little long-term result; and the fall of Crete in 1669, after a siege lasting twenty-two years, had effectively put an end to Venice's imperial ambitions in the eastern Mediterranean. True, the Venetians had fought back and, in the century's last quarter, had even managed briefly to regain a few of their former possessions (scoring, as they did so, a direct hit on the Parthenon); but by 1718, when their frontiers were drawn for the last time, they found themselves – apart from their provinces on the Italian *terra firma* – with only Istria and Dalmatia, northern Albania and the Ionian islands and finally, south of the Peloponnese, the little island of Cythera.

Then, in the early eighteenth century – whether by accident or design remains uncertain – the Most Serene Republic set itself upon a completely different course. It assumed the mantle of pleasure capital of Europe – and in doing so, during the final decades of its existence, set in train a dramatic revival of financial prosperity. This, fortunately, was the age of the Grand Tour. From all over northern and western Europe – but above all from England – young noblemen descended on Italy with the ostensible purpose of completing their education. Rome, inevitably, was their principal objective, with all the opportunities it offered for the study of the great monuments of antiquity; but there were few indeed who did not return by way of Venice, where Carnival lasted longer, the gambling was for higher stakes and the courtesans were more obliging and highly skilled than anywhere else on the continent. For those visitors of more intellectual tastes, there were books, pictures and sculptures to be bought and churches and palaces to be admired, to say nothing of the music and opera for which Venice was famous throughout the civilized world. The city was the most comfortable in Italy, and by far the most beautiful; and by a further lucky coincidence it boasted a number of hugely talented men who in the past fifty years had brought the art of townscape painting to a point of excellence never achieved before or since. It was fortunate too that the greatest of these *vedutisti*, Antonio Canal – generally known as Canaletto – should have selected as his agent an Englishman, a certain Joseph Smith, who had come to Venice in 1700 at the age of eighteen and was to remain there till his death seventy years later. In 1742 Smith was appointed British Consul, in which capacity he was careful to make the acquaintance of all the richer Englishmen passing through the city – and to ensure that they all received an invitation to the Master's studio. Thus it was that when – somewhat wiser and a good deal poorer – the young *milords* eventually returned to their homeland, a mild dose of the clap must have seemed a small price to pay for a brace of Canalettos and the memories of the happiest and most exciting weeks of their lives.

Smith was a remarkable man, one of the leading figures of eighteenth-century Venice. Canaletto was not his only client: he also negotiated sales on behalf of Marco and Sebastiano Ricci, of Francesco Zuccarelli and of the greatest portraitist in pastel who ever lived, Rosalba Carriera. We can only regret that, living as he did among artists, none of them ever painted his likeness; among his Venetian contemporaries there are few men of his distinction of whose appearance we know so little. The dedicatee of Canaletto's only published set of engravings, he was himself an avid collector. In 1762 he sold his complete collection of pictures and *objets d'art* to George III for £20,000;* and when, three years later, the King followed this tremendous purchase with another, buying all the Consul's books and manuscripts *en bloc* for £10,000, he laid the foundations for the British Library as we know it today. With the proceeds Smith immediately began a new collection – he was then eighty-three – which by his death five years later had grown to such a size that its own sale took thirteen days.

★

When Consul Smith died in 1770, the Republic had just over a quarter of a century to live. It was still putting on a brave show. The future Tsar Paul I and his wife – travelling under the romantic aliases of Count and Countess of the North – paid a visit in January 1782, and the celebrations in their honour were as lavish as ever: on one evening during their stay, a touch from the hand of the Countess was enough to set a huge artificial dove speeding around the Piazza, sparking off a hundred torches as it went and finally coming to rest on an eighty-foot-high replica of the Arch of Titus in Rome. But the fabric of the state was crumbling, and all thinking Venetians knew it.

The root of the problem, whatever it might be, was certainly not economic. With no wars fought since 1718, with trade flourishing and with a constant flood of well-heeled visitors pouring into the city, Venice was enjoying a period of unusual commercial prosperity and economic growth. Her citizens – some 160,000 of them – were in all probability as happy and contented as they had ever been. What, then, had happened? Quite simply, she had lost her self-respect. No longer was she an international force to be reckoned with, no longer did she see herself as a significant player on the world stage. Her war fleet, that fleet which in former times had made her the unrivalled mistress of the Mediterranean, was now reduced to about twenty vessels; her menfolk, once famous across the oceans for their navigation and seamanship, were now

---

* 'The most spectacular acquisition by an English royal collector since Charles I's agent had brought off his coup in Mantua in the 1620s' (Oliver Millar, *Italian Drawings and Paintings in the Queen's Collection*, London, 1965).

better known as panders and procurers, gamblers and pimps. Dedicated now only to the relentless pursuit of pleasure – and to the purveying of that pleasure to others – Venice had neglected those very institutions that had made her great, and had perhaps even enabled her to survive: her naval and military strength and – arguably most important of all – her unique political structure.

Alone among the states of Europe, Venice by the mid eighteenth century had maintained her constitution essentially unchanged for over a thousand years. Twice only – in 1310 and again in 1355 – had it been threatened, and on both occasions the upheavals, such as they were, had been dealt with in a matter of hours. It was admittedly oligarchic: the vast majority of Venetians had always been without the franchise and had no say in the government of the Republic. Few on the other hand complained. The civil service was open to all; commerce and the craftsmanship for which the city was famous provided a source of pride and satisfaction as well as rich material rewards; and it was almost universally accepted that the government had the best interests of its citizens at heart.

But the body politic was not as healthy as it seemed. There was, first of all, the curious reluctance of the Venetian upper classes to marry. Of the fourteen Doges who reigned in the hundred years between 1675 and 1775, eleven were bachelors; and if we look at the aristocracy as a whole, much the same pattern is revealed – at the time of which we were speaking, well over 60 per cent remained unattached. The underlying philosophy is clear: the family must continue; and it must continue rich. One son was therefore required to marry, and to beget enough legitimate male heirs to ensure the first of these requirements; the other sons would remain single, thus – by preventing the dispersal of wealth – fulfilling the second.* This reluctance had two dangerous consequences. The first was that sometimes a carefully laid plan would go wrong: several old

---

* This enforced bachelorhood may well have accounted for the number of professional courtesans in Venice. It certainly explains the quantity of 'orphanages' and convents, since the blow fell hardest on the upper-class girls of the city, at least two-thirds of whom failed to find husbands.

and distinguished families became extinct in this way; the second was that the nobility suffered from an ever-widening split between rich and poor. This in turn meant a dramatic increase in the so-called *barnabotti*, that class of impoverished noblemen who were too poor or too uneducated to occupy any but the lowest adminis-trative positions, and whose dissatisfaction was growing steadily more vocal. In an effort to infuse new blood, seats on the Great Council – since 1298 exclusively reserved for those families whose names were at that time entered in the Golden Book – were now openly offered for sale to approved and suitably affluent outsiders; but this practice too showed itself to be deeply divisive. Doge Paolo Renier, who assumed the ducal throne on 14 January 1779, described the situation as well as anyone:

> If any state has need of unity, it is ours. We have no forces, neither on land nor at sea. We have no alliances. We live by good fortune, by accident, putting our trust solely in that reputation for prudence that the government of Venice has always enjoyed. Here, and here only, lies our strength.

But prudence, too, seemed to be in short supply. Renier himself – who was married to a Greek tightrope walker – had a reputation for sharp practice and was commonly rumoured to have bought the Dogeship by bribing 300 members of the Great Council. Moreover, he found himself pitted against unscrupulous political bosses who frequently wielded a good deal more real power than he did himself – violent reactionaries such as Andrea Tron, popularly known among Venetians as *il Paron*,★ or embittered *barnabotti* such as Giorgio Pisani who openly accused the government of criminal mismanagement, decadence and corruption. Such men in former centuries would have been unknown, or – had they dared to raise their heads – would have been dealt with quietly and expeditiously by the government. By the 1770s, though the state still retained vestiges of its old authority – Pisani was finally arrested and

★ *Il padrone, le patron,* the boss.

imprisoned for ten years on the mainland – it had largely forfeited the respect of its citizens. This it would not regain.

Even when Venice's power was at its zenith, Napoleon would have been a formidable adversary; in her present condition she stood no chance against him. Her emissaries, Francesco Donà and Lunardo Giustinian, who followed him hotfoot across Italy and Austria and finally found him at Graz, were deceived by his bluster and horrified by his threat to be 'an Attila to the state of Venice'; their report to the Doge and the Signoria only confirmed the general view that war was imminent, the Republic doomed. On Tuesday 9 May 1797 Villetard, the French chargé d'affaires, handed over an ultimatum demanding *inter alia* the establishment of a provisional municipality in place of the Republic, whose insignia was to be burnt at the foot of a Tree of Liberty erected in the centre of the Piazza; and three days later the Great Council assembled, in what was to be its final session, to consider this document. Soon afterwards shots were heard outside, and panic spread through the chamber. The source of the commotion proved to be nothing more than a few Dalmatian soldiers who, expelled by the French, were discharging their muskets in a farewell salute to the city; but by now reassurances were useless and the debate was abandoned. Some – though by no means all – the members of the Council were persuaded to delay their departure long enough to cast their votes; few, however, remained to hear the result. The resolution to accept the ultimatum was carried by 512 to 20, with five abstentions.

The 120th and last Doge of Venice, Lodovico Manin, made no attempt to flee. Almost alone among his fellow patricians, he had maintained a quiet calm amid the hubbub – a calm born, perhaps, of fatalism and despair, but a calm none the less that enabled him to keep his dignity, even while the last frail structure of the Republic crumbled about him. In the sudden stillness that followed the breakup of the meeting he slowly gathered up his papers and withdrew to his private apartments. There, having laid aside his ducal *corno*, he carefully untied the ribbons of the close-fitting cap of white linen always worn beneath it, the *cuffietta*, and handed it to his valet with those sad words which, more than any others, seem to symbolize the fall of Venice: '*Tolè, questa no la dopero più*' – 'Take this, I shall not be needing it again.'

The crowds who had gathered outside the Palace showed a good deal more spirit than their rulers. They had watched, astonished, the precipitate flight of the Council members from the building, and the news of the resolution spread quickly through the city. Within minutes the people were streaming from all sides into the Piazza, shouting '*Viva la Repubblica!*' and '*Viva San Marco!*', sacking the houses of what they called the 'Jacobins' and even the shop of a pork-butcher in S. Moisè who had been imprudent enough to display a pro-French poster. Only when the officer in charge of internal security, Bernardino Renier, had brought up a regiment of artillery to the Rialto Bridge and opened fire down the Grand Canal was order finally restored.

★

The French troops under General Louis Baraguey d'Hilliers entered Venice on Monday 15 May – the first foreign army in all its history to set foot in the city. On the following day the newly established Venetian Municipality took office for the first time and immediately addressed a letter to Napoleon – a letter that tells us virtually all that we need to know about it. It began as follows:

> To the provisional Municipality of Venice, now installed after the voluntary abdication of the former Great Council, in joyful exaltation and imbued with most heartfelt gratitude towards its great and magnanimous liberator, the general commanding the invincible Army of Italy, no duty is more urgent than that of raising its voice to proclaim to all Europe that it owes its liberty to the glorious French nation and to the immortal Bonaparte.

Soon afterwards the Municipality turned its attention to the Lion of St Mark. 'It is not appropriate,' declared one of its members, 'that the gentle and pacific character of the people of Venice should be represented by a wild beast whose dripping fangs threaten only massacre and ruin.' Orders were accordingly given to one Giacomo Gallini, head of the stonemasons' guild, to remove or efface every lion in the city – as had already been done by the French, with hideous efficiency, throughout the *terra firma*. We can only be thankful that Gallini proved less conscientious: though he accepted his pay – 982 ducats – relatively few lions were touched.★ The fact that such action was even contemplated is indication enough of the mentality of French and Venetians alike all through that night-mare summer; curiously enough, however, the emblem of the lion continued to appear on the edicts of the Municipality. The only difference was that instead of the words *Pax tibi Marce evangelista meus* (Peace unto you Mark my evangelist) the book held in his paw now carried the slogan *Diritti e doveri dell' uomo e del cittadino* (Rights and duties of man and citizen) – prompting a waggish gondolier to express relief that, after so many centuries, the lion had at last turned the page.

The following Ascension Day, which fell on 25 May, was the first for 797 years on which the Venetians did not perform their annual ceremony of *lo Sposalizio* – the Marriage with the Sea. There were however other celebrations on Whit Sunday, 4 June, which demonstrated all too clearly the level to which Venice had sunk within a month of the Republic's end. Those who, prompted more by curiosity than enthusiasm, made their way to the Piazza on that day had already grown accustomed to the Tree of Liberty – that towering wooden pole, surmounted by the symbolic scarlet Phrygian cap (which bore more than a passing resemblance to the ducal *corno*) rising incongruously from its centre. To this had now been added three large tribunes, ranged along the north, south and west sides of the square. The western one, which was intended for the sixty members of the Municipality, bore the inscription LIBERTY IS PRESERVED BY OBEDIENCE TO THE LAW; the other two, destined for the French and other less distinguished Italian authorities,

---

★ The most serious casualty was the representation of Doge Francesco Foscari kneeling before the Lion, which formed the centrepiece of the Porta della Carta at the main entrance to the Doge's Palace. It was the work of Bartolomeo Bon (*c.*1376–*c.*1467), the leading Venetian sculptor of the day. The existing panel is a nineteenth-century replacement.

respectively proclaimed that DAWNING LIBERTY IS PROTECTED BY
FORCE OF ARMS and ESTABLISHED LIBERTY LEADS TO UNIVERSAL
PEACE. The entire Piazzetta was similarly bedecked, with an outsize
banner in praise of Bonaparte stretched between the two columns.

   After General Baraguey d'Hilliers and the Municipality had taken
their places, the bands began to play – there were four of them,
disposed at intervals around the Piazza, comprising a total of well
over 300 musicians – and the procession began. First came a group
of Italian soldiers, followed by two small children carrying lighted
torches and another banner with the words GROW UP, HOPE OF
THE FATHERLAND. Behind them marched a betrothed couple
(DEMOCRATIC FECUNDITY) and finally an aged pair staggering
under the weight of agricultural implements, bearing words 'refer-
ring to their advanced age, at which time liberty was instituted'.

   The procession over, the President of the Municipality advanced
to the Tree of Liberty where, after a brief ceremony in the Basilica,
he proceeded to the most dramatic business of the day: the symbolic
burning of a *corno* and other emblems of ducal dignity – all obligingly
provided for the purpose by Lodovico Manin himself – and a copy
of the Golden Book. He and his fellow *municipalisti*, together with
the General and the senior members of his staff, then led off the
dancing round the Tree of Liberty, while the guns fired repeated
salutes, the church bells rang and the bands played '*La Carmagnole*'.
The celebrations ended with a gala performance of an opera at the
Fenice Theatre, which had been completed less than five years
before.

   There is, or seems to be, a law of politics whereby the degree of
freedom and democracy actually enjoyed by a given state varies
in inverse ratio to the volume and vehemence with which it is
proclaimed. The so-called 'democratic' government which wielded
power in Venice for the next eight months was, for all its trumpet-
ings, nothing of the kind. The sixty members of the Municipality
did not even enjoy the pretence of a popular mandate. They
were appointed by the French; the people of Venice were neither
consulted in advance nor called upon to ratify the appointments
afterwards. During the government's short life no election was ever

held; indeed, there was little point in holding one, since – although few people participating in those flatulent Whit Sunday festivities were aware of the fact – already six weeks before, on 18 April, at the castle of Eckenwald, just outside Leoben in Styria, a provisional peace had been signed by Napoleon (in the name of the Directory, which he had not bothered to consult) and Austria. He had taken this unexpected step since he was determined that he and no one else should be the conqueror of the Habsburg Empire; and there seemed a distinct possibility that his chief rival, the brilliant young General Lazare Hoche, who was now rapidly advancing through Germany, might reach Vienna before him. The only way in which Hoche could be stopped was by an armistice, for the quick conclusion of which Napoleon was ready to pay a heavy price; and by the terms of the ensuing agreement Venice and the Veneto, together with Istria, Dalmatia and all Venetian mainland territory bounded by the Oglio, the Po and the Adriatic were transferred to Austria. Only Bergamo, Crema, the lands between the Oglio and the Adda and the Ionian islands were to be retained by the French as part of their newly formed Cisalpine Republic.

But Napoleon had no intention of making the Emperor Francis a present of a rich and influential city; and there was still a chance of milking Venice of everything he could lay his hands on. Hence the so-called Treaty of Milan, which was signed on 16 May by Venetian deputies in the name of a Republic that had four days previously ceased to exist and was never ratified by the Directory in Paris. Outwardly it proclaimed peace between France and Venice, confirming the abolition of the hereditary aristocracy and the other political institutions of the former Republic and providing for a garrison of French troops 'to maintain order and the security of persons and property'; but it also contained five secret clauses according to which Venice would not only pay an indemnity of 3 million *livres tournois* and another 3 million in kind, together with three ships of the line and a frigate, fully armed, equipped, crewed and provisioned; she was obliged also to surrender – for transmission to Paris – twenty of her finest paintings and 500 manuscripts, all to be chosen by a committee appointed by the French general commanding. The selectors were persuaded to leave Tintoretto's *Last Judgement* in the Doge's Palace and Titian's great *Assumption of the Virgin* in the Frari; but they insisted, alas, on taking Paolo Veronese's glorious *Marriage at Cana* from the refectory of S. Giorgio Maggiore. It still hangs in the Louvre today. The manuscripts included 172 Greek codices, nearly all from the library of Cardinal Bessarion★ and 320 printed volumes from the Dominican Convent of S. Maria del Rosario on the Zattere, 219 of these being incunabula dating from before 1500.

Within a month of its formation the Municipality, overwhelmed by the incessant French demands for money and material, was in serious financial distress. Desperately searching for new sources of wealth, its eyes lit on the Treasury of St Mark's; and early in August it summoned a committee of four jewellers to produce estimates for all the most valuable items. The jewellers, however, maintained that they could not make accurate assessments unless the pieces were broken down into their component parts; and there followed several nightmare weeks during which some of the greatest treasures in all Europe were deliberately and systematically destroyed, with literally thousands of diamonds, rubies, sapphires and amethysts wrenched from their settings and superb pieces of gold and silver melted down. They included five large roses of solid gold, presents from various Popes to the Doges of Venice, and twelve pectoral crosses bearing a total of 5,573 pearls and precious stones. We can only be thankful that the *Pala d'Oro*, that great golden altarpiece, escaped destruction. By some miracle it was assumed by the *municipalisti* to be of plated metal.

★

It was not surprising that the Venetians, watching helplessly while their city was plundered and having somehow to find board and lodging for the 10,000 French troops who were now billeted among

★ The Greek churchman who, having accompanied the Byzantine Emperor John VIII to the Council of Florence in 1437, converted with him to Catholicism and later became a cardinal. Before his death he left his entire library to the Venetian Senate.

them, soon began to realize the enormity of what had occurred. By now, too, all their old institutions and traditions were being swept away, or changed beyond recognition. There was a new penal code and a new civil code; the entire judiciary was reorganized on the lines of current revolutionary thinking; the number of public officials – there had admittedly been far too many – was dramatically reduced, causing wide unemployment; taxation on the other hand was equally dramatically increased. No wonder that throughout the summer dissatisfaction grew, to the point where the authorities became seriously concerned. A proclamation dated 22 July warned against the number of seditious pamphlets in circulation, the disrespect shown to national uniforms, the vituperative denunciations of the municipal government, even the open mockery of several of its members. It was now decreed that all subversive activity – even the shouting of *Viva San Marco!* – would be punishable by death; any hotel-keeper who did not immediately report suspicious conversations on the part of his guests would be liable to five years' imprisonment. And yet somehow these provisions had little effect, and the atmosphere in the city remained dangerously tense until, in mid-October, the Venetians sustained a blow greater even than the loss of their beloved Republic.

The terms of the Leoben agreement had never been announced in Venice. In any case it had been merely a preliminary. Now, however, its provisions – only slightly amended – were incorporated into the formal treaty of peace between France and Austria, concluded on 17 October 1797 in Lodovico Manin's villa at Passariano in Friuli but known to history by the name of the nearby village of Campoformio.* The secret could no longer be kept. The Venetians now learned that they were to be handed over to Austria – news that they received first with incredulity and then with horror. Hostilities between the *municipalisti* and the Republicans were forgotten; they were all Venetians now. They might have lost their Republic, but Bonaparte had promised them at least their

* Or, more properly, Campoformido. 'Campoformio' is in fact a borrowing from the local dialect.

freedom and independence; suddenly, without consulting them or indeed even informing them, he had sold them like chattels to the Emperor of Austria. On the 27th a public plebiscite was held, to answer the following questions:

1. Were the people of Venice prepared to await, in ignorance and silence, the fate which threatened them?
2. Were they also prepared to take an oath to maintain the liberty of their country, their children and their descendants?
3. Would they take part in a national congress, to be held in Milan?
4. And would they persuade the provinces of the *terra firma* to do the same?

The result was 12,725 votes in favour of prompt and decisive action, and 10,843 against; but it was too late. Venice's fate was sealed. And now the serious depredations began. Over the next few weeks the French occupiers worked round the clock to leave nothing movable behind for their successors. They commandeered all the ships they could find, loading into them whatever gold and silver was left in the city, including that from the altars of the churches and even the trimmings on the *Bucintoro*, the magnificent state barge, rowed by 168 oarsmen, in which the Doge and Senate had sailed out every Ascension Day for the Marriage with the Sea; those few vessels that were in construction in the Arsenal were either quickly completed and dispatched to Toulon or, if work on them was insufficiently advanced, destroyed on the spot. Tons of hemp, miles of rope, acres of canvas, even the huge cauldrons for the boiling of pitch were carried away. Every piece of artillery in the city was shipped off to France or Corfu to prevent its falling into Austrian hands. The victualling yards, too, were ransacked: it is reported that two and a half million biscuits were put up for public sale, and 44,000 *moggia*★ of salt. Banks suspended payments; long-term loans were called in. On 7 December 1797 the people watched with dismay as the four bronze horses of St Mark's, which had stood for more than five centuries above the great west portal

★ A *moggio* was generally equal to eight bushels.

of the Basilica, were lowered to the ground; they too were destined for Paris, where they were eventually placed on the Arch of the Carrousel in the Tuileries. The city's oldest lion, that which for even longer had crowned the eastern column on the Piazzetta, followed them, finding its new home on the Champ de Mars.

For all this looting, however outrageous, the French had their reasons, however unacceptable. They wished to impoverish Venice before passing it over to the Austrians; and they wished to enrich themselves. But there were other acts committed in the Arsenal for which there could be no justification. They did not need to destroy the models of the ships which they left behind them, nor the fine plasterwork of the more important rooms; they did not need to attack the fine marble staircase with sledgehammers; nor, on 9 January 1798, to take axes to the *Bucintoro*.

On Sunday 18 January the last of the French army departed; and on that same day arrived the Austrian vanguard, to take formal possession of the city. Three days later the new occupiers held an official reception in the Doge's Palace, with the former Doge Lodovico Manin among the guests. There may have been a few among his compatriots optimistic enough to believe that the Austrians might restore the Republic and its former system of government; if so, they were quickly disillusioned. The only state in Italy which had never once in all its history been subjected to foreign domination – indeed, had always been looked upon as the last refuge of Italian liberty – now found itself, to its shame and disgust, a relatively unimportant province of the Habsburg Empire.

★

This first occupation of Venice by Austria was to last only seven years; its story can be quickly told. The commander-in-chief of the imperial army of Italy, General Oliver von Wallis, promulgated his orders swiftly and without fuss. Every Venetian, wherever he might be, was to swear loyalty to the Emperor. Every city in the Veneto was to return to those political institutions that had been in force on 1 January 1796. Venice herself was to revive her hereditary aristocracy, of whom 900 assembled on 23 February in the Sala dello Scrutinio of the Doge's Palace, but in ordinary clothes rather than their former robes of office. From these was chosen what was described as a Corpo de' Nobili Patrizi Possessori, to be known as the Congregazione Delegata. This would constitute the effective government of the city. At its head was Giovanni Pietro Grimani, the Republic's last Ambassador in Vienna and one of the few Venetians who actually approved of the annexation. He was soon joined by the Cavaliere Francesco Pesaro, a former Procurator of St Mark's, who bore the title of Imperial Commissioner, with full powers over 'all political, civil and financial affairs' in Venice and the *terra firma*.

All these men doubtless did their best to set their city on its feet again; and the Venetians soon had to admit that, with taxation now much reduced and an end to the shameless extortions practised by Napoleon's troops, the Austrian yoke was a good deal lighter than the French. Nevertheless we have da Ponte's testimony quoted at the start of this chapter that ten months after the Austrian take-over Venice was still but a pale reflection of what she had been only two years before. Her recent political upheavals alone were a more than sufficient explanation; but she had also suffered a serious economic collapse. This had begun as a result of the deplorable behaviour of the departing Napoleonic army, which had effectively emptied the Treasury; but it had been aggravated by several other factors, including a run on the banks, the forced conversions of ducats into lire and the inevitable decline in industry and commerce. All this had been disastrous to the nobles and the richer members of the bourgeoisie, many of whom had decamped to their mainland estates, with the results so clearly foreseen by Casanova in the letter quoted at the head of this chapter. Public offices, too, were far fewer than they had been in the days of the *Serenissima*. The diplomatic service for example, which alone had provided several hundred profitable posts, had ceased to exist. For the general populace, one of the most vital sources of wealth, international tourism, had dried up. The rich young *milords* came no longer. The Grand Tour was over.

On the mainland the situation was even worse – to the point where the Congregazione Delegata became seriously concerned at the number of beggars and vagabonds who were pouring into the city in search of food. Orders were given for their immediate expulsion, with the threat of heavy fines to be imposed on any boatmen found bringing such people across the lagoon;* but these measures proved largely ineffective, and the steady stream of undesirables continued. The result was a serious epidemic of typhoid. The disease seems to have been introduced into the provinces of the *terra firma* by the French troops, who had succumbed in such numbers that there were no longer beds for them in the hospitals; many had been billeted on the local populations, among whom the virus had rapidly spread. The epidemic hit Venice in the summer of 1802 and by a hideous coincidence was accompanied by hundreds of cases of severe poisoning, following the importation into the city of large quantities of infected meat.

These sad years were, however, punctuated by a single remarkable event, unparalleled in Venetian history: an event which made the city, now no longer the capital of a Republic, the temporary capital instead of the Church of Rome. Pope Pius VI had died on 29 August 1799, an exile – some might have called him a prisoner – in Valence. He was almost paralysed, and too ill to say mass; death had come to him as a blessed release. Well-meaning but weak and narrow-minded, he had failed totally to realize the magnitude of the changes that were taking place in Europe, and the necessity of moving with the times. At the outbreak of the French Revolution he had had to see the old Gallican Church suppressed – largely at the instigation of Talleyrand, himself a bishop – and the confiscation of all pontifical and church properties in France, including, early in 1791, the formerly papal city of Avignon. A few months later the Paris mob had burnt him in effigy at the Palais-Royal. After the French invasion of Italy and the defeat of the papal forces he, like the Venetians, had been forced to sign a treaty with Napoleon in 1797; but in February 1798 the French occupied Rome, proclaimed a Republic and demanded that he renounce his temporal authority. On his refusal he was arrested and carried off to France to die.

* Access to Venice was then only by water. The existing bridge dates from 1841–6.

In their continued endeavour to strip the Pope of his temporal power, it was clear that the French would interfere with the coming election if they possibly could, either by imposing their own candidate or by making trouble within the conclave. Clearly therefore the Curia could not meet in Rome, and looked around for an alternative location where it would be safe from foreign influences. Venice was the obvious answer, isolated by her lagoon and now able to call upon the Austrian navy for additional protection as necessary. The Emperor's permission was sought – and on 12 October accorded, with a further guarantee that all expenses would be met by the imperial treasury.

Over the next six weeks more and more cardinals appeared in the city – they included the 74-year-old Cardinal Henry, Duke of York, younger brother of Bonnie Prince Charlie – and on 1 December the conclave began in the Benedictine abbey of S. Giorgio Maggiore. All thirty-three cardinals present were lodged in the monastic buildings; but despite the extreme discomfort they suffered in largely unheated accommodation through more than three months of a Venetian winter, they were unable to decide on the next Pontiff until 14 March 1800, when the election was announced of Cardinal Barnaba Chiaramonti, Bishop of Imola, as Pius VII. To the Emperor in Vienna the choice of a man who, fifteen months before, had preached a Christmas sermon in praise of 'that Liberty which is so dear to God and to mankind' was something less than ideal. He had no choice but to accept the decision of the conclave, but made known his displeasure by forbidding the papal coronation to take place, as had been expected, in St Mark's. Instead, the ceremony was performed in the church of S. Giorgio Maggiore; and the traditional *urbi et orbi* message, which would have echoed so resonantly across the Piazza, was delivered from the Abbot's window overlooking the terrace in front of the church, to little more than a handful of people gathered beneath. It was, perhaps, the Papacy's greatest humiliation since the Middle Ages.

But at least it continued to exist. The Venetian Republic was dead – and continued, even now, to be despoiled. Towards the end of 1799 the greatest private library in Venice, that of the former Doge Marco Foscarini, was confiscated by Austria as a result of non-payment of taxes by his great-nephews. The manuscript codices were sent off to the Imperial Library in Vienna, where they still remain; the printed books, listed in a catalogue that ran to 296 pages, were sold off piecemeal. Many other treasures, many other collections, were similarly to disappear in the years that followed.

Venice, then, as the nineteenth century began, presented a sorry picture indeed. Her character too had changed, as well it might. Gone were the days and nights of wine and roses; the god Mammon had been dethroned. All Venice had left was her beauty, still almost unimpaired, and her memories. And yet, in a strange way, these were enough. Not only did they keep her alive, but gradually, as the new century got under way, they were once again to attract men and women from all over the world to the city – no longer the simple seekers after pleasure (for there were by then many European cities in which far more varied delights were available) but those who instead sought inspiration of the kind that only Venice could give. They, with Venice herself, are the subject of this book; but before we come to them we must briefly return for a closer look at the man who dominated the first years of the new century even more completely than he had the last years of the old: Napoleon Bonaparte.

2. Napoleon
(1807)

L'anema ti ga intrepida, alto el talento;
El cor magnanimo, e l'ardimento
Più forte ancora del nostro leon.
Torna presto Napoleon!

Your spirit is brave, your abilities high,
You have greatness of heart, and your courage
Exceeds even that of our Lion.
Come back soon, Napoleon!

Gondoliers' song

On a bitterly cold December day in 1805, near Austerlitz in Moravia, a French army of 68,000 commanded in person by the Emperor – for so he had proclaimed himself exactly one year before – defeated some 90,000 Russians and Austrians under General Mikhail Kutuzov. It was one of Napoleon's most perfect victories, bringing Austria to her knees and forcing her to conclude, on the 26th, a peace treaty at Pressburg (now Bratislava) by which she returned to him, *inter alia*, all the Venetian territories she had acquired at Campoformio. And so it came about that on Sunday 19 January 1806 – eight years and a day after the arrival of the Austrians – the French returned to Venice, now incorporated into the recently formed Kingdom of Italy. On 3 February arrived the new Viceroy: the Emperor's 25-year-old stepson, Eugène de Beauharnais. Despite the generous promises he made in the name of his stepfather, the Venetians' feelings can well be imagined. They had hated their Austrian masters; but the French – whose treatment of their city during the previous occupation was still fresh in their minds – they resented even more; and they found additional humiliation in the fact that the capital of the now greatly expanded Kingdom remained at Milan, while Venice was now demoted to being nothing more than the *capoluogo*, or chief town, of the Department of the Adriatic.

The years that followed brought them little comfort. In January 1806 Napoleon adopted de Beauharnais as his son and gave him the title of Prince of Venice – a further insult to all good Venetians. The continental blockade which he declared in November of that year may have been directed against England but its impact on Venice was far greater, coming as it did just at the moment when she was striving to rebuild her mercantile strength; and the English counter-blockade which began soon afterwards effectively put an end to all Mediterranean commerce, throwing the Venetian economy into ever steeper decline. Meanwhile in the city itself – and this was for many Venetians more demoralizing still – the French had embarked on a policy the savagery of which, even now, sends shivers down the spine.

It took the form of a frontal attack on the religious institutions of Venice. The first blow was struck on 28 July 1806, when a viceregal decree ordered the immediate suppression of thirty-four monasteries and convents in the city itself and the islands of the lagoon, including those of S. Giorgio Maggiore, S. Giobbe and S. Francesco del Deserto. Over the next three years eighteen secular churches went the same way – among them S. Severo, S. Gregorio and S. Geminiano at the west end of the Piazza. Yet even this was only a beginning: in 1810, following a new decree by the Emperor, another twenty-five monastic institutions were dissolved. Later that same year, the reorganization of the city of Venice into thirty-two parishes led to the closing of fifteen more churches; this time they included S. Angelo and S. Aponal, S. Marina and S. Margherita, S. Sofia and S. Stin. We can only be grateful that the suppression of a monastery or convent did not necessarily involve the closure of its church; had it done so, we should have also lost SS. Giovanni e Paolo and the Frari, S. Giorgio Maggiore, S. Zaccaria, S. Maria dei Miracoli and S. Francesco della Vigna.

The 385 *scuole* – those devotional or charitable institutions that were so important a feature of Venetian life – suffered a similar fate. The buildings of the six *scuole grandi* – those of S. Marco, S. Rocco, S. Giovanni Evangelista, S. Maria della Carità, S. Maria della Misericordia and S. Teodoro – have fortunately all been preserved; but the vast majority of the remainder, together with their furnishings and works of art, have disappeared without trace.★ It could be argued that of these *scuole*, as of the churches and monasteries, there had been far too many; indeed, the government of the Republic had made a first attempt at reducing them some thirty years before. Nothing, however, could justify the scale of the French operation, nor the lack of any adequate arrangements to preserve the buildings – many of which were turned over to the occupying forces – or their contents: thus S. Anna was converted into a gymnasium, S. Marina into a hostelry, the ancient monastery of S. Maria delle Vergini into a military prison. At least a dozen fine churches for which no alternative use could be found were arbitrarily demolished. They included Pietro Lombardo's exquisite early Renaissance S. Andrea, on the island of Certosa; the little fourteenth-century S. Vio, in which was the tomb of Venice's most brilliant portraitist, Rosalba Carriera; and – most tragic loss of all – the great Gothic church of S. Maria dei Servi where, in one of the apse chapels, lay the bones of Fra Paolo Sarpi, the Servite friar who had guided the Republic through her greatest religious crisis in the early seventeenth century. No one, it seems, even bothered to rescue them.†

★

At that time the Emperor had still never set foot in the city; there was therefore much curiosity – and even more trepidation – when,

★Even great pictures associated with the life of St Mark were looted – going this time to Milan: a humiliation to the Venetians greater even than if they had gone to Paris. They included the vast canvas by Gentile Bellini – assisted by his brother Giovanni – of St Mark preaching in Alexandria, and a superb Tintoretto of the rediscovery of the body of the Evangelist after its concealment in a column of the Basilica. Both are still in Milan and can be seen in the Brera.
† The ruins of S. Maria dei Servi were offered to Ruskin – 'ground and all, or stone by stone' – in 1852.

in the last days of 1807, His Imperial Majesty paid his first and only visit. It lasted from Sunday 29 November to Tuesday 8 December. He had come from Milan, where he had managed to spend some hours with his mistress, the celebrated contralto Giuseppina Grassini,* and had spent the previous night in the Villa Pisani at Strà. Exhausted, and in one of those black humours which terrified everyone around him – he had been barely civil to Beauharnais, to his own sister Maria Elisa and to his two brothers-in-law when they had come to greet him in Vicenza – on his arrival at the villa he had drunk his evening glass of milk and then retired at once to bed, pausing only to look briefly at the famous ballroom with its vast ceiling by the 66-year-old Giambattista Tiepolo.† On the following morning he heard mass in the chapel and then, at half past two in the afternoon, at the head of a long procession of coaches and escorted by a regiment of exotically uniformed mame-luke troops carrying long gilded lances, set off in driving rain for Fusina, the point of departure for Venice. Here he received an official welcome from the *podestà*, Daniele Renier – son of the penultimate Doge – while two negro pages knelt before him, bearing a cushion on which lay the symbolic keys of the city, one of silver, one of gold. Finally he boarded the first of five *peotte*,‡ and the little fleet – escorted, we are assured, by a vast quantity of other boats of all shapes and sizes – set off across the windswept lagoon.

Meanwhile, in Venice, his new subjects awaited the man who, seemingly effortlessly, had brought their thousand-year Republic to a sudden and humiliating end. He was a superman: so much they knew. Worse, he was a hostile superman. He had no love for them

* Ten years later, in Paris, she was similarly to bestow her favours upon the Duke of Wellington – a remarkable left-and-right.
† He had seen it some ten years before, when he had spent a few days at Strà with his wife, Josephine. On that occasion, on being told that the painting was a fresco, he had remarked: 'A pity: if it had been on canvas it would have looked superb at Fontainebleau!'
‡ Hugely ornate ceremonial boats, rowed by twelve oarsmen and carrying roughly the same number of passengers. Their modern equivalents can still be seen today at the *regata storica*, held annually on the first Sunday in September.

or for their city, on which he had threatened to wreak a destruction on the scale of that wrought by Attila almost fourteen centuries before. Already his armies had done untold damage, both to their monuments and to their long-held traditions; was this to be only a foretaste of what now lay in store? And if so, how were they to defend themselves? Even while their Republic was still in existence, their attempts to do so had been pitiable; now, a decade later, disastrously impoverished and yet further demoralized at the hands of two separate conquerors, they were more helpless still. What new cataclysm must they now expect?

One feeble ray of hope remained. All that the Emperor knew about the city was based on hearsay, on the books and papers which had been put before him and from which he had drawn such unwarranted conclusions. When he had seen Venice's beauty for himself, when a few responsible Venetians had had an opportunity to talk to him personally and plead the Venetian cause, was it not possible that he might change his mind? They were well aware on the other hand that, having chosen to come in late November, he would be seeing the city at its worst – grey, cold and damp. Besides, even if he did relent, even if he did allow himself to be at least in some degree seduced, there was no chance that he would restore its independence or even put an end to its subjection. Nor was there any long-term hope for the future, for he was still only thirty-eight: he might easily have forty years or more to rule.

It was perhaps just as well that by the time the Emperor and his entourage reached the monastery of S. Chiara – which stood roughly on the site of the present Piazzale Roma – darkness had already fallen, since many of the decorations put up for the occasion had succumbed to the wind and rain and were hanging in dripping tatters from the houses. Huge flares did however reveal the outlines of the hundred-foot-high triumphal arch – considerably larger than those of Constantine the Great and of Septimius Severus in Rome – that had been erected in wood, plaster and papier mâché across the Grand Canal between the now demolished church of S. Lucia and that of S. Simeone Piccolo. Slowly the procession passed the entire length of the Canal. From time to time Renier would indicate points of interest, but Napoleon remained resolutely unimpressed. He had always hated Venice, whose old aristocracy he insisted on believing – without a shred of evidence – to be the most vicious and corrupt in Europe. Every remark by the *podestà* received at best a grunt, at worst a cutting reply. Having just passed beneath the Rialto Bridge, Renier pointed out the magnificent Palazzo Dolfin-Manin,* where the last Doge, Lodovico Manin, had died a broken man. 'Judging by the richness of his villa at Passariano,' said the Emperor, 'where I stayed ten years ago, he was obviously a Croesus. Yet the poor people who lived around him were naked and hungry!' Renier forbore to point out that Manin had died in abject poverty, having been relieved of vast sums by the army of the Revolution.

Not a moment too soon for the poor *podestà*, the procession arrived at last at the Piazzetta, where the Emperor disembarked, passing between the two columns and onward into the Piazza itself, where three vast tricolours hung, limp and sodden, from the great ceremonial flagstaffs in front of the Basilica. There, turning left, it made its way along the arcade of the Procuratie Nuove, which de Beauharnais had appropriated for the Royal Palace. At the entrance Napoleon dismissed his suite, refusing to attend the dinner that had been arranged for him, and demanded to be taken at once to his apartment on the first floor. There he retired immediately to his room – to read, we are told, the *History of the Council of Trent* by Fra Paolo Sarpi† in the author's own copy, specially removed for his benefit from the Marciana Library.

★

The weather the next morning – Monday 30 November – showed

---

* Built by the Procurator Giovanni Dolfin to the designs of Jacopo Sansovino between 1536 and 1575, it was neoclassicized by Lodovico Manin after 1787. It is now occupied by the Banca d'Italia, and can easily be recognized by the B.I. monogram on its mooring posts.
† (See p. 22 and, for a fuller account of Sarpi, *A History of Venice*, Chapter 39.) Napoleon, whose relations with Pope Pius VII were at the time distinctly uneasy, would have warmly applauded his anti-papal sentiments.

no sign of improvement; nor, indeed, did the Emperor's temper as
he gazed out over a sulky, colourless lagoon.* But fortunately, as
the Venetians soon came to realize, he was no longer in a destructive
mood. Whatever he might have thought of the Most Serene
Republic, that Republic no longer existed. His task now was to
take in hand the city which, as the second most important in his
Italian Kingdom, must be rendered stable and efficient under a
capable – and largely French – administration. The next nine days
would not after all show him as an avenging Angel of Darkness;
they were to be days of inspection, of familiarization, of getting
things done. For us today, reading of Napoleon's only Venetian
visit some 200 years after the event, it might be seen as something
of an anticlimax; but we can be sure that the people of Venice saw
it in a very different light; and by the time of his departure there
probably lurked, in many a Venetian heart, feelings not only of
relief but of grudging admiration as well.

At nine o'clock, after a hurried breakfast, his audiences began.
With him – though, we may be sure, a little behind and at a slightly
lower level – was the recently created King Maximilian I of Bavaria
with his wife and daughter (who was married to de Beauharnais).
One by one, the Viceroy presented the senior French officers,
followed by the Venetian members of the Council, the judges and
magistrates, and the architects and planners responsible for the two
most important building works ordered more than a year before by
the Emperor, sight unseen. The first of these was at the western
end of the Piazza itself, where the ancient church of S. Geminiano,
which occupied the centre of the range facing the Basilica, was

* But at least he could see it, which he would have been unable to do a year or
two before. The vast Granaries of Terranova which stood between the Procuratie
Nuove and the Riva had recently been demolished by Eugène de Beauharnais
and replaced by the gardens which still exist today. This brought much-needed
light into the Palace and gave it the superb view over the lagoon; but – as the
paintings of Canaletto and his friends make only too clear – the Granaries, though
severely plain and functional, made – quite apart from their considerable historical
interest – an important architectural statement; their loss must be added to the
debit side of Napoleon's account.

already half demolished. Moved from its original position about half-way along the Piazza – an inscription in the pavement marks the spot – when the great square was doubled in size under Doge Sebastiano Ziani in the late twelfth century, the church had been remodelled in the 1550s by Jacopo Sansovino, who was buried there and whose son had later described it as 'perhaps the most ornate in the city, being faced both inside and out with precious marbles and Istrian stone, exceedingly rich, and perfectly conceived as a structure'. Later it had acquired a vast number of fine paintings, sculptures and works of art, becoming one of the most spectacular small treasure-houses in the city.

This was the building that Eugène de Beauharnais, with his stepfather's consent, had decided to sacrifice in the interests of extending the Royal Palace in the Procuratie Nuove around the south-west corner of the Piazza and all the way along the west side, providing it with a new ceremonial staircase and, on the upper floor, with a grand ballroom. Six months before, on 19 May, the last service had been held in the church and all its countless treasures dispersed. Among them was the tomb of John Law, the Scottish financial genius who had risen to become French Controller-General of Finance under Louis XV. As such he had been second in importance only to the King himself, until, after the sudden collapse of his 'Mississippi Scheme' in 1720, he had been forced to flee the country. After years of wandering he had finally settled in Venice, where he had died on 2 March 1729. Now, seventy-eight years later, the military governor of the city chanced to be none other than Law's great-nephew James, who had taken the title – from the name of the family estate just outside Edinburgh – of Comte de Lauriston; and on the closure of the church he had immediately arranged for the remains of his great-uncle to be transferred to the neighbouring church of S. Moisé, where they still lie today.

Napoleon, who had considerable admiration for Law, seems to have warmly approved his general's action; but he was more interested still in the second major work that he had set in train – the provision of a proper cemetery for Venice. Burials in a city so waterlogged and liable to flooding had always been something of a problem; there was no more room left in the churches, and church-yards were virtually unknown. The Emperor's most favoured local architect, Giannantonio Selva – who some years before had designed the Fenice Theatre – had accordingly put forward a proposal to make a city cemetery of the little island of S. Cristoforo between the Fondamenta Nuove – effectively Venice's northern shoreline – and the far larger island of Murano, further out in the lagoon. Some advance work had been done, largely to consolidate the banks, but before long the project – which included the demolition of the fifteenth-century church of S. Cristoforo della Pace – had been allowed to lapse owing to lack of sufficient funds. This was not the sort of thing that Napoleon liked to hear. Then and there he dictated a decree making available 100,000 lire for the completion of the work; two years later the cemetery was ready.*

The audiences over, the Emperor and his vast suite proceeded down the centre of the Piazza to St Mark's, for a special mass of welcome and thanksgiving. Once again, the Venetians made every effort to display an enthusiasm which they can have been far from feeling, seating him on the great golden throne which was normally reserved exclusively for the Patriarch and singing a hymn specially composed for the occasion: '*Domine salvum fac imperatorem et regem nostrum Napoleonem*'. Their guest, on the other hand, made no attempt at all to conceal his impatience as he grimly sat out the hour-long service. Almost before the last notes of the organ had died away he was on his feet: striding out through the north door, walking the length of the west front of the Basilica – with little more than a glance at the now empty platform where the bronze horses had stood before their removal to the Tuileries – and stopping only at the foot of the campanile, where he was told once again of

* It was to serve its purpose admirably for thirty years; in 1837, however, when there was no more space on the island for further graves, the narrow channel separating it from the nearby island of S. Michele was filled in. The name – indeed, the very existence – of S. Cristoforo was quickly forgotten as it became absorbed into its larger neighbour, and Mauro Coducci's exquisite early Renaissance church of S. Michele, until 1810 the nucleus of one of Venice's most important abbeys, became little more than a setting for funerals.

that memorable day in 1609 when Galileo had taken the Doge and the Signoria up to the top of the tower to demonstrate his recently invented telescope. Making his way thence down the Piazzetta to the Molo, the Emperor then took ship for the Arsenal for a brief tour of inspection there before returning to the Palace for lunch.

Never, except on state occasions, was Napoleon more than ten minutes at table. Since he was invariably served first, his suite barely had time for a mouthful before he was off again, this time to inspect the defences – such as they were – along the Lido. In the days of the *Serenissima*, the fortifications surrounding the three narrow entrances to the lagoon had been formidable indeed; but they had been largely dismantled during the first French occupation and there was now little to prevent an English fleet sailing up the Adriatic and forcing an entry if it had a mind to do so. Disembarking at Punta S. Nicolò on the northern tip, the Emperor rode through dunes and scrub the entire ten-mile length of the island to Alberoni and the Malamocco port* in the far south. Only then did he give his orders: the defences were to be completely rebuilt, starting at once.

By now night had fallen, bringing with it a thick rolling fog that covered the lagoon in an impenetrable blanket and tried the navigational skills of the helmsman to the utmost. The journey back seemed interminable, and the boat tied up before the Palace only just in time for the Emperor to change for the evening re-ception and to greet his guests. These countless receptions were, he knew, unavoidable; they were also important for his popularity, in that they enabled him to meet as many of his subjects as possible. Coming, however – as they almost always did – after a long and physically exhausting day, he found them a strain and, very often, a considerable irritation. He was not in the best of tempers when he finally retired to bed.

The next morning – it was Tuesday 1 December – saw another extensive tour of the defences: this time, however, he concentrated

---

* The Italian word *porto*, in this connection, means simply the narrow gap between one of the long sandbank islands and the next.

on those constructions which had been designed to protect Venice from the onslaughts of nature rather than of any human enemy. Known as the *murazzi* and built between 1744 and 1782, they consisted of a series of immense sea walls and breakwaters which ran along the entire Adriatic shore of the island of Pellestrina from the Malamocco port to that of Chioggia – a total length of about thirteen miles.* Here once again, Napoleon immediately agreed to a major public works programme under the control of Selva, providing for all necessary repairs to the walls themselves and the dredging and cleaning of the major canals, which would permit ships of up to seventy-four cannon to sail directly to the Arsenal itself.

After a brief lunch with his brother Joseph, King of Naples, who had arrived that morning in Venice, the Emperor dismissed his entire suite. His programme for the afternoon remains something of a mystery; but he was certainly at the Fenice Theatre that evening for the most important social event of his entire visit: a gala performance of a work specially written for the occasion by one Lauro Corniani degli Algarotti† entitled *The Justice of Jove*, with another grand reception to follow. Both entrances to the theatre, the water entrance and that on the Campo S. Fantin, were lit with so many blazing torches that – according to one eye-witness – it seemed like noonday; the auditorium was hung from floor to roof with sky-blue satin trimmed with silver, while from the royal box itself there rose a huge canopy of dark-green velvet, supported on Napoleonic eagles.

The actual performance seems to have been rather less impressive. It consisted, predictably enough, of a wildly sycophantic masque in which the gods of Olympus themselves acknowledged the supremacy of the Emperor, while assorted nymphs and blessed spirits sang his praises. It was, we read, cheered to the echo.

★

---

* Despite their tremendous strength, the *murazzi* were smashed to bits by the great storm and floods of 4–5 November 1966. They were rebuilt and further reinforced a few years later.

† I have searched for this composer in five separate works of reference; he is listed in none of them.

Wednesday 2 December 1807 was an important day for the Bonapartes – the third anniversary of Napoleon's imperial coronation;
and the French authorities were determined to celebrate it in style.
His face still black as thunder, the Emperor received the formal
congratulations of Eugène de Beauharnais and other members of
his suite, and was given a handwritten letter from Josephine – with
whom his relations were already under considerable strain – written
in Paris five days before and brought to Venice by special messenger.
Then, at ten o'clock precisely, he was at the site of the new Via
Eugenia – now Via Garibaldi – which was being constructed at the
eastern end of the city over the former Rio di S. Anna, as part of a
plan to give the city its first public park. Once again, Giannantonio
Selva was the presiding genius. It was an ambitious project, and
indeed a large green open space was urgently needed; but the price
was to be high. Four religious buildings were to be demolished –
the lovely Renaissance S. Nicolò di Castello, with its neighbouring
seminary and home for retired sailors; the Gothic S. Antonio Abate,
with its paintings by Lorenzo Veneziano and Carpaccio and its
tomb of Vettor Pisani, hero of the victory over the Genoese at
Chioggia in 1380;* a convent of Capuchin nuns, known as the
Concette; and finally the early fourteenth-century church and monastery of S. Domenico. A fifth, S. Giuseppe di Castello, is said to
have been saved only thanks to the fervent pleading of Beauharnais's
wife and Vicereine, the beautiful but deeply devout Augusta
Amelia, daughter of the King of Bavaria.

From Via Eugenia it was little more than a minute's walk to
the Arsenal where, on the Emperor's second visit, he attended
the launch by the Vicereine of two corvettes, the *Fama* and the
Speranza, destined for his own navy. The ceremony over, he and
his entourage were treated to the traditional Venetian spectacle
of the *Forze d'Ercole*, in which some fifty *arsenalotti* leaped on to
each others' shoulders to form a human pyramid. Then, having

* All that is left of this once-beautiful church can be seen near the bridge over
the Rio S. Giuseppe, just before you reach the entrance to the Biennale. It is a
magnificent arch by the military engineer and architect Michele Sanmicheli
(1484–1559).

first unveiled a huge bronze bust of himself, he strode off to the Admiral's barge for lunch. The anniversary celebrations continued throughout the afternoon with a regatta on the Grand Canal, watched by the Emperor from a balcony of Palazzo Balbi.★ Later that evening, he appeared several times with his brother Joseph at a window of the Royal Palace to acknowledge the cheers of a vast crowd on the Piazza – illuminated for the occasion, according to the *Quotidiano Veneto*, by 4,094 torches, with candelabra bearing a total of 1,116 candles. It must have been a wonderful sight, for a time; all too soon, however, a sudden December downpour extinguished the lot.

The uncertain weather conditions now led to another of those seasonal inconveniences to which Venice has long been liable: *acqua alta*, or the tidal flooding of the Piazza and other low-lying areas of the city.† The morning of Thursday 3 December presented the Emperor with the unexpected sight of the people of Venice making their way across their principal public square knee-deep in water. He himself, however, headed in his state barge for the glass factories on the island of Murano, where he bought for Josephine a magnificent cup, painted in enamel with Arcadian and mythological scenes, and another for the Austrian Archduchess Marie Louise – whom he was already considering as a possible second wife. That evening, after a long afternoon meeting with treasury officials both French and Venetian, he attended a state ball at the Fenice, given by the Municipality in his honour.

Much of the next two days was spent touring the lagoon. On Friday there were visits to S. Erasmo – with its eighteenth-century fortress – and Burano, the two *lazzaretti* and various other small

---

★ Palazzo Balbi stands on the Dorsoduro side at the first – northward – curve of the Canal. To this day it marks the winning post of the *regata storica*, held in September each year. Two superb Canalettos of the regatta in the National Gallery, London, show it clearly, on the extreme left of each picture; it is easily identifiable by the two obelisks on the roof. A wall plaque records Napoleon's visit.

† Seasonal, at least, in Napoleon's day. Since then, *acqua alta* has increased dramatically in frequency and can nowadays occur during any month of the year.

islands; not one of these sites was in itself of any real importance, but Napoleon seems to have been genuinely anxious to see all he could and to gain a proper understanding of the city – which was, after all, totally unlike any other – before taking the several important decisions which were awaiting him. Apart from the major projects mentioned earlier in this chapter, there were several others which had been initiated by Beauharnais and which he himself had already approved in principle, but various aspects of which still needed detailed discussion. Among them was the establishment in 1807 of an Academy of Fine Arts in the former church, convent and *scuola* of the Carità (where the present Accademia remains today); the provision of a commercial area at the far end of the planned extension of the Riva degli Schiavoni, around the present Campo S. Giuseppe di Castello; the conversion of the Scuola Grande di S. Marco, with the neighbouring Dominican convent and the hospice of S. Lazzaro dei Mendicanti, into a military hospital;* the deposit of the State Archives in a building just to the north of the Frari, on the site of the suppressed church of S. Nicoletto della Lattuga;† a broad avenue along the Giudecca, leading to a public garden and an open ground for military parades; and the transformation of the island of S. Giorgio Maggiore into a free port – a project which was to result, a few years later, in the construction of the lovely little harbour, with its twin lighthouses, that we know today.

On Saturday morning, 5 December, the Emperor was rowed over to S. Giorgio to see for himself the site of the proposed free port. He then paid brief visits to the church, cloister, refectory, library and finally the historic room in which, nearly eight years before, Cardinal Barnaba Chiaramonti had been elected Pope Pius VII‡ – that same Pope whom he had obliged to attend his coronation in 1804, but whom he had not permitted to perform it. In

---

* It was to become the principal public hospital of Venice in 1819.

† 'Little St Nicholas of the Lettuce' was an early fourteenth-century church, so-called because of the miraculous cures obtained by eating the lettuces in the Franciscans' garden.

‡ See p. 18.

the afternoon he went on to visit Torcello and its cathedral, followed by Burano, S. Erasmo and the two *lazzaretto* islands – a demanding itinerary even with a modern motorboat. Returning exhausted and chilled to the marrow, he sent word that he would not be attending that evening's performance at the Fenice of Racine's *Iphigénie*, by a company from the *Comédie française* recently arrived from Paris.

The next day being Sunday, he attended mass, not at St Mark's – which he was beginning to know all too well and which he anyway considered hideous – but in the Palladian church of the Redentore on the Giudecca, which must have been a good deal more to his taste. Refreshments followed in the refectory of the local Franciscan friars, after which he paid a visit to the Marciana Library. Here a collection of papers was produced for his inspection, suggesting that the Bonapartes were descended from the ancient Roman family of Bona Pars and had thus had a long and distinguished history before they settled in Corsica. To Napoleon, always sensitive about his background, such documents were of immense interest; on his departure he left 23,000 Italian lire to the library, 'for new acquisitions'.

At this time too he showed his appreciation of the two most distinguished living Venetians – the poet Ugo Foscolo and the sculptor Antonio Canova – by awarding them high honours. Foscolo had been born in 1778 on the Ionian island of Zante, at that time part of the Venetian Empire. In 1797 he had composed an ode in praise of Napoleon; and though his hopes had been initially dashed by the Treaty of Campoformio he had never entirely lost his faith, and had later even served as a volunteer in the French army. His was a voice which all Italians heard with admiration and respect. If his sympathies could be won back, he would prove a valuable asset; and the Emperor knew it. For Antonio Canova, on the other hand, he had no ulterior motives. Born in 1757 in the hills around Asolo, Canova had been brought to Paris by the Emperor as early as 1802; both his heroic statue of the naked Napoleon as Mars, over eleven feet high – the marble version hilariously fills the stairwell of Apsley House in London – and his recumbent figure of the Emperor's almost equally unclothed sister,

Pauline Borghese, were, by the time of which we are speaking, rapidly approaching completion.

One of the Emperor's first acts on his arrival in Venice had been to strike from his programme the proposed official visit to the Doge's Palace. As everyone knew, he had always detested the Most Serene Republic; and he had wished to emphasize the fact by refusing to set foot in its chief civic building. This refusal, however, had created a bad impression among the Venetians. Realizing his mistake, he had not only restored the visit to the programme but had announced his intention of presiding over a meeting of the Municipality in the Sala del Gran Consiglio itself; and it was this meeting that now took place. The agenda was in no way remarkable – it concerned street lighting, the institution of a secondary school or *liceo*, the construction of new bridges, the excavation of a canal previously filled in and – somehow inevitably – the donation of a bust of the Emperor to the Marciana Library; but Napoleon had a surprise for the assembly. Just before he adjourned the meeting an announcement was made that the heavy debts incurred by the Republic in the last sad years before its fall were to be assumed by the Kingdom of Italy. Not a single one of those present stood to gain a penny from this magnificent-sounding concession; but the announcement was greeted, we are told, with loud and enthusiastic applause.

★

Napoleon's stay in Venice was rapidly drawing to its close. His departure had been fixed for the morning of Tuesday 8 December, and the whole of the previous day was taken up with the necessary preparations. The first of the high officials formally to take his leave was the Patriarch, to whom the Emperor confirmed his decision to change the status of the Basilica of St Mark. Never, since the first St Mark's was built in the ninth century to accommodate the body of the Evangelist – stolen in 828 by two Venetian merchants from its shrine in Alexandria and brought in triumph to Venice★ – had the building been the cathedral of the city. That title was enjoyed

★ See *A History of Venice*, Chapter 3.

by the distant and always somewhat obscure church of S. Pietro di
Castello; St Mark's, technically, had been nothing more than
the private chapel of the Doge, for the very good reason that
the precious relic, remaining as it did in a building under the
jurisdiction of the state rather than the Church, was protected from
any attempt by the Papacy to appropriate it. Now, however, the
Doge was no more. Any conceivable danger to the Evangelist could
be safely ignored; and so S. Pietro lapsed still further into obscurity
while St Mark's at last assumed its place as the cathedral church
of Venice.

His Eminence was followed by delegations from the Municipality and the Magistrature and several other groups. These included
representatives of the *arsenalotti* and the gondoliers, and – interest-
ingly enough – of the Jewish community, who particularly wished
to thank the Emperor for having removed the barriers and gates by
which, in the days of the Republic, the ghetto had been segregated
from the rest of Venice. Then, in the afternoon, it was the turn of
the French – the Governor of the city, the commanders of the
garrison and *gendarmerie*, the senior naval officers from the squadron
anchored in the Bacino and other distinguished residents. The
Venetian nobility had to wait till the evening when, in the course
of yet another interminable reception at the Fenice, they too
were to have the opportunity of bidding their Emperor farewell.
Relatively few of them in fact did so: Napoleon, quickly tiring of
the small-talk and the smiles, made (as so often) his excuses and
headed back in his barge through the bitter cold – the temperature
having by now fallen to minus nine degrees centigrade – to the Palace.

Tuesday 8 December dawned bright and clear, though as cold
as ever. In order to avoid the same immense and unruly crowds
that had gathered to greet the Emperor after his arrival – or possibly
to provide a reason for their absence – it had been announced that
he would not be leaving Venice until the afternoon; it was in fact
at ten in the morning that he emerged from the Palace into the
Piazza with his stepson and – pausing only for a last look at the rapidly
rising Ala Napoleonica at its western end – walked the length of
the Piazzetta to the Molo, where he boarded the same *peotta* that

had carried him down the Grand Canal ten days before. He returned along its full length and headed not for Fusina but for the small port of Marghera where, with the minimum of ceremony or delay, he entered his waiting carriage. Beauharnais made to get in beside him, but Napoleon raised an arm. He had, he said, decided to go to Treviso; Eugène was excused from accompanying him. They would meet at Christmas in Paris.

He never returned to Venice. Probably, he never wanted to. Italy, which had played such a vital part in his early career, was henceforth to be of comparatively little interest in his eyes. For the defunct Republic he had never had anything but contempt, while the city's enduring beauty seems to have been lost on him. When it first fell into his grasp he had seen it primarily as a treasure-house to be looted. Later, to give him his due, he had inaugurated several ambitious projects which proved to be of lasting benefit. As well as providing the city with public gardens and the new cemetery,★ he extended the Riva degli Schiavoni as far as the Arsenal, made S. Giorgio Maggiore a free port, dredged the Malamocco Canal and gave Venice its first effective municipal lighting. On the other hand, although he never proved quite the Attila that he had threatened to be, he was responsible for more destruction and depredation than anyone else in Venetian history. For a few years – a very few – gondoliers may have celebrated him in their songs; but soon, we may be sure, a note of sarcasm crept in and gradually the songs themselves were forgotten.

Today, in St Mark's Square, the deeply undistinguished Ala Napoleonica still stands as a memorial to his vanity. It is crowned with fourteen statues of Roman Emperors; but between the seventh and the eighth there is a wide gap – which, it need hardly be said, was intended to accommodate a fifteenth – considerably larger than the rest – of Napoleon himself. The building work was completed in 1814, when he was (or so it was generally assumed) out of harm's way on Elba; but what might have been called the topping-out

★ Its first occupant was a 36-year-old governess by the name of Andrianna Bozza, who was buried there at 1 p.m. on 1 July 1813.

ceremony, with the erection of that massive statue, was indefinitely postponed. To the occasional inquiry, the Venetians would always reply, with a perfectly straight face, that the statue itself was ready; unfortunately, nobody could quite remember where they had put it.

★

Postscript: Some twenty years ago, on an impulse, I bought a little book in Venice called I dieci giorni di Napoleone I a Venezia, *by a certain Ugo Fugagnollo. I skimmed through it at the time, but it was only when I began to research this chapter that I studied it with any care. It is not very good – its cheap, inflated journalese quickly becomes tiresome. More irritating still, it has no footnotes or bibliography: the author gives us no sources for any of his statements. Nevertheless he seems to have done his homework, meticulously – and on the whole correctly – detailing the Emperor's programme on each day of his visit and filling out his account with liberal quotations from the contemporary press.*

I say 'on the whole' because what distinguishes Signor Fugagnollo's account from our other authorities is an intriguing thread of romance which runs through his book. There was, he assures us, in Venice at the time – staying at Palazzo Sandi in the Campo dell' Albero – a mysterious lady called Countess Nahir de Lusignan, with whom the Emperor was having a passionate affair. Her name was distinguished enough: the Lusignans were a great crusading family who had ruled for nearly 300 years in Cyprus and also, more briefly, in Armenia. But the main branch of the family had died out at the end of the fifteenth century and Nahir, we are told, was born in Alexandria, the daughter of a doctor to the Mameluke rulers of Egypt and an Indian mother. If Fugagnollo is to be believed, Napoleon was mad about her; unfortunately they were able to spend only a single night together as she was laid low with severe bronchitis for most of his stay. When he left she agreed, against her doctor's advice, to meet him at the villa at Passariano; he waited three days for her, but she never turned up. Later she is said to have returned to Alexandria and married an English diplomat – whose name, alas, is not given.

I have scoured the London Library and two libraries in Paris for references to this lady, but have found not a single mention of her. I have also consulted two of the greatest experts on *Venetian history, my friend Count Alvise Zorzi*, author of several superb books on the city and Republic, and his brother Marino, now Director of the Marciana Library. Neither has a particularly high regard for Fugagnollo – who died some years ago – and both have expressed the opinion that the mysterious Nahir was nothing but a figment of his imagination. This view is shared by perhaps the world's foremost authority on Napoleon – whom I have also consulted – Professor Jean Tulard of the Sorbonne. So formidable an array of expertise should surely clinch the matter; but there are one or two questions – or so it appears to me – that remain to be answered. Why should Fugagnollo, whose account is otherwise factual and shows every sign of painstaking research, suddenly introduce into his narrative, with no warning or explanation, a completely imaginary character, giving her additional substance with considerable circumstantial detail? Was it simply to inject a little spice into his story? And if so, why should he spoil it all with the bronchitis? Why, moreover, should he invent for her so extraordinary a name? 'Lusignan' may be familiar to us all, but 'Nahir' – though occasionally met with in the Muslim world – is unknown in Christendom.

And so – perhaps ludicrously – in the back of my mind, a lingering and probably quite illogical shadow of doubt remains. That is why, although I have removed the lovely – if ultimately disappointing – Nahir from the text above, I have felt justified in allowing her a postscript to this chapter. Should any of its readers come across any reference to her, however tenuous, I hope they will let me know.

3. Byron
(1816–19)

> . . . it is not so gay as it has been, and there is a monotony to many people in its Canals and the comparative silence of its streets. To me who have been always passionate for Venice, and delight in the dialect and naiveté of the people, and the romance of its old history and institutions and appearance, all its disadvantages are more than compensated by the sight of a single gondola.
>
> > Byron to James Wedderburn Webster,
> > 8 September 1818

On Thursday 25 April 1816, fleeing from the threat of bankruptcy and his disastrous marriage – he had signed the final deed of separation four days before – George Gordon Lord Byron, aged twenty-eight, left England for the last time with his personal physician, Dr John Polidori. They travelled in his huge Napoleonic coach, large enough to accommodate a bed, a travelling library and a profusion of china, plate and household linen, its sides painted boldly with his family crest. Its owner planned to stop briefly in Geneva, where his friend John Cam Hobhouse would be joining him; but his true destination was Venice, which – as he was to confess to Thomas Moore – 'has always been the greenest island of my imagination'. He was exhausted and far from well – his liver in particular was giving cause for concern after years of heavy drinking – but his character and proclivities were unchanged. No sooner had they reached their inn at Ostend – called, rather grandly, the Cour Impériale – than, as Polidori recorded in his diary, 'Lord Byron fell like a thunderbolt upon the chambermaid.'

The party arrived in Geneva on 27 May, having been overtaken on the road by Byron's tiresomely importunate mistress, Claire Clairmont – who, though he did not know it, was already carrying his child – her stepsister Mary Godwin and Mary's lover, Percy Bysshe Shelley, with whom she had eloped two years before. (They were to marry at the end of December.) It was there that the two poets met for the first time. Each was immediately fascinated by the other, and a friendship was cemented which was to end only with Shelley's death. Byron soon moved into the Villa Diodati at Cologny, on the southern shore of the lake, where – much to his later regret – he resumed his former relations with Claire, who was living with her friends at Montalègre, less than a quarter of a mile away; but her constant clamouring for attention soon became an embarrassment, and by the end of July he was refusing to see her alone. Hobhouse and his friend Scrope Davies arrived at last on 26 August, and it must have been an immense relief to Byron when Claire, with Shelley and Mary, left for England three days later.

He and Hobhouse remained for almost another six weeks in Geneva, setting off again on 5 October. Taking the Simplon Pass over the Alps, they arrived a week later in Milan, where they spent another month. Finally on 3 November they embarked in Hobhouse's carriage on the last lap of their journey, stopping briefly in Verona, Vicenza and Padua, and reaching Mestre on the night of the 10th – a Sunday. There, in driving rain, they embarked in a gondola for Venice. In those days no gondola was complete without the little black box, known as the *felze*, which enclosed the seats in the centre; they therefore remained dry, but could see nothing through the tiny windows till the lights told them that they had entered the city. Hobhouse noted in his diary:

> The echo of the oars★ told us [we] were under a bridge and a boat-man cried out to us – 'the Rialto' – shortly afterwards we landed under the *Hotel of Great Britain* on the great canal and were shown up a magnificent flight of stairs into rooms whose gilding & painted silks showed they belonged to better people in better times . . .

★ For such long distances two gondoliers were usually required.

Byron took to Venice at once. A week after his arrival he wrote to his publisher John Murray:

> Venice pleases me as much as I expected – and I expected much. It is one of those places which I know before I see them, and has always haunted me the most – after the East. I like the gloomy gaiety of their gondolas and the silence of their canals. I do not even dislike the evident decay of the city, though I regret the singularity of its vanished costume . . . however there is much left still.

They did not stay long at the hotel. Byron soon found private accommodation over the shop of a draper named Segati in the Frezzeria, a narrow *calle* running northwards from S. Moisè just to the west of the Piazza. This was the scene of his first – though by no means his last – Venetian love affair. He wrote on 17 November to Thomas Moore:

> . . . I have fallen in love, which, next to falling into the canal (which would be of no use, as I can swim) is the best or the worst thing I could do. I have got some extremely good apartments in the house of a 'Merchant of Venice', who is a good deal occupied with business, and has a wife in her twenty-second year. Marianna (that is her name) is in her appearance altogether like an antelope. She has the large, black, oriental eyes, with that peculiar expression in them which is rarely seen among *Europeans* – even the Italians – and which many of the Turkish women give themselves by tinging the eyelid – an art not known out of that country, I believe. This expression she has *naturally* – and something more than this. In short, I cannot describe the effect of this kind of eye – at least upon me.

The attraction seems to have been mutual: six and a half weeks later, on 2 January 1817, he reported to Murray:

> I am very well off with Marianna, who is not at all a person to tire me; firstly because I do not tire of a woman *personally*, but because

they are generally bores in their disposition, & secondly because she is amiable & has a tact which is not always the portion of the fair creation, & 3dly she is very pretty, & 4thly – but there is no occasion for further specification. I have passed a great deal of my time with her since my arrival at Venice, and never a twenty-four hours without giving and receiving from one to three (and occasionally an extra or so) pretty unequivocal proofs of mutual good contentment.

It is hardly surprising, in the circumstances, that Hobhouse – who was, unlike his friend, a compulsive sightseer – felt rather out of things and soon took himself off on an extended tour of Italy. Byron, on the other hand, quickly adopted a daily routine. 'By way of divertisement', he wrote to Moore,

I am studying daily, at an Armenian monastery,★ the Armenian language. I found that my mind wanted something craggy to break upon; and this – as the most difficult thing I could discover here for an amusement – I have chosen, to torture me into attention . . . I try, and shall go on; but I answer for nothing, least of all for my intentions or my success.

In a letter written at about the same time to Murray, he wryly remarked: 'The lady has, luckily for me, been less obdurate than the language, or, between the two, I should have lost my remains of sanity.'

The language, on the other hand, proved obdurate indeed; Byron's tutor, Father Pasquale Aucher,† himself later reported: 'He

---

★ This monastery still exists on the island of S. Lazzaro degli Armeni, just off the Lido. Founded in 1717, it is now probably – with St James's Cathedral in Jerusalem – the most important repository of Armenian religion and culture outside Armenia. It boasts a most impressive modern library, and the monks are delighted to show visitors 'Byron's Grammar', together with several other Byronic mementos.
† Father Aucher was a remarkable man who spoke ten languages fluently. He had spent two years in England and in 1824 was to publish an Armenian translation of *Paradise Lost*.

did not make very rapid progress. He was often very pettish, and complained a good deal of the hardships he experienced in trying to learn it.' As a gesture of thanks, however, Byron paid for the printing of the *Armenian and English Grammar* on which Father Aucher had been for some time engaged, and to which he also contributed a short preface. In it he writes:

> These men [the monks of S. Lazzaro] are the priesthood of an oppressed and a noble nation, which has partaken of the proscription and bondage of the Jews and of the Greeks, without the sullenness of the former or the servility of the latter. This people has attained riches without usury, and all the honours that can be awarded to slavery without intrigue. But they have long occupied, nevertheless, a part of 'the House of Bondage', who has lately multiplied her many mansions. It would be difficult, perhaps, to find the annals of a nation less stained with crimes than those of the Armenians, whose virtues have been those of peace, and their vices those of compulsion. But whatever may have been their destiny – and it has been bitter – whatever it may be in the future, their country must ever be one of the most interesting on the globe; and perhaps their language only requires to be more studied to become more attractive.
>
> If the Scriptures are rightly understood, it was in Armenia that Paradise was placed – Armenia, which has paid as dearly as the descendants of Adam for that fleeting participation of its soil in the happiness of him who was created from its dust. It was in Armenia that the flood first abated, and the dove alighted. But with the disappearance of Paradise itself may be dated almost the unhappiness of the country, for though long a powerful kingdom, it was scarcely ever an independent one, and the satraps of Persia and the pachas of Turkey have alike desolated the region where God created man in his own image.

Unfortunately this preface was omitted from the *Grammar* when it finally appeared, Father Aucher having objected to the reference to the Turks on the grounds that the huge majority of his compatriots – though not, of course, the monks of S. Lazzaro – lived under their protection. On learning of the refusal Byron flew into one of his terrifying rages, but to no avail. His name, with Father Aucher's, on the title page of the book should perhaps be seen rather as a gesture of reparation than as an indication of his proficiency in the language: he himself admitted that by the time he made the offer he had 'about mastered thirty of the thirty-eight cursed scratches of Mesrob the Maker of Alphabets,* and some words of one syllable'.

*

Emotionally and intellectually, it appears, Venice had more than enough to offer; in other respects life in the city was dreary indeed. The Austrian occupation – which Byron deplored but accepted without protest – had put an effective damper on social gatherings: of the several *salons* which had existed during the last years of the Republic only one of any importance remained – that of the Contessa Isabella Teotochi Albrizzi. The Countess was a remarkable woman. Born in 1760 on the island of Corfu, she had first come to Venice as the loudly protesting wife of a certain Carlo Antonio Manin; but their unhappy marriage had been annulled in 1795 and in the following year she had married Count Giuseppe Albrizzi, member of a fine old Venetian family with a magnificent palace at S. Aponal. He had died in 1812, so that in Byron's day she was a widow in her middle fifties, passionately interested in literature and the arts and a friend of all artists and writers. Hobhouse had dubbed her 'the Madame de Staël of Italy', though even he had to admit that something had been lost in the copying process; nevertheless she was much admired by such luminaries as Antonio Canova (for one of whose works she provided the illustrations) and Ugo Foscolo – the latter being one of her several lovers.

For the first year of Byron's stay in Venice he regularly attended *conversazioni* in Palazzo Albrizzi; but he made no other efforts to mix in Venetian society, and though he already spoke passable

---

* St Mesrob (354–441), with his friend St Isaac I, promoted a cultural and religious revival in Armenia. In 406 he invented the first thirty-six of the thirty-eight characters in the Armenian alphabet.

Italian he tended to be too self-conscious to do so in public, except
when absolutely necessary. Thus, to most Venetians, this strange
milord inglese was a figure of mystery and – for some considerable
time – of fascinated speculation. His night-long debaucheries were
famous, particularly after the Carnival of January and February
1817 which had left him physically exhausted; and endless stories
were told about his impetuous generosity, his sudden rages and his
tendency to violence. It was said that he could never bear to see a
woman eating (which was not entirely untrue; he certainly hated
it) and that he had never seen the Piazza San Marco because he
refused to be watched as he limped across it (which was patently
ridiculous). We are told too that when he went for his daily ride
on the Lido a small crowd was always waiting on the quay beside
the Jewish cemetery, simply to see him.

During the Venetian Carnival the almost universal wearing of
masks by the leisured classes and the wealthy visitors to Venice
made possible a degree of sexual licence even greater than that
which prevailed for the rest of the year. In 1817, despite Marianna
and the numerous other women who regularly beat a path to his
door, Byron flung himself into it wholeheartedly. How he managed
during those hectic weeks to finish *Manfred*, the verse drama which
he had begun in Switzerland six months before, is not immediately
easy to understand; less surprising, perhaps, is the emotional and
physical exhaustion which produced in the days immediately following the end of the festivities on 18 February, the most perfect
short lyric he ever wrote:

> So, we'll go no more a-roving
>   So late into the night,
> Though the heart be still as loving,
>   And the moon be still as bright.
>
> For the sword outwears its sheath,
>   And the soul wears out the breast,
> And the heart must pause to breathe,
>   And love itself have rest.

> Though the night was made for loving,
> And the day returns too soon,
> Yet we'll go no more a-roving
> By the light of the moon.

Perhaps because of his weakened physical state, Byron fell victim in March to a low fever, which continued for a month; in search of a change of air, he decided to travel south – via Bologna, Ferrara and Florence to Rome, where he planned to meet Hobhouse. The journey was several times postponed, partly because of furious scenes by Marianna and partly because he had heard that Rome was

> pestilent with English – a parcel of staring boobies, who go about gaping and wishing to be at once cheap and magnificent. A man is a fool who travels now in France or Italy, till this tribe of wretches is swept home again. In two or three years [i.e. when foreign travel was possible again after the Napoleonic wars] the first rush will be over, and the Continent will be roomy and agreeable again.

He finally set out in mid-April, arriving in Rome on the 29th. Hobhouse, who had been there for some months already, was eager to show him round, but he seems to have preferred riding in the Campagna, soaking up the atmosphere in preparation for the Fourth Canto of *Childe Harold*, to 'poring over churches & antiquities'. He did however see 'a live Pope and a dead Cardinal – Pius 7th has been burying Cardinal Bracchi . . . both of them looked very well indeed'; he attended the public beheading of three robbers, noting that this form of execution seemed 'altogether more impressive than the vulgar and ungentlemanly dirty "new drop" as practised in England'; and he sat to the celebrated Danish sculptor Thorwaldsen for the marble bust that can now be seen in John Murray's publishing house at 50 Albemarle Street. (He rejected out of hand Hobhouse's suggestion that the brow should be crowned with laurel: 'I won't have my head garnished like a Christmas pie with holly – or a cod's head and fennel, or whatever the damned weed is they strew round it.')

By the end of May he was back in Venice, where Marianna was waiting to welcome him. But the summer heat was increasing daily, and like all the wealthier Venetians he was determined to escape it; he therefore took a six-month lease on the Villa Foscarini dei Carmini, on the left bank of the Brenta in the village of La Mira. Formerly a convent, it possessed, he reported to Hobhouse, 'more space than splendour . . . & not much of that; and like all the Venetian ex-marine habitations too near the road – they seem to think that they can never have enough dust to compensate for their long immersion'. Still, it suited him. He kept four horses in the stable and rode regularly along the Brenta in the late afternoon, occasionally crossing in his gondola to the Lido to swim in the Adriatic. At night, after Marianna had left him, he would settle down to *Childe Harold*, writing 126 stanzas of the Fourth Canto in just five weeks. On 31 July Hobhouse arrived to join him.

It must have been some time in early August when the two were riding together that they met two unusually good-looking peasant girls with whom they got into conversation. One, whose name was Margarita Cogni, appeared to welcome Byron's advances to her; but – as he wrote later to Murray – 'Hobhouse's charmer took fright (I don't mean at Hobhouse but at not being married, for here no woman will do anything under adultery) and flew off'. As for Margarita,

she said that she had no objection to make love with me, as she was married and all married women did it; but that her husband (a baker) was somewhat ferocious and would do her a mischief . . . In a few evenings we arranged our affairs, and for two years . . . she was the only one who preserved over me an ascendancy, which was often disputed & never impaired. As she herself used to say publicly, 'It don't matter – he may have five hundred [other women] but he will always come back to me.' The reasons for this were firstly her person – very dark, tall, the Venetian face, very fine black eyes – and other qualities which need not be mentioned. She was two and twenty years old, and never having had children had not spoilt her figure, nor *anything else* – which is I assure you a great desideration in a hot climate where they grow relaxed and doughy and *flumpity* in a short time after breeding . . . In other respects she was somewhat fierce and 'prepotente' – that is, overbearing – and used to walk in when ever it suited her . . . and if she found any women in her way she knocked them down.

Before long, inevitably, word of this new liaison reached Marianna, who was ill advised enough to threaten her new rival. She soon saw, however, that she had met her match:

Margarita threw back her veil and replied in very explicit Venetian: 'You are not his wife: I am not his wife. You are his *donna*, and I am his *donna*. Your husband is a cuckold, and mine is another; for the rest, what right have you to reproach me? If he prefers what is mine to what is yours, is it my fault?'

It was November before Byron and Hobhouse returned to Venice. The horses were moved to the Lido, 'so that I not only get a row in my gondola, but a spanking gallop of some miles daily along a firm and solitary beach, from the fortress to Malamocco, the which contributes considerably to my health and spirits'. In the evenings there were visits to the opera or the theatre, or *conversazioni*; but now they had a more informal – and far more amusing – alternative to those of Palazzo Albrizzi. The Contessa Marina Querini Benzon was by now in her sixties. Twenty years before she had celebrated the fall of the Republic by dancing with Ugo Foscolo round the Tree of Liberty, dressed in a short Athenian tunic which had caused considerable scandal; at much the same time she had inspired one of Venice's most popular love songs, '*La biondina in gondoleta*', which can still be heard of an evening along the canals. By 1817, however, her figure was not what it had been – owing in large measure to her passion for hot polenta. During the winter months, hefty slices of this typically Venetian delicacy would be concealed in her ample bosom, and those sitting next to her in her gondola would be astonished to see wisps of smoke curling up from her cleavage. At about this time, too, she suddenly decided to marry her lover of thirty years' standing, the seventy-year-old Count Giuseppe Rangone. She shamelessly enjoyed all the good things of life, and her enthusiasm was infectious; no wonder everyone loved her.

Hobhouse left Venice on 8 January 1818 for London, taking with him the Fourth Canto of *Childe Harold*. That winter, with Margarita Cogni making regular visits from La Mira, Byron's affair with Marianna came to an end. This in turn enabled – or possibly obliged – him to leave the apartment in the Frezzeria, and he began to look around for something rather grander. His eye first fell on the Palazzo Gritti – now the famous hotel – on the Grand Canal; but he and Count Gritti failed to agree on a price, and in March he finally settled for a two-year lease on one of the three adjacent palaces of the Mocenigo family, on the S. Marco side of the Grand Canal just after its first sharp turn.★ The cost was 4,800 francs – rather less than £200 sterling – a year.

★

At the beginning of April 1818 Byron received a message from the Shelleys, who had just arrived in Milan with Claire Clairmont and his baby daughter, Allegra, now fifteen months old, accompanied by a Swiss nurse called Elise. They planned to take a villa for the summer on Lake Como, where they suggested that Byron should join them. Not surprisingly, he refused: the last thing he wanted to do was to renew his relationship with his former mistress, who he knew was still hopelessly in love with him and was all too obviously trying to use the baby as a means of worming her way back into his affections. On the other hand, he was genuinely eager to see his child; as a compromise, he accordingly proposed that Claire should send her and Elise to Venice. Unfortunately the Palazzo Mocenigo was not yet ready for him, while the Frezzeria apartment, with its small, dark rooms loud with the cries of women either ecstatic or

---

★ The palazzo now bears a plaque, erected some years ago by the Byron Society. It stands almost directly across the Canal from the *vaporetto* station of S. Tomà.

hysterical, was clearly out of the question. He therefore boarded them out for a few weeks with the British Consul, Richard Belgrave Hoppner – second son of the portrait painter – and his Swiss wife; but when he finally moved into the Mocenigo towards the end of May he immediately brought them to join him.

Now at last he could live in a manner suitable to his station. He quickly built up his domestic staff to fourteen, all of them Italian except his faithful English valet, Fletcher; he also started his menagerie, writing to Hobhouse a few months later: 'I have got two monkeys, a fox & two new mastiffs. Mutz [the tailless shepherd dog that he had had since soon after his arrival in Venice] is still in high old age. The monkeys are charming.' His human friends, however, were few, and almost exclusively English. Chief among them were the Hoppners, who seem to have been flattered by his attentions and not in the least shocked by the behaviour for which he was now notorious throughout Venice. Through them he met one or two others including Alexander Scott, a wealthy young English bachelor who would join him on his evening rides along the Lido; but he showed little disposition to broaden his circle of acquaintance. There was by now a steady stream of English travellers passing through the city; but such was his reputation that many of them would simply cut him dead, forbidding their wives and daughters to shake his hand or to look in his direction, while even those who left their cards on him usually received only the most cursory acknowledgement.

His principal foreign friend was a somewhat ruffianly ex-soldier, French but of Italian extraction, who called himself the Cavalier Angelo Mengaldo. In some respects Mengaldo infuriated him. He was arrogant and a liar, forever boasting of his courage, his physical strength and his sexual prowess; on the other hand he was a genuine lover of literature and poetry, and in addition a passionate Bonapartist who claimed to have fought at the Emperor's side throughout the recent wars and to have swum both the Danube and the Beresina under fire. It was this last boast that particularly attracted Byron. He himself was a superb swimmer. In the water his lameness was of no consequence: there he could compete physically with others. More than once, on leaving Palazzo Albrizzi, he would dismiss his gondola and dive in full evening dress into the Rio della Madonetta to swim home. It was therefore somehow inevitable that sooner or later he and Mengaldo would organize a swimming contest. There was a practice race in mid-June from the Lido to St Mark's, in which Mengaldo, Hoppner and Scott all competed; none of them was half-way to the finishing post when Byron reached the Piazzetta. But that was only a rehearsal. The great event took place on the afternoon of Thursday 25 June 1818, with Mengaldo Byron's only competitor. Starting once again from the Lido, the Englishman was already a clear 500 yards in the lead by the time he reached the Salute. Shortly afterwards Mengaldo gave up; Byron, on the other hand, continued the length of the Grand Canal. 'I was in the sea from half-past four till a quarter past eight without touching or resting,' he wrote to Hobhouse; 'I could not be much fatigued, having had a *piece* [i.e. a woman] in the forenoon, and taking another in the evening at ten of the clock.'

The pieces came and went – 'at least 200, of one sort or another', by his own computation. Many of them would fling themselves at him for monetary gain, for in Venice he had a reputation for generosity; but many others simply found him irresistible – although, as he himself admitted, he was now balding and running seriously to fat. Apart from a single dose of gonorrhoea acquired during the Carnival ('the first gonorrhoea I have not paid for'), the life seemed to suit him; it might, on the other hand, have been thought rather less suitable for little Allegra and her nurse. True, in a palazzo the size of the Mocenigo they could have apartments of their own well removed from those of her father; nevertheless there seem to have been some embarrassing moments, since in early August they returned to the Hoppners. By that time, too, Claire was receiving letters from Elise that caused her serious alarm. On 22 August she arrived secretly with Shelley in Venice and went straight to the Consulate.

The following afternoon Shelley called on Byron to discuss the situation, allowing him to understand that Claire was in Padua. Their friendship seemed to carry on precisely where it had left off,

and the two were in high spirits when they left together to ride on
the Lido. On their return they continued to talk until the early
hours of the morning. In the course of their conversation Byron
explained that he had recently leased the Hoppners' villa at Este,
just to the south of the Euganean Hills; why, he suggested, did not
the Shelleys, with Claire, Allegra and Elise, settle there for the rest
of the summer? Fortunately for him, they agreed to do so; as he
later reported to his sister, Augusta Leigh:

> Allegra is well – but her mother (whom the Devil confound) came
> prancing the other day over the Appenines to see her *child* – which
> threw my Venetian loves (who are none of the quietest) into great
> combustion; and I was in a pucker till I got her to the Euganean
> hills where she & the child now are – for the present. I declined
> seeing her for fear that the consequence might be an addition to
> the family . . .

The worsening atmosphere at the Mocenigo seems to have been
principally due to the fact that Margarita Cogni – now generally
known as *la Fornarina*, 'the baker's wife' – had taken over the
running of the palace and was now ruling it with a rod of iron,
terrorizing the servants and putting a firm stop to their constant
peculations, cutting Byron's expenditure by more than half. But
her reign did not last long.

> She became quite ungovernable some months after, and a concur-
> rence of complaints . . . compelled me to part with her . . . I told
> her quietly that she must return home . . . and she refused to quit
> the house. I was firm, and she went, threatening knives and revenge.
> I told her that I had seen knives drawn before her time, and that if
> she chose to begin there was a knife – and fork also – at her service
> on the table and that intimidation would not do. The next day,
> while I was at dinner, she walked in (having broke open a glass door
> that led from the hall below to the staircase by way of prologue)
> and advancing strait up to the table snatched the knife from my
> hand, cutting me slightly in the thumb in the operation . . . Fletcher

seized her by the arms and disarmed her. I then called my boatmen
and desired them to get the gondola ready and conduct her to her
own house again, seeing carefully that she did herself no mischief
by the way. She seemed quite quiet and walked down stairs. I
resumed my dinner. We heard a great noise, I went out – and met
them on the staircase, carrying her upstairs. She had thrown herself
into the Canal . . . They had got her out without much difficulty
or damage except the salt water she had swallowed and the wet-
ting she had undergone . . . I had her sent home quietly after her
recovery, and never saw her since except twice at the opera, at a
distance among the audience. She made many attempts to return –
but no more violent ones.

With Margarita gone, the women came thicker and faster than
ever. Even Shelley was scandalized. He wrote to Thomas Love
Peacock that Byron was

familiar with the people the gondolieri pick up in the streets. He
allows fathers & mothers to bargain with him for their daughters
. . . He says he disapproves, but he endures.

Byron himself admitted to Hobhouse:

Some of them are countesses, and some of them are cobblers' wives;
some noble, some middling, some low, & all whores . . . I have had
them all and thrice as many to boot since 1817 . . . I shall not live
long, and for that reason I must live while I can . . . 'for the night
cometh'.

One evening during the first days of April 1819 Byron went with
his friend Alexander Scott to a *conversazione* in the palazzo★ of the
Contessa Benzon. He had already been there some time when a

★ The palazzo, like nearly all the historic palazzi of Venice, still stands, much as
the Contessa left it. It can be seen on the S. Marco side of the Grand Canal,
between the Rio Michiel and the S. Benedetto *traghetto*.

strangely ill-matched couple entered the room: a distinguished but supercilious-looking gentleman of about sixty, with red hair and whiskers, accompanied by a girl who could not have been more than a third his age. She was short, and possibly a little plump; but she had a radiant complexion under a mass of auburn hair, beautiful eyes and teeth and a magnificent bosom. They were announced as the Conte and Contessa Alessandro Guiccioli, from Ravenna. When his hostess offered to introduce him, Byron at first refused, on the grounds that he did not wish to meet any more ladies: 'if they are ugly it is because they are ugly, and if they are pretty because they are pretty'. But he soon relented, sat down beside the young Countess and began to talk.

This was in fact Teresa Guiccioli's second meeting with Byron; he had escorted her to see Canova's statue of Helen at the Palazzo Albrizzi a year or so before. That first encounter, however, seems to have made little impression on either of them; this second was the most memorable experience of her life. She saw him, she later wrote, 'as a celestial apparition'. He for his part was not yet totally captivated, but as they discussed Dante and Petrarch he was increasingly struck by her intelligence; her youthfulness and enthusiasm did the rest. He wrote on 6 April to Hobhouse:

> . . . I have fallen in love with a Romagnola Countess from Ravenna, who is nineteen years old, and has a Count of fifty* whom she seems disposed to qualify, the first year of marriage being just over . . . She is pretty, but has no tact; answers aloud, when she should whisper; talks of age to old ladies who want to pass for young; and this blessed night horrified a correct company at the Benzona's, by calling out to me '*mio Byron*' in an audible key, during a dead silence . . . What shall I do? I am in love, and tired of promiscuous concubinage, and have now an opportunity of settling for life.

Before they parted, he asked to meet her alone on the following day. For what followed, we have the authority of a curious

---

* At this time the Count was in fact fifty-eight.

'Confession', apparently written at some later date by Teresa to her husband, telling the full story of her relationship with Byron.★ 'I was so imprudent,' she writes,

> as to agree, on condition that he would respect my honour: he promised and we settled on the hour after dinner in which you took your rest. At that time an old boatman appeared with a note, in an unknown gondola, and took me to Mylord's gondola, where he was waiting, and together we went to a *casinò*† of his. I was strong enough to resist at that first encounter, but was so imprudent as to repeat it the next day, when my strength gave way – for B. was not the man to confine himself to sentiment. And, the first step taken, there was no further obstacle in the following days.

Indeed, there was active complicity; for the Guiccioli household included a former governess with whom Teresa habitually practised her French. This lady, Fanny Silvestrini, was herself carrying on an affair with the Count's steward, Lega Zambelli; perhaps for that reason she proved the ideal confidante – delivering notes and messages, protecting the couple's secret meetings in the lagoon and, after the Guicciolis left Venice, providing an accommodation address for Byron's letters.

For alas, this initial idyll was to last only ten days. One evening Teresa followed Byron into his box at the opera and told him, during a performance of Rossini's *Otello*, that her husband had decided to move to one of his country estates in the Po delta and that they were leaving almost at once. All Byron could do was promise to rejoin her in Ravenna as soon as possible. There would, it appeared, be nothing inherently difficult about such a reunion:

★ 'Its peculiar mixture of truth and lies and its remarkable skill in skating over thin ice are characteristic, but it is difficult to account for its having been written at all, except on the supposition that Guiccioli extracted it from her, to disprove what was being said of him by the Gamba family' (Iris Origo, *The Last Attachment*).

† The small apartment kept by many Venetian gentlemen to entertain ladies in private. The accent falls on the last syllable.

though their liaison was the talk of Venice, Teresa's husband showed no signs of jealousy, assuring Byron that he would always be welcome at Palazzo Guiccioli.

Byron, for his part, was not so sure. For all his considerable intelligence and charm, Count Guiccioli had a reputation for cunning; he also had a past that many might have considered distinctly unsavoury. Some years before, certain shady business dealings had landed him in prison in the Castel S. Angelo in Rome; his accuser had been murdered in the street a few days after his release. During the recent occupation of the Romagna by the French he had collaborated wholeheartedly with them – preferring, as he put it, to put himself at the head of the *canaille* rather than to lose his own head to it; then, after the return of the province in 1815 to papal authority, he had immediately transferred his allegiance to Pius VII. His immense wealth he owed to his first wife, the Contessa Placidia Zinanni, who was much older than he was and from whose shortcomings he had found consolation in one of his housemaids, who had duly borne him six children. When at last his wife protested, he had sent her away – the wife, not the housemaid – to a distant country house, from which she returned to die in mildly suspicious circumstances having, it need hardly be said, left him her entire fortune. He then married the housemaid; but on the night that she in her turn died, in 1817, it was noticed that he went to the theatre as usual, and there were many who believed that she too had been helped by her husband to her grave. Teresa was thus his third wife. She was the daughter of one of his oldest friends, Count Ruggero Gamba Ghiselli. According to Guiccioli's own grandson, the couple's first meeting – which had taken place one evening in Palazzo Gamba in Ravenna – had been something less than romantic. The light being poor, the elderly suitor had seized a candle and walked round and round his intended bride, 'exactly as if he were buying a piece of furniture'.

There was no question of the lovers' seeing each other again until the Guicciolis returned to Ravenna; Byron, in any case, was in no hurry. He seems to have been genuinely surprised – perhaps even a little amused – at the depth of his feeling for Teresa, but he could still see her objectively. On 24 April, some ten days after her departure – while he was writing to her almost daily in his fluent if endearingly inaccurate Italian – he could confide in his friend Douglas Kinnaird:

> I have fallen in love within the last month with a Romagnuola Countess from Ravenna, the spouse of a year of Count Guiccioli – who is sixty, the girl twenty. He has eighty thousand ducats of rent and has had two wives before; but he is sixty. He is the first of Ravenna nobles; but he is sixty. She is fair as sunrise – and warm as noon – we had but ten days to manage all our little matters in beginning, middle and end, & we managed them . . . She is a sort of Italian Caroline Lamb, except that she is much prettier, and not so savage. But she has the same red-hot head, the same noble disdain of public opinion, with the superstructure of all that Italy can add to such natural dispositions.

Nor did his feelings for Teresa have the slightest effect on his way of life. On 18 May we find him writing to Murray:

> In going, about an hour and a half ago, to a rendezvous with a Venetian girl (unmarried and the daughter of one of their nobles), I tumbled into the Grand Canal, and, not choosing to miss my appointment by the delays of changing, I have been perched in a balcony with my wet clothes on ever since, till this minute on my return I have slipped into my dressing-gown. My foot slipped in getting into my Gondola to set out (owing to the cursed slippery steps of their palaces) and in I flounced like a Carp, and went dripping like a Triton to my Sea-nymph and had to scramble up to a Grated window
>
>> 'Fenced with iron within and without
>> Lest the Lover get in, or the Lady get out.'

Teresa answered all his letters; but her replies were vague, and left him somehow unsatisfied. It was some time before he discovered that her references to a fever in fact referred to a miscarriage – for which, however, he knew that he had not been responsible, since she had confessed to him when their affair began that she was already three months pregnant. (What he did not know was that Count Guiccioli was probably not responsible either, Teresa having only six months after her marriage taken a previous lover: a certain Count Cristoforo Ferri, described by one who knew him as 'a licentious brazen satyr'.) Meanwhile he was becoming increasingly uneasy about her apparent unwillingness to give him proper instructions about joining her in Ravenna. For some time Hobhouse had been warning him of the risks entailed by this new liaison; but Byron was fatalistic:

> The adventure is so far past preventing – that we had consummated our unlawful union with the proper rites four days and daily, previously to *her* leaving Venice. She was with child, too, previous to this ingrafting and to our connection, but miscarried at Pomposa on the road to Ravenna on her return, and is now on her recovery. For anything I know, the affair may terminate in some such way as you hint at, for they are liberal with the knife in Ravenna . . . Be that as it may, everything is to be risked for a woman one likes.

He finally set off for Ravenna on 1 June, leaving Allegra in the care of the Hoppners and still by no means easy in his mind. Before he had even reached Padua, he was writing to Hobhouse again:

> La G.'s instructions are rather calculated to produce an *éclat*, and perhaps a scene, than any decent iniquity . . . to go to cuckold a Papal Count who, like Candide, has already been 'the death of two men, one of whom was a priest' in his own house, is rather too much for my modesty when there are several other places at least as good for the purpose. She says they must go to Bologna in the middle of June, so why the devil then drag me to Ravenna?

A few days later, finding no letter from his mistress awaiting him in Bologna – 'where I am settled like a sausage and shall be broiled

like one if this weather continues' – he was on the point of returning
to Venice; but on the morning of 8 June he changed his mind and
resolved to go on. Two days later he drove into Ravenna.

★

Teresa, he discovered, had suffered a relapse and was confined to
bed with a high fever. On the day after his arrival Count Guiccioli,
friendly as ever, had personally called on him at the Albergo
Imperiale on the Via di Porta Sisi – despite its name it was a mean
little inn and none too clean, but it was the best Ravenna could offer
– and had driven him to the palace to see her. He was to remain at her
bedside throughout; but, although over the next few days he was
allowed to call on her as often as twice a day, the two were never
alone together. Within a few days he was desperate with frustration:

> My love: pray instruct me how I am to behave . . . I have no life
> now, except in you. My peace is lost in any case – but I should
> prefer death to this uncertainty . . . I feel inexpressibly unhappy . . .
>   It is impossible for me to live long in this state of torment. I am
> writing to you in tears – and I am not a man who cries easily. When
> I cry my tears come from the heart, and are of blood.★

On 6 June the situation improved slightly: Teresa's fever had left
her, and the doctor allowed her to go out. Somewhat surprisingly
perhaps, she and Byron were allowed to travel alone to the pine-
woods that lie between Ravenna and the sea; but her husband,
with a party of friends, followed closely in another carriage. The
situation remained intolerable; and a week later, on the 14th, Byron
wrote suggesting elopement as the only way out:

> If trouble arises there is only one adequate remedy; that is to go
> away together. And for this a great Love is necessary – and some

★ Byron's letters to Teresa are all written in Italian. The English translations are
presumably by Iris Origo, from whose superb account of the affair, *The Last
Attachment*, they have been taken.

courage. Have you enough? I can already anticipate your answer. It will be long and divinely written – but it will end in a negative.

It was, and it did: partly, perhaps, because the lovers soon resumed their former relations in the palazzo itself. Byron wrote to Hoppner on 2 July:

> . . . *She* manages very well – though the locale is inconvenient (no *bolts* and be d—d to them) . . . and *no* place but the great Saloon of his own palace – so that if I come away with a stiletto in my gizzard some fine afternoon I shall not be astonished. I can't make *him* out at all; he visits me frequently and takes me out (like Whittington, the Lord Mayor) in a coach and *six* horses. The fact appears to be that he is completely *governed* by her; for that matter, so am I . . . By the aid of a Priest, a Chambermaid, a young Negro-boy and a female friend we are enabled to carry on our unlawful loves . . .

One reason for the Count's continued cordiality became apparent when, soon after the above letter was written, he took Byron aside and discreetly inquired whether it might be possible for him to be granted an honorary British vice-consulship. Romagna was now, after its Napoleonic interlude, once again a papal state, and he had reason to believe that the authorities in Rome were once again showing rather too much interest in his affairs. Diplomatic immunity might well offer the most certain means of avoiding another visit to the Castel S. Angelo. Byron did what he could, writing first to Hoppner and later to Murray; but neither was able – or perhaps prepared – to help, and the matter progressed no further.

Early in August the Count decided to go off with his wife to his palace in Bologna (now known as the Palazzo Savioli). Byron followed, refusing an invitation to stay with them and putting up instead at the Albergo Pellegrino, from which he made long visits every afternoon. Three weeks later, however, when the Guicciolis moved on to yet another estate, he did not accompany them but remained in Bologna, where Teresa had given him the key to the palace. Now he was perhaps unhappier than at any time since the affair began. On the 23rd he wrote to Hobhouse that he was

> so nervous that I cry for nothing – at least today I burst into tears all alone by myself over a cistern of Gold fishes, which are not pathetic animals . . . I have had no particular cause of grief, except the usual accompaniments of all unlawful passions; I have to do with a woman rendered perfectly disinterested by her situation in life, and young and amiable and pretty – in short as good and at least as attractive as anything of the sex can be with all the advantages and disadvantages of being scarcely twenty years old, and only two out of her Romagnuolo Convent at Faenza. But I feel, and I feel it bitterly, that a man should not consume his life at the side and on the bosom of a woman – and a stranger . . . and that this Cicisbean existence is to be condemned. But I have neither the strength of mind to break my chain, nor the insensibility which would deaden its weight – I cannot tell what will become of me . . .

In his misery he wrote to the Hoppners, asking them to send him Allegra. This unusual expression of interest in his daughter seemed to take Mrs Hoppner by surprise, not that she had shown very much of it herself; she was forced to admit that in the course of the summer she had farmed the three-year-old out with no fewer than three other families, while the nursemaid whom Byron had so carefully provided had disappeared without trace. When Allegra arrived early in September, her father was horrified to discover that she spoke not a word of English or even proper Italian; her only language was Venetian. But he was enchanted by her, and by the time the Guicciolis returned towards the end of the month his spirits were much improved.

The same could not be said, however, for Teresa's health. She had not really been well since May, and her symptoms – 'a perpetual cough and intermittent fever' – suggested a distinct possibility of consumption. Byron strongly urged a visit to Dr Francesco Aglietti in Venice. Aglietti had been responsible for numerous learned publications, not only on medicine but also on philosophy, geology and Renaissance painting; he was however first and foremost a doctor, and Byron swore by him. Once already – soon after his own arrival – he had brought Aglietti at his own expense to Ravenna to see Teresa, and he firmly believed that the doctor had cured her; now, surely, he could do so again. To the delight of the two lovers, the Count agreed at once. He himself was obliged to return to Ravenna, and seemed only too happy to allow Byron to escort his wife to Venice.

Allegra and the servants went on ahead; Byron and Teresa travelled for form's sake in separate coaches, but stayed at the same inn on each of the two nights they were on the road. Before reaching Padua they made a brief pilgrimage to Arquà in the Euganean Hills, where Petrarch had lived the last five years of his life, where he had died in 1374 and where his tomb looks much as it always did. When the road became too steep and narrow they left their coaches and climbed on foot to the poet's ruined house. Teresa recited some of his verses and they both signed – Byron for the second time – the visitors' book, which can still be seen there. The following morning, at the Padua inn, they were much embarrassed to find Countess Benzon and her recently married husband, Count Rangone; any hopes they might have had of avoiding further scandal in Venice were now destroyed. They must have known, on the other hand, that the damage was already done; and after spending a few hours at La Mira they both went that same night to Palazzo Mocenigo – Teresa openly ignoring her promise to stay in the apartment that her husband had had prepared for her.

★

It seems to have been one of Francesco Aglietti's great strengths as a doctor that he always prescribed the treatment his patients most wanted. He gave it as his confident opinion that there was nothing wrong with Teresa that would not be cured by a complete change of air, and recommended a trip to Lakes Garda and Como. This she duly reported to her husband, pointing out that Byron was anyway keen to see the lakes and had kindly offered to escort

her there. There was also good news, she added somewhat dis-
ingenuously, about the much desired vice-consulship. One of
Byron's friends, to whom he had written on the subject, had
promised to submit a petition at once and do everything in his
power to ensure its success. How far this last point affected the
Count's decision we shall never know; he replied, at any rate, that
if the proposed trip would restore his wife to health, he saw no
objection to it. By the time his letter arrived the two had settled
happily in La Mira. (Whether poor Allegra went with them we are
not told, but it seems unlikely.)

They were still there on Thursday 7 October when Byron's old
friend Thomas Moore arrived. Moore wrote in his journal:

. . . left Padua at twelve and arrived at Lord Byron's country house
La Mira near Fusina at 2 – he was but just up & in his bath – soon
came down to me – first time we have met these five years – grown
fat, which spoils the picturesqueness of his head . . . The Countess
Guiccioli whom he followed to Ravenna came from thence with
him to Venice by the consent it appears of her husband (a rich old
fellow, but of the worst possible character, who poisoned his first
wife & has had a man assassinated – and she is now domesticated
with Lord B. at La Mira . . . it would have been safer to stick to his
Fornarinas.) Found him in high spirits & full of his usual frolicksome
gaiety – He insisted upon my making use of his house in Venice
while I stay, but could not himself leave the Guiccioli.

He drest and we set off together in my carriage for Venice – a
glorious sunset when we embarked at Fusina in a Gondola, & the
view of Venice, and the distant Alps (some of which had snow
reddening on them in the last light) was magnificent – but my
companion's conversation, which though highly ludicrous & amusing was any thing but romantic, threw my mind & imagination into
a mood not at all agreeing with the scene – arrived at his Palazzo
on the Grand Canal – he having first made the gondolier row round
in order to give me a sight of the Piazzetta – where he gave orders,
with the utmost anxiety & good nature, for my accommodation
. . . he ordered dinner from a Traiteur's & stopped to dine with me.

Mr Scott arrived – thinks Byron will not be able to get rid of the Countess, unless he will cash those bills for the husband, which this high minded *marito* wished . . . Byron however swears he will not cash the bills, and lays a wager of two sequins with Scott that he will get rid of the Countess notwithstanding . . .

At nine o'clock he set off to return to La Mira & I went with Mr Scott to two theatres . . . actors all disagreeable – Forgot to mention that Byron introduced me to his Countess before we left La Mira – she is blonde & young – married only about a year – but not very pretty – he said to me this evening: 'I say, Tom, you might have been my salvation – for if you had come here a little sooner, I'll be damned if I would have run away with a red-haired woman of quality.'

Moore stayed in Venice just four days. They were not altogether a success:

The Piazetta [*sic*] of S Mark, with its extraordinary Ducal palace, & the fantastical Church, & the gaudy clock opposite altogether makes a most barbaric appearance & is to my mind any thing but great – the only redeemming [*sic*] beauty of it is the Mint opposite the Palace – the architecture is certainly chaste and elegant – The disenchantment one meets with at Venice! – The Rialto so mean! – the canals so stinking! . . .

From the Contessa d'Albrizzi we went to Madame Bensona, who they tell me is one of the last of the Venetian ladies of the old school of nobility – thoroughly profligate, of course, in which she but resembles the new school – her manners very pleasant & easy – She talked to me much about Byron – bid me scold him for the scrape he had got into – said that till this '*il se conduisait si bien*' . . .*
Introduced me to another old Countess, who when I said how much I admired Venice, answered '*Oui, pour un étranger tout ça doit être bien drôle.*'†

---

* 'He behaved himself so well.'
† 'Yes, to a foreigner all this must seem pretty funny.'

On his departure on 11 October Moore called again at La Mira, where he saw Teresa once more ('looked prettier than she did the first time') and where Byron gave him his Memoirs 'to make whatever I please of them'. The two then rode together along the Brenta as far as Strà, where they separated. They were never to see each other again.

It is clear enough from Byron's remarks to Moore and Scott that he was rapidly growing bored with Teresa. The evenings, he confessed to Hoppner towards the end of October, were 'surely longer than the nights', adding that Guiccioli was expected in a week's time, when 'I am requested to consign his wife to him, which shall be done – with all her linen.' The Count in fact appeared in Venice on 1 November, having announced – somewhat surprisingly – his intention of staying with Byron at Palazzo Mocenigo, perhaps as a way of emphasizing the friendship that existed between them and so putting an end to Venetian gossip. Byron wrote:*

> . . . he found his wife considerably improved in health, but hating him so cordially, that they quarrelled violently. He had said nothing before, but at last, on finding this to be the case, he gave her the alternative, *him* or *me*. She decided instantly for *me*, not being allowed to have both, and the lover generally having the preference. But he had also given her a paper of rules to which he wished her to assent, all of them establishing his authority.

The Count's list of seventeen 'Indispensable Rules' is far too long to quote in full. To give just two examples, however, Rule 1 reads, 'Let her not be late in rising, nor slow over her dressing, nor fussy over lacing and washing, with danger of injuring herself.' Rule 10 is simply, 'Let her receive as few visitors as possible.' Teresa replied to this grotesque memorandum with just six short 'Clauses in Reply to Yours', the first reading, 'To get up whenever I like'; but she added a postscript:

* Letter to Douglas Kinnaird, 16 November 1819.

Not even all this would be enough for us to live together peacefully, etc., if you should refuse to grant me the following:

1. A horse, with everything necessary for riding;
2. *The right to receive, without discrimination, any visitor who may come.*

In despair, the Count appealed to Byron himself.

He actually came to *me*, crying about it, and I told him, 'if you abandon your wife I will take her undoubtedly; it is my duty – it is also my inclination – in case of such extremity; but if, as you say, you are really disposed to live with, and like her as before, I will not only not carry further disturbance into your family, but even repass the Alps; for I have no hesitation in saying that Italy will now be to me insupportable'.

To Teresa, this was betrayal; but, as Byron put it,

What could I do? On the one hand to sacrifice a woman whom I loved, for life; leaving her destitute and divided from all ties in case of my death; on the other hand to give up an *amicizia* which had been my pleasure, my pride and my passion. At twenty I should have taken her away, at thirty, with the experience of *ten such years*! – I sacrificed myself only; and counselled and persuaded her, with the greatest difficulty, to return with her husband to Ravenna – not absolutely denying that I might come there again – else she refused to go.

And so, on 10 November, Count and Countess Guiccioli returned to Ravenna; and Byron, heartily sick of Italy and Venice – 'an oyster with no pearl' – prepared also to head for home: 'as I left England on account of my own wife, I now quit Italy for the wife of another'. No sooner had he taken this decision, however, than Allegra – who was by now back in the Mocenigo – fell ill with what Dr Aglietti diagnosed as the *doppia terzana*, a severe form of malaria. Thanks to his ministrations she soon recovered, and on

25 November was pronounced well enough to travel; but Byron, having once delayed his departure, began to procrastinate. The date was postponed, and then postponed again, and when at last it came, on 9 December, he lost his nerve. Fanny Silvestrini described what happened:

> He was already dressed for the journey, his gloves and cap on, and even his little cane in his hand. We were all waiting for him to come downstairs – his boxes being already aboard the gondola. At this moment Mylord, to give himself an excuse, declared that if it struck one o'clock before everything was in order (his guns were the only thing not quite ready) he would not leave that day. The hour struck, and he remained. Evidently he did not have the heart to go.

Nor did he ever see England again. Before long there came alarming news from Ravenna: Teresa's father, Count Gamba, wrote to say that his daughter had suffered a dramatic relapse, which was causing the whole family grave anxiety. He begged Byron to return at once, assuring him that Count Guiccioli fully associated himself with the request. For Byron, it was all he needed. He wrote at once to Teresa:

> . . . Love has won. I have not been able to find enough resolution to leave the country where you are, without seeing you at least once more . . . I believed that the best course, both for your peace and for that of your family, was for me to leave, and to go *very far away*; for to remain near and *not* approach you, would have been impossible for me. But you have decided that I am to return to Ravenna. I shall return – and do – and *be* – what you wish. I cannot say more.

On 21 December 1819 he left Venice, and on Christmas Eve he was back in a snow-covered Ravenna, to be welcomed – by Gambas and Guicciolis alike – with every show of warmth.

★

Neither Byron nor Teresa Guiccioli ever returned to Venice; so the rest of this mildly ridiculous story – which certainly does neither of the protagonists much credit – has no real place in this book. Perhaps the most surprising thing about it is the fact that Byron, now accompanied by his infant daughter and his usual menagerie of assorted animals, remained in Ravenna for very nearly two more years, still occupying the upper floor of Palazzo Guiccioli for four months after the Gambas – including Teresa, who was now formally separated from her husband – had been exiled to Tuscany.★ Meanwhile the furious Count still prowled about the *piano nobile* – the first floor – apparently unable, or at least unwilling, to evict him. In the summer of 1821 Byron sent Allegra, now four, to a Capuchin convent some fifteen miles away at Bagnacavallo, and never saw her again; she died the following year, not having received a single visit from her father.

Finally, on Monday 29 October 1821, he climbed into his huge coach, leaving behind those denizens of his menagerie that he could not face taking with him,† and with considerable reluctance – as he wrote to Moore, 'if my bed had not been stripped of linen, I should have remained cowering under the covers' – set off for Pisa, where the Gambas had now settled, and where Percy and Mary Shelley had been living for the past two years. Even in the comparatively free Tuscan atmosphere the proprieties were maintained: he and Teresa might see each other in company during the day, but their lovemaking continued only in secret, and at night. It was an aimless and basically unsatisfactory existence, enlivened only by frequent domestic dramas and scarcely improved by the fact that Teresa still spoke virtually no English and the Leigh Hunt family – who arrived in strength in June 1822 – not a word of Italian; and there is no telling how long it might have continued but for the tragedy in early July when Shelley, his friend Edward Williams and

★ Henry James, visiting Ravenna in 1874, wondered how he could have stood the place for so long. It could have been possible, he suggested, 'only by the help of taking a great deal of disinterested pleasure in his own genius'.
† They included 'a Goat with a broken leg, an ugly peasant's dog, a Bird which would only eat fish, a Badger on a chain, and two ugly old Monkeys'.

their eighteen-year-old boat boy Charles Vivian were drowned off Leghorn.★

After this the unhappy little circle broke up. When, at the end of August, the Gambas were informed that as political exiles under a papal ban they were no longer welcome in Tuscany, they removed to Genoa, whither Byron soon followed them. Not, however, for long. Since his days in Ravenna he had been toying with the idea of travelling to Greece and perhaps settling there, devoting what might quite possibly be the remainder of his life to the cause of Greek independence; and by the early summer of 1823 his mind was made up. His greatest anxiety was of breaking the news to Teresa; typically, he entrusted the task to her brother Pietro, who had insisted on accompanying him. Her reaction was every bit as dramatic as he had feared: 'a death sentence', she wrote, 'would have seemed less terrible'.

In the early evening of Sunday 13 July 1823 a small boat carried Byron, with three friends, four servants and three dogs, to a chartered brig, the *Hercules*, that was to take them to the Ionian islands, while Teresa and Mary Shelley watched tearfully from the shore. Bad weather – a flat calm followed by a raging storm – delayed their departure by another three days; but by then, to their relief, the two women were well on the way to Bologna. One of Teresa's last letters to her lover had ended with the prophetic words 'I know that we shall never see each other again.'

As we all know, they never did. Byron was to die at Missolonghi on 19 April 1824, aged thirty-six. Teresa, on the other hand, lived to be seventy-three. She remarried at forty-seven, but her cult of Byron grew more and more exaggerated. Over the fireplace in her *salon* there hung a full-length portrait of him, and she would stand for hours gazing at it, murmuring: '*Qu'il était beau! Mon Dieu, qu'il était beau!*' For the rest of her life, however, she determinedly maintained that their relations had been platonic – never anything more than what she described as 'a warm and enthusiastic friendship'; by the end she seemed to believe it herself. In 1868, just five

★ The now obsolete English word for the city of Livorno.

years before she died, she produced her own account of their friendship. *Lord Byron jugé par les témoins de sa vie* was published anonymously, but although its authorship was known to everyone it was not a success. Even her publisher was obliged to admit: '*Je n'ai jamais réalisé jusqu'à ce jour combien Lord Byron peut être ennuyeux*' – 'I never realized until today just what a bore Lord Byron can be.'

4. Ruskin
(1835–88)

I would endeavour to trace the lines of this image before it be
for ever lost, and to record, as far as I may, the warning which
seems to me to be uttered by every one of the fast-gaining
waves, that beat, like passing bells, against THE STONES OF
VENICE.

Ruskin, Introduction to *The Stones of Venice*

'Thank God I am here,' wrote John Ruskin in his diary on 6 May
1841, 'it is the paradise of cities.' He was at this time twenty-two
years old, but still dominated by his elderly, deeply religious Scottish
parents: his mother and cousin had actually accompanied him to
Oxford, where they had remained throughout his three years as an
undergraduate. His studies had been interrupted when he had fallen
disastrously in love with Adèle Domecq, the daughter of his father's
partner in a firm of sherry importers; and on finding that his feelings
were unrequited he had suffered an alarming form of nervous
prostration. It was principally to distract him that his parents had
decided on an extended tour of western Europe.

But western Europe was very different from what it had been a
quarter of a century before. On Monday 18 October 1813 – less
than three years before Byron and Hobhouse arrived in Venice –
the French had lost the battle of Leipzig and Napoleon had seen
the collapse of his Empire. Six months later he had abdicated
unconditionally and submitted to banishment on the island of Elba.
The continental map clearly had to be redrawn; and in the autumn
of 1814 representatives of all the principal European nations met in
Vienna to do so. They were still deliberating when, on 1 March
1815, the Emperor escaped from Elba, and by the time they broke

up in early June he had once again established himself at the Tuileries; there must have been many, in Vienna and elsewhere, who wondered whether the Final Act of the Congress was worth the paper it was printed on. In fact they had no cause for alarm: only a week afterwards he met his nemesis at Waterloo. Europe breathed again.

The Venetians, however, who had had no one in Vienna to speak on their behalf, saw little enough reason to rejoice. Once again they found themselves under Austrian rule: a not very significant part of the imperial province of Venetia–Lombardy, which comprised not only their own former territories but also the ex-duchies of Milan and Mantua and part of the previously papal territory of Ferrara. Officially the province had two capitals, Milan and Venice, with the Austrian Governor spending six months of the year in each; but it was generally accepted that of the two Milan was incomparably the more important. They consoled themselves only with the reflection that anything was better than Napoleon, who had exploited them mercilessly, both for money and manpower. Besides, was not the Habsburg Emperor Francis II★ almost an Italian? Had not his father, Leopold II, been Grand Duke of Tuscany before he became Emperor? And had he not himself been born in Florence, living there for the first seventeen years of his life? Married to a Neapolitan, he at least could surely be trusted to understand Italian aspirations, even if he could not share them.

Alas, they were to be disappointed. As time went on, it became obvious that Francis was a reactionary autocrat of the most bigoted kind, and that the Austrian government intended to rule with a firm hand. Taxation remained cruelly high. Conscription, too, which had been bad enough under the French, was increased from four years to eight; to those who had the misfortune to be called up, it was of little comfort to know that they represented a smaller

---

★ As the last of the Holy Roman Emperors he was Francis II, the designation by which he is usually known; but as the first Emperor of Austria he was also Francis I.

proportion of the population than in French days. The Austrian ports of Trieste and Fiume★ had relegated Venice to third place among the ports of the northern Adriatic. Worst of all, for the average educated Venetian, was the censorship. Nowhere, either in the press or in printed books, was it permitted to express remotely liberal ideas. Even in conversation it was as well to be cautious: government informers were everywhere, and it sometimes seemed that the walls themselves had ears. The result, inevitably, was a plethora of secret societies, all plotting clandestinely against the Austrian oppressors – societies whose activities were finally to lead to revolution.

In other respects – and always providing that their Venetian subjects were prepared to behave themselves – the Austrians did what they could to rebuild the city's economy, which Napoleon had left in ruins. In 1830 they declared all Venice a free port, but this proved less successful than had been hoped; of far greater lasting benefit was the opening, on 13 December 1842,† of the 222-arched, mile-and-a-half-long railway bridge connecting Venice with the mainland. It could hardly have been built at a worse moment: less than seven years later, during the siege, it was severely damaged – and narrowly escaped total destruction – by Austrian shells. But in the long run it was to prove a godsend: before it was built, Venice was normally reached as Byron and Hobhouse had reached it, by gondola from Mestre or Fusina and across the Bacino of St Mark to the Piazzetta – a journey of some four hours or more. Now, from Mestre, it was the matter of a few minutes. Thus the bridge effectively terrestrialized Venice, at the same time spinning it around: its principal gateway was now by what had formerly been, as it were, the tradesmen's entrance – in the north-west of the city rather than the south-east.

By the time the railway bridge was built, the Emperor Francis had been long in his grave. He had died on 2 March 1835 – surprisingly popular with his Austrian subjects but hated by liberals

---

★ Now known by its Croatian name of Rijeka.
† It was not formally inaugurated until 11 January 1846.

throughout Europe – leaving his throne to his son Ferdinand, who was little better than a half-wit and utterly unfit to rule. Effective power passed to the elderly Chancellor, Prince Metternich, who continued the old reactionary policies and was largely responsible for the steadily increasing unrest wherever the writ of the Habsburgs ran – and indeed beyond. This was the prevailing mood in Venice when, on 8 February 1841, John Ruskin arrived with his parents at the Danieli Hotel.

★

It was already his second visit to Venice; on the first, six years before when he was only sixteen, he had been moved to poetry – of a kind:

> I've tried St Mark's by midnight moon and in Rialto walked about
> A place of terror and of gloom which is very much talked about,
> The gondolier has rowed me by the house where Byron took delight
> The palace too of Foscari is very nearly opposite.

Later he had announced to Mr and Mrs Ruskin that he 'meant to make such a drawing of the Ducal Palace as had never been seen before' – a task which he 'proceeded to perform by collecting some hasty memoranda on the spot and finishing the design elaborately out of his head at Treviso'. But this second tour, which lasted for ten days, was even more important for him. 'Everything,' he wrote, 'was equally rich in rapture on the morning that brought us in sight of Venice, and the black knot of gondolas in the canal of Mestre is more beautiful to me than a sunrise full of clouds all scarlet and gold.'

Typically, young Ruskin soon found himself staring at two of the principal corner sculptures of the Doge's Palace – they portray the Fall of Man and the Drunkenness of Noah – and wondering why they should be 'representations of human weakness'. He was still worrying about them thirty years later: this was, perhaps, the beginning of those endless philosophizings about Venice – her history, her significance, her decline and decay – which were to occupy him at intervals throughout his life. At this time, however, he was still probably looking at the city through the eyes of Byron, and even more through those of his great hero, Joseph Mallord William Turner, who had first seen Venice in 1819. Turner was a close friend of the Ruskin family, and little John had first begun to associate him with Venice on his thirteenth birthday, when he had been given a copy of Samuel Rogers's *Italy*, the first part of which had been published in 1822 and which was delightfully illustrated with little vignettes taken from Turner's pictures; soon afterwards his father had bought, directly from the artist's studio, one of his most important paintings of the Grand Canal.

Byron, in *Childe Harold*, had been acutely conscious of the recent fall of the Venetian Republic to Napoleon in 1797; it had occurred, after all, only nineteen years before his own arrival. To Samuel Rogers, on the other hand – who had devoted to Venice seven whole chapters of his poem – her history and her political fate were alike immaterial; for him she was something magical, mystical, that had risen 'like an exhalation from the deep':

> There is a glorious city in the sea;
> The sea is in the broad, the narrow streets
> Ebbing and flowing, and the salt sea-weed
> Clings to the marble of her palaces.

As is clear from his early, highly atmospheric drawings and watercolours, this was also the vision of the young Ruskin. Only on his third visit, in September and October 1845 – when for the first time he was 'heartless enough', as he rather revealingly put it, to travel without his parents – did the scales begin to fall from his eyes. That visit, which lasted for five weeks, during which he was accompanied only by his valet and general amanuensis, John Hobbs, formed part of a seven-month tour of France, Switzerland and Italy; it was then that he acquired that passion for the high mountains that was to remain with him all his life. In Venice they were joined by his friend and old art master, the painter James Duffield Harding. Ruskin suffered his first shock before he had even reached Venice: in the previous four years the railway bridge had been built across

1. The Four Horses of St Mark carried off by the French army (artist unknown)

2. The Ruskin party in Venice, June/July 1872. From left to right: Ruskin, Mrs J. C. Hillyard, Mrs Joan Severn, Arthur Severn, Constance Hillyard, Albert Goodwin. Ruskin had just received a telegram from the La Touches calling him to London: his companions' fury at this disruption to their holiday is evident in their expressions

3. The Market in Campo S. Giacomo di Rialto

4. (*above right*) The Piazzetta. The Doge's Palace is on the left, the Marciana Library on the right

5. (*below right*) *Rose la Touche*: portrait by Ruskin

6. Portrait of Rawdon Brown (artist unknown), now in the Marciana Library

7. Horatio Brown

8. John Addington Symonds in 1864, soon after his marriage

9. Daniele Manin

10. Field Marshal Radetzky

11. Palazzo Vendramin

12. *Katharine de Kay Bronson*: watercolour by Ellen Montalba, *c.* 1892

13. Mr and Mrs Curtis in the Palazzo Barbaro

14. Constance Fenimore Woolson

15. Robert Browning
in 1889

the lagoon from Mestre, bringing the new steam trains right into the city. In a letter to his father he described it as

> the Greenwich railway, only with less arches and more dead wall, entirely cutting off the whole open sea & half the city, which now looks as nearly as possible like Liverpool . . . When we entered the Grand Canal I was yet more struck, if possible, by the fearful dilapidation which it has suffered in these last five years . . . It began to look a little better as we got up to the Rialto, but, it being just solemn twilight as we turned under the arch, behold, all up to the Foscari palace – *gas lamps!* on each side, in grand new iron posts of the last Birmingham fashion . . .

At this rate, he felt, there would soon be nothing left.

Nor was it just the modernization of the city that horrified him; it was what seemed to him the tragic decay of all the loveliest buildings or – even worse – their ham-fisted restoration and so-called cleaning. Immediately he set about recording the fast-vanishing details of all the buildings he saw as threatened, in drawings which were no longer romantic and atmospheric as on his previous visits, but careful and meticulous. It was painfully slow work – helped, however, by a fascinating new invention, the daguerreotype:

> Now at Venice I found a French artist producing exquisitely bright small plates (about 4 ins. square) which contained under a lens the Grand Canal or St Mark's Place, as if a magician had reduced the reality to be carried away into an enchanted land. The little gems of pictures cost a napoleon each; but with 200 francs I bought the Grand Canal from the Salute to the Rialto . . .
>
> Daguerreotypes taken by this vivid sunlight are glorious things. It is very nearly the same thing as carrying off the palace itself – every chip of stone and stain is there – and of course there is no mistake about *proportions*. I am very much delighted with these and am going to have some more made of pet bits. It is a noble invention, say what they will of it.

It was on this visit too, that he made what was to prove an even more important discovery: that of the genius of Tintoretto, made manifest in those sixty-nine tremendous canvases at the Scuola Grande di S. Rocco.

> I have had a draught of pictures today enough to drown me. I never was so utterly crushed to the earth before any human intellect as I was today, by Tintoret . . . He took it so entirely out of me that I could do nothing at last but lie on a bench and laugh . . . As for *painting*, I think I didn't know what it meant till today – the fellow outlines you your figure with ten strokes, and colours it with as many more. I don't believe it took him ten minutes to invent and paint a whole length . . .

'But for this visit,' he wrote later, 'I should have written *The Stones of Chamounix* instead of *The Stones of Venice*.'

The Stones was still a few years in the future; but by this time Ruskin already had the first two volumes of *Modern Painters* to his credit; and it was as the dazzling young author and art critic already making a name for himself that he was described by his friend the lawyer F. J. Furnivall:

> Ruskin was a tall, slight young fellow whose piercing frank blue eyes looked through you and drew you to him. A fair man, with rough light hair and reddish whiskers, in a dark blue frock coat with velvet collar, bright Oxford blue stock, black trousers and velvet slippers – how vivid he is to me still . . . I never met any man whose charm of manner at all approached Ruskin's. Partly feminine it was, no doubt; but the delicacy, the sympathy, the gentleness and affectionateness of his way, the fresh and penetrating things he said, the boyish fun, the earnestness, the interest he showed in all deep matters, combined to make a whole which I have never seen equalled.

This was the John Ruskin who on Monday 10 April 1848, at the age of twenty-nine, married an outstandingly pretty Scottish girl called Euphemia Chalmers Gray, known to her family and friends as Effie. It was she who had suggested a journey to Venice, and her husband had been only too ready to agree; but alas, less than three weeks before the wedding, on 22 March, revolution had broken out in the city, just as it had – or was shortly to do – at various points throughout Europe. John took his bride instead for a three-month honeymoon – if it can so be described, since the marriage was always to remain unconsummated – to northern France. Whether Effie – who was still only nineteen – enjoyed the twelve to fourteen hours a day spent visiting the medieval buildings of Normandy is open to doubt; but the result was *The Seven Lamps of Architecture*, published the following year.

The 1848 Revolution in Venice started auspiciously enough.★ The Austrian forces of occupation were driven out, and the popular leader Daniele Manin proclaimed the second Venetian Republic. It was a heroic venture, but it could not last. In April 1849 the counter-attack began, with the Austrian army submitting the city not only to a sea blockade but to a continuous bombardment from the mainland. Ruskin had been horrified, writing to Effie on the 25th: 'If they knock down Venice I shall give up all architectural studies and keep to the Alps: they can't knock down the Matterhorn.' Fortunately Venice survived; but on 22 August, when food and ammunition were alike exhausted and cholera was rapidly spreading, Manin was obliged to surrender.

Just six weeks later, on 3 October, Ruskin, Effie, her friend Charlotte Ker and his valet John Hobbs – now, to avoid confusion, always known as George – embarked on their much delayed journey to Venice. They travelled via Geneva, Chamounix, Milan, Brescia and Verona, finally reaching their destination on 10 November. Effie wrote to her mother:

We had a delightful sail across the Lagune from Mestre on Saturday having passed Vicenza and Padua on the railway. Formerly it brought you into Venice across the Lagune but parts of the Bridge

★ See Chapter 6.

were thrown down during the Bombardment and they are now repairing it. If I was Radetzky★ not one stone of it should be left on another. It completely destroys your first impressions of Venice and it cost the Italians £150,000, and no good has come of it so far & the everlasting shame besides of turning half their Churches into Mills because they can't be troubled to keep them in order, covered with invaluable Frescoes of Titian, Giorgione, the Bellinis & others and giving all that money for a Railway bridge, but they have been dreadfully punished already . . .

They stayed at Ruskin's favourite hotel, the Danieli. Originally one of the palaces belonging to the noble family of Dandolo, it had been taken over in 1822 by Joseph da Niel, a Swiss; he had converted part of it into a hotel, to which he had given a rough approximation of his own name. Much of it had now been requisitioned by the Austrian army; but the Ruskins somehow managed to secure a large double bedroom on the western corner of the *piano nobile* with an adjoining dressing room and sitting room. Neighbouring rooms were taken for Charlotte and for Hobbs. The total cost was sixteen English shillings a day, with seven shillings and sixpence each a day for meals.

It was an odd time to come to Venice: the Ruskins were almost certainly the first foreign visitors to arrive since the collapse of the Revolution. The Austrian army had just reoccupied the city, everything was still in chaos after the fighting, and piles of Austrian cannon still blocked both the narthex of St Mark's and the arcade of the Doge's Palace. The city's economy had ground to a halt: grim signs of unemployment were everywhere; the homeless lay packed together at the foot of the bridges. 'The lower population here are exactly like animals in the way they live,' wrote Effie somewhat heartlessly, 'and the fishermen's families live in rooms without an article of furniture and feed in the streets.' She was enchanted, none the less, and wrote to her mother:

★ The Austrian Field Marshal Johann Josef Radetzky, Military Governor of Venetia-Lombardy.

It is the most exquisite place I have ever seen . . . [The Piazza] is like a vast drawing room lighted enough by the gas from the arcades all round the square under which sit all the Ladies & gentlemen at their coffee, iced water and cigars with a dense crowd in the centre of men, women, children, soldiers, Turks, magnificent Greek costumes and sky above studded with innumerable twinkling stars . . .

. . . It is so delicious to think that you can never be run over, no carriages, carts, horses, barrows or anything but people and gondolas. The last is the most luxurious conveyance in the world if you can fancy yourself moved through canals of oil. There is no more motion on the green canals and you lie all your length on soft cushions and pass other people in the same happy ease as yourself. I often wish you were all here for nothing could be more enjoyable.

Meanwhile winter was setting in – a winter which proved to be the coldest Venice had had for twenty years: the snow lay thick on the *campi* and the lagoon froze over. In the Danieli, as everywhere else, there was little or no heating; on 10 December Effie wrote to her father:

. . . we sit in a very large room, and although we are at a dreadful expense for wood as each basket costs 2/6 and there is no other kind of heat but charcoal which is unhealthy, we cannot keep ourselves warm all these rainy days but by exercise; John stands at one end of the room and I at the other, we catch each other's balls and it is so exciting and warming that we do not tire until we are very hot. We have also a kind of cricket, and a kind of shell-practice. This is extremely difficult and we are hardly able to succeed as it is throwing the ball in the air to strike a particular point in its descent.

For several hours each day, however, Ruskin defied the cold; and for the next four months he continued the work that he had begun on his previous visit, teetering on high ladders and scaffolds (which he paid for himself), making literally thousands of detailed analytical drawings of mouldings, decorations and sculptures, producing a record of Venetian architecture of a kind that had never before been attempted. He later informed his father that he had minutely examined buildings covering five square miles, had read some forty volumes of archives and had made hundreds of architectural drawings. On 24 February 1850 Effie wrote to her mother:

> John excites the liveliest astonishment to all and sundry in Venice and I do not think they have made up their minds yet whether he is very mad or very wise. Nothing interrupts him and whether the Square is crowded or empty he is either seen with a black cloth over his head taking Daguerreotypes or climbing about the capitals covered with dust, or else with cobwebs exactly as if he had just arrived from taking a voyage with the old woman on her broom-stick. Then when he comes down he stands very meekly to be brushed down by Domenico quite regardless of the scores of idlers who cannot understand him at all . . .

Meanwhile, he was only too happy for Effie and Charlotte to enjoy themselves. Since both were outstandingly attractive, they were immensely popular with the young Austrian officers – to whom, after recent events, no well-brought-up Venetian girl would have dreamed of speaking. 'Many are the cigars,' wrote Effie, who spoke German and was even more unashamedly pro-Austrian than her husband, 'that are taken out of the mouths as we pass.' There was, inevitably, any amount of innocent flirtation, which in her letters home she hardly bothers to conceal; to her mother, as early as 24 November, she writes:

> Charlotte and I are quite used to it now, but the first night when we were followed into the Hotel, although George was with us, by some Austrian Officers, we thought it very funny, but now we are accustomed to it. I half expect we shall get letters from some of them next but this is joking and John thinks it most delightful and when he takes us to the Opera he is quite lively as long as the Lorgnettes are all turned to our box but when they are not during

the Ballet, which is much patronized and a superior thing to our ballet, he says, 'How tiresome,' and goes to sleep in the back of the box to Charlotte's and my infinite amusement. We never saw any body like him, so perfectly devoid of jealousy.

Soon to become her greatest friend among the Austrians – indeed, her greatest friend in all Venice – was Charles Paulizza, First Lieutenant of the Austrian Artillery. In the same letter Effie continues:

> . . . [John] sometimes does enjoy himself. The other day he took Paulizza, Charlotte and I to Torcello. George, John and the two Gondoliers rowed us so that we went very fast. The day was cloudy but we were afraid to put off the day in case another opportunity should not occur again; the sun broke forth warmly and the after-noon was charming . . . At three o'clock we sat down in the same place as before, leaning against the old Monastery of the Brothers of Torcello now filled with slag; a black lizard roused by the sun's heat fell from above on my shoulder but was gone before I hardly saw it. George laid out the cloth upon which he spread cold fowls, Parmesan cheese, Italian bread, beef, cakes, Muscat and Champagne wines – and a copper vessel full of cold water from the draw well completed our bill of fare. John & Paulizza were in the greatest spirits and nothing could be merrier than the two. After dinner, to show us that the Champagne which they certainly did not take much of, had not gone into their heads, they ran races round the old buildings and so fast that one could hardly see them . . .

More than one critic has been struck by the contrast between Effie's enthusiastic accounts of her social success and her sad and sexless marriage. It has been pointed out, for example, that Ruskin

> wrote of Venice with a passion which betrays more than intellectual interest; his paintings reveal an engagement with the mystery and sensuality of the city, and his fascination with the tides suggests that the organic, pulsing, female nature of Venice communicated itself

strongly to him. It is as if the Ruskins' marriage was being consummated through Venice's female symbolism while it was denied in
their conjugal bed.★

For an example of this passionate writing, it is hard to know
what to choose: there are so many of them, one or two so well
known that they are almost in danger of becoming hackneyed.
Here is one perhaps a little less familiar, because it actually describes
Turner's painting of the city rather than the city itself:

> Those azure, fathomless depths of crystal mystery, on which the
> swiftness of the poised gondola floats double, its black beak lifted
> like the crest of a dark ocean bird, its scarlet draperies flashed from
> the kindling surface, and its bent oar breaking the radiant water into
> a dust of gold. Dreamlike and dim, but glorious, the unnumbered
> palaces lift their shafts out of the hollow sea – pale ranks of motionless
> flame – their mighty towers sent up to heaven like tongues of more
> eager fire – their grey domes looming vast and dark, like eclipsed
> worlds – their sculptured arabesques and purple marble fading
> farther and fainter, league beyond league, lost in the light of distance.
> Detail after detail, thought beyond thought, you find and feel them
> through the radiant mystery, inexhaustible as indistinct, beautiful,
> but never all revealed; secret in fulness, confused in symmetry, as
> nature herself is to the bewildered and foiled glance, giving out of
> that indistinctness, and through that confusion, the perpetual new-
> ness of the infinite and the beautiful. Yes, Mr Turner, we are in
> Venice now.†

All the time, however, one is aware of the astonishing contrast
between Ruskin's passion for the city and his contempt for its
inhabitants. In one of his daily letters to his father he wrote:

★ Dr Denis Cosgrove, *The Iconography of Landscape: Essays on the Symbolic Representation, Design and Use of Past Environments.*
† The late Tony Tanner commented: 'The quickening self-excitation of the
passage is little short of orgasmic. The last line can be read as a climactic cry of
exultation, or a deep sigh of ease after consummation.'

Round the whole square in front of the church there is almost a continuous line of cafés, where the idle Venetians of the middle classes lounge, and read empty journals: in the centre the Austrian bands play during the time of vespers, their martial music jarring with the organ notes – the march drowning the miserere, and the sullen crowd thickening round them – a crowd which, if it had its will, would stiletto every soldier that pipes to it. And in the recesses of the porches, all day long, knots of men of the lowest classes, unemployed and listless, lie basking in the sun like lizards; and un-regarded children – every heavy glance of their young eyes full of desperation and stony depravity, and their throats hoarse with cursing – gamble, and fight, and snarl, and sleep, hour after hour, clashing their centesimi upon the marble ledges of the church porch . . .

In March 1850 the Ruskins returned to London; and exactly a year later, in March 1851 – the year of the Great Exhibition – was published the first volume of *The Stones of Venice*, together with three large folios entitled *Examples of the Architecture of Venice, Selected and Drawn to Measurement from the Edifices*. The very first sentence gives us the substance of the whole book:

Since first the dominion of men was asserted over the ocean, three thrones, of mark beyond all others, have been set upon its sands: the thrones of Tyre, Venice and England. Of the First of these great powers only the memory remains; of the Second, the ruin; the Third, which inherits their greatness, if it forget their example, may be led through prouder eminence to less pitied destruction.

Ruskin, in short, sees Venice as a terrible warning – since England, he believes, has inherited something of Venice's mantle. England too is a mercantile power, a free nation that has flourished for some 800 years, enriched by commerce, governed by a secular monarch and parliament, and with a complicated system of political checks and balances designed to prevent autocratic rule. He sees Venetian history as falling into three distinct parts: first, the growth of the Republic from its foundation in the fifth century – at least, if we

are to believe the legend – to the Serrata del Maggior Consiglio in
1297. This was the moment when membership of the Great Council
– effectively the parliament – was restricted by law to members of
the noble families of the Republic. The second part constitutes
Venice's apogee, which he places during the century and a quarter
between 1297 and the death of Doge Tommaso Mocenigo in 1423
(or perhaps five years earlier) – he is frequently confused about this,
even self-contradictory; and the third, the decline, which he dates
from 1423 to the end of the Republic in 1797 – if indeed that
decline is not still continuing as he writes. It is a depressing thought
that Venice should have been on her downward path some years
before the birth of Giovanni Bellini; but this, none the less, is what
Ruskin asks us to believe.

> From pride to infidelity, to the unscrupulous and insatiable pursuit
> of pleasure, and from this to irremediable degradation, the transitions
> were swift, like the falling of a star.

For 'degradation', of course, read 'sex' – the bugbear that haunted
Ruskin throughout his life. He could not forgive Venice for having
been, in the seventeenth and eighteenth centuries, the Venice of
Casanova, the pleasure capital of Europe, the Las Vegas of its day.

> By the inner burning of her own passions, as fatal as the fiery rain
> of Gomorrah, she was consumed from her place among the nations;
> and her ashes are choking the channels of the dead, salt sea.

The three periods, Ruskin points out, were almost exactly reflected
by the three styles of Venetian architecture – the Byzantine, the
Gothic and the Renaissance; and one of the chief aims of *The Stones
of Venice* is to show up what he calls 'the baseness' of the last of
these – and by extension, of the architecture of Europe over the
past 500 years.

When this first volume was published, the remaining two were
still in rudimentary form: and in the autumn of 1851 their author
returned to Venice with Effie – but alas for her, no Charlotte this

time – to complete his researches. This was to be their longest visit: they stayed in the city from 1 September till 29 June 1852. The first week they spent in Palazzo Businello, near the Rialto Bridge, with a friend from their previous visit, the English antiquarian Rawdon Brown;* then on the 9th they moved to what is now the Gritti Palace Hotel but was then the property of a certain Baroness Wetzlar, an elderly Hungarian lady who had been persuaded by Brown to make available a spacious apartment consisting of the five main rooms at the eastern end of the first floor, with three servants' rooms and a kitchen below, all for £17 a month. 'For the first time in my life I feel to be living really in my own house – I never lived at any place that I loved before', Ruskin wrote, somewhat insensitively, to his father. There they stayed till their lease expired on 15 May 1852, after which they moved to the Hotel San Marco on the north side of the Piazza. This turned out to be less of a success: all Effie's jewellery was stolen a month later.

Just before the Ruskins left the city on 29 June, John had written to his father, 'I don't think I shall want to come here again in a hurry.' In May 1857, in a letter to his new friend Charles Eliot Norton, he was to explain why:

I went through so much hard, dry, mechanical toil there, that I quite lost, before I left it, the charm of the place. Analysis is an abominable business: I am quite sure that people who work out subjects thoroughly are disagreeable wretches – One only feels as one should when one doesn't know much about the matter: If I could give you, for a few minutes – just as you are floating up the canal just now, the kind of feeling I had when I had just done my work – when Venice presented itself to me merely as so many 'mouldings', – and I had few associations with any building but those of more or less pain and puzzle & provocation – Pain of frost-bitten finger and chilled throat as I examined or drew the windowsills in the wintry air; puzzlement from said windowsills which didn't agree with the doorsteps – or back of house which

* See Chapter 5.

wouldn't agree with front – and provocation, from every sort of
soul or thing in Venice at once: from my Gondoliers, who were
always wanting to go home, and thought it stupid to be tied to a
post in the Grand canal all day long; and disagreeable to have to
row to the Lido afterwards; – From my Cook, who was always
trying to catch lobsters on the doorsteps – and never caught any:
from my valet de Place – who was always taking me to see nothing;
and waiting by appointment – at the wrong place: from my English
servant, whom I caught smirking genteelly on St Marks Place, and
expected to bring home to his mother quite an abandoned character:
from my tame fish, who splashed the water all over my room, and
spoiled my drawings; from my little Sea-horses, who wouldn't coil
their tails about sticks when I asked them; from a fisherman outside
my window, who used to pound his crabs alive for bait every
morning just when I wanted to study morning light on the Madonna
della Salute; from the sacristans of all the churches, who used never
to be at home when I wanted them – from the bells of all the
churches which used always to ring most when I was at work in
the steeples; from the tides – which never were up, or down, at the
hour they ought to have been; from the wind, which used to blow
my sketches into the canal, & one day blew my gondolier after
them; from the rain, which came through the roof of the Scuola de
San Rocco, from the sun, which blistered Tintoret's Bacchus &
Ariadne every afternoon at the Ducal palace, and from the Ducal
palace itself – worst of all – which wouldn't be found out, nor tell
me how it was built. (I believe this sentence had a beginning
somewhere, which wants an end someotherwhere – but I haven't
any end for it – so it must go as it is; but apropos of fish – mind you
get a fisherman to bring you two or three cavalli di mare, & put
them in a basin in your room, and see them swim. But don't keep
them more than a day, or they'll die, put them into the canal again).
There was only one place in Venice which I never lost the feeling
of joy in; at least the pleasure which is better than joy: and that was
just halfway between the end of the Giudecca & St George of the
Seaweed, at sunset. If you tie your boat to one of the posts there,
you can see at once the Euganeans, where the sun goes down, and

all the Alps, and Venice behind you by the rosy sunlight: there is
no other spot so beautiful. Near the Armenian convent is however
very good also; the city is handsomer – but the place is not so simple
and lovely.

I have got all the right feeling back now, however; and hope to
write a word or two about Venice yet, when I have got the
mouldings well out of my head – and the Mud . . .

Volumes II and III of *The Stones* were published in 1853. The first
volume had had disappointing sales, and Ruskin's father – who was
meeting virtually all the considerable expenses – had advised his
son to make its successors 'more poetical'. Certainly they contain
even more fine writing than Volume I; but they also go far, far
further over the top. The Renaissance, Ruskin maintains, was
Venice's undoing: its luxury, its self-indulgence and above all its
paganism had set in motion an irreversible artistic decline. And the
symptoms of this decline were plainly visible in both the art and
the architecture:

The whole mass of the architecture founded on Greek and Roman
models, which we have been in the habit of building for the last
three centuries, is utterly devoid of all life, virtue, honourableness,
or power of doing good. It is base, unnatural, unfruitful, unenjoyable
and impious. Pagan in its origin, proud and unholy in its revival,
paralysed in its old age, yet making prey in its dotage of all the good
and living things that were springing around it in their youth . . .
an architecture invented, it seems, to make plagiarists of its architects,
slaves of its workmen and sybarites of its inhabitants; an architecture
in which intellect is idle, invention impossible, but in which all
luxury is gratified, and all insolence fortified; the first thing we have
to do is to cast it out, and shake the dust of it from our feet for ever.
Whatever has any connection with the five orders, whatever is
Doric, or Ionic, or Tuscan, or Corinthian, or Composite, or in any
wise Grecized or Romanized; whatever betrays the slightest respect
for Vitruvian laws, or conformity with Palladian work – that we are
to endure no more.

He hated the style, too, for what we would nowadays call its elitism:

> The Renaissance architect says 'I will give you no gay colour, no pleasant sculpture, nothing to make you happy; for I am a learned man. All the pleasure you can have in anything I do is in its proud breeding, its rigid formalism, its perfect finish, its cold tranquillity. I do not work for the vulgar, only for the men of the academy and the court.'

Palladio himself is cursorily dismissed as being 'completely lacking in architectural imagination'.

Reading passages like these, it is hard to believe that in the chapter on 'Castel-Franco' which he added to the otherwise much abridged 1877 'Traveller's Edition' of *The Stones of Venice*, Ruskin attributes what he calls 'the non-acceptance of the book's teaching' to 'the entire concealment of my personal feelings throughout'. Less surprising, perhaps, is the remark made by the ever-sensible Dr Baedeker: 'The intelligent reader will temper Mr Ruskin's extreme and sometimes extraordinary statements with his own discretion.'

But *The Stones* carried another message too. Ruskin believed that the art and architecture of a people depended, 'for their dignity and pleasurableness in the utmost degree, upon the vivid expression of the intellectual life which has been concerned in their production'. In the middle ages, he pointed out, a craftsman working in the Gothic style enjoyed freedom in his work; he carved a capital as he pleased. After the Renaissance, which imposed classical rules on architecture, workers became little better than machines, condemned to mindless activity and eventually to mass production, turning out objects which might be perfectly finished but which were devoid of soul. This idea brought with it a growing concern for the welfare of the working classes. Ruskin had already written in *The Seven Lamps of Architecture* that the most important question to ask when contemplating stonework was, 'Was the carver happy while he was about it?' In *The Stones of Venice* he went further, going beyond the criticism of works of art to discuss the society that produced them. The quality of the one, he believed, depended on the quality of the other.

Perhaps Ruskin's chief defect, if we look at *The Stones* as a work of architectural criticism, is his extraordinary lack of interest in volume. If architecture is about anything, it is surely about the enclosure of space: it must, in its very essence, be three-dimensional. But Ruskin was not an architect, and seems to have simply ignored most of the practical problems with which professional architects have to deal. His great work, for all its thoroughness and immense length, tells us remarkably little about the interiors of the buildings it describes, or even, more often than not, about their ground plans. (We are given plans of the Doge's Palace, the cathedral of Torcello and S. Donato on Murano; but there is none of the Basilica of St Mark or of any other building in the city.) He far prefers to analyse colour, surface texture and decoration. And he is unrepentant. Of St Mark's he writes:

> It is on its value as a piece of perfect and unchangeable colouring, that the claims of this edifice to our respect are finally rested [my own – not Ruskin's – incredulous italics] and a deaf man might as well pretend to pronounce judgment on the merits of a full orchestra, as an architect trained in the composition of form only, to discern the beauty of St Mark's. It possesses the charm of colour in common with the greater part of the architecture, as well as of the manufac- tures, of the East; but the Venetians deserve especial note as the only European people who appear to have sympathized to the full with the great instinct of the Eastern races. They indeed were compelled to bring artists from Constantinople to design the mosaics of the vaults of St Mark's, and to group the colours of its porches; but they rapidly took up and developed, under more masculine conditions, the system of which the Greeks had shown them the example: while the burghers and barons of the North were build- ing their dark streets and grisly castles of oak and sandstone, the merchants of Venice were covering their palaces with porphyry and gold.

After all, he points out,

> The whole architecture of Venice is architecture of incrustation . . .
> the Venetian habitually incrusted his work with nacre: he built his
> houses, even the meanest, as if he had been a shell-fish – roughly
> inside, mother-of-pearl on the surface [?]: he was content, perforce,
> to gather the clay of the Brenta banks, and take it into brick for his
> substance of wall; but he overlaid it with the wealth of the ocean,
> with the most precious of foreign marbles. You might fancy early
> Venice as one wilderness of brick, which a petrifying sea had beaten
> upon till it coated it with marble: at first a dark city – washed white
> by the sea foam.

When he begins to interpret decoration, his enthusiasm carries
him even further – further, indeed, than most of us are prepared
to accompany him: in Chapter XXVII of the first volume, for
example, he analyses six different cornices based on floral or leaf
ornament, two of which he describes as 'the Christian element
struggling with the formalism of the Papacy'. 'That officialism of
the leaves and their ribs means Apostolic Succession and I don't
know how much more, and is already preparing the way for the
transition to the old heathenism and the Renaissance.' Another,
rather more naturalistic cornice he unhesitatingly identifies as 'Prot-
estantism – a slight touch of dissent, hardly amounting to a schism,
in those falling leaves'.

Ruskin's hatred of Roman Catholicism comes through again
and again, to the point where one begins to wonder how he seems
so effortlessly to reconcile it with his admiration for the high
morality of the medieval Venetians, all of them, of course, Catholics
to a man. The probable answer lies in the traditional Venetian
attitude to the Papacy, which was informed from earliest times by
a robust republicanism and feeling for independence. It was first
demonstrated after the arrival in Venice of the body of St Mark,
stolen from Alexandria in 828. The Venetians did not consign it to
their cathedral, S. Pietro di Castello, since by doing so they would
have subjected it to papal authority; instead, they built a special

basilica to receive it, the predecessor of the present St Mark's, making it clear at the outset that the new building – which was connected to the Doge's Palace by an interior passage – was technically the private chapel of the Doge. Venice's greatest treasure was thus, from the outset, the property of the civil power. This sturdy independence was to continue long after the end of the Middle Ages, and indeed all through what Ruskin saw as the age of decadence; the most obvious example was Venice's open defiance of a papal interdict (in fact the fourth in her history) in May 1606, when Doge Leonardo Donà – advised by the Servite friar Paolo Sarpi – ordered all churchmen, from patriarchs to the humblest vicars, to ignore the ban of the Church. They were to continue as before with the cure of the souls of the faithful and the celebration of the mass, praying in particular that God would lead the Pope to see the error of his ways. For Ruskin the Venetians had always been proto-Protestants, centuries before their time.

His loathing of Renaissance architecture also enabled him to admire St Mark's as a building at a time when it was seen by most of his contemporaries to be utterly barbaric. As we all know nowadays, it is quite the reverse: Byzantine architecture of the highest possible sophistication, modelled on Constantine's Church of the Holy Apostles in Constantinople. Together with Ravenna, which was the capital of the Byzantine Exarchate of Italy from 540 to 727 but which then completely severed its Byzantine connections, Venice remains the most Byzantine city in western Europe, and one which willingly gave its allegiance to the Emperor in Constantinople for the first three centuries of its existence. Thanks to those two and a half miles of shallow water – and, let it never be forgotten, shallow water is a far more effective defence than deep – which separated them and protected them from their enemies on the mainland, the Venetians never, in those early centuries, felt part of Italy. They were merchants, first, last and always; they kept their eyes fixed firmly on the East, the source of all their wealth, and above all on the richest, most sumptuous city in the world, Constantinople. Small wonder, then, that even after they had declared their independent Republic in 727 they remained, for another five

centuries and more, under the cultural and artistic influence of
Byzantium.

Thanks entirely to his love for St Mark's, John Ruskin was
perhaps the first western European to champion Byzantine art
and architecture, and of course the Byzantine art of mosaic,
which can be studied there more thoroughly than anywhere else
in the Orthodox world. He writes of the mosaics, it must be
admitted, slightly patronizingly; but he accepts and admires
their power:

> The whole church may be seen as a great Book of Common Prayer;
> the mosaics were its illuminations, and the common people of the
> time were taught their Scripture history by means of them . . . They
> had no other Bible, and – Protestants do not often enough consider
> this – *could* have no other. We find it somewhat difficult to furnish
> our poor with printed Bibles; consider what the difficulty must have
> been when they could be given only in manuscript . . . I have to
> deprecate the idea of [the mosaics] being in any sense barbarous . . .
> They have characters in them of a very noble kind; nor are they by
> any means devoid of the remains of the science of the later Roman
> Empire. The character of the features is almost always fine, the
> expression stern and quiet, and very solemn, the attitudes and
> draperies always majestic in the single figures, and in those of the
> groups which are not in violent action; while the bright colouring
> and disregard of chiaroscuro cannot be regarded as imperfections,
> since they are the only means by which the figures could be rendered
> clearly intelligible in the distance and darkness of the vaulting. So
> far am I from considering them barbarous, that I believe of all works
> of religious art whatsoever, these, and such as these, have been the
> most effective.

So much for the Byzantine style; Volume II then brings us
to what is arguably the most important chapter in the entire
book: Chapter VI, 'The Nature of Gothic'. Ruskin stresses
above all

its perpetual change, both in design and execution, [its ornament standing out] in prickly independence and frosty fortitude, jutting into crockets and freezing into pinnacles; here starting up into a monster, there germinating into a blossom, anon knitting itself into a branch, alternately thorny, bossy, and bristly, or writhed into every form of nervous entanglement . . . It is that strange *disquietude* of the Gothic spirit that is its greatness; that restlessness of the dreaming mind, that wanders hither and thither among the niches, and flickers feverishly around the pinnacles, and frets and fades in labyrinthine knots and shadows along wall and roof, and yet is not satisfied, nor shall be satisfied.

Not unlike, perhaps, John Ruskin himself.

Of all the Gothic buildings in Venice, the greatest is the Doge's Palace – for Ruskin, 'the central building of the world'.

It had always appeared to me most strange that there should be in no part of the city any incipient or imperfect types of the form of the Ducal Palace; it was difficult to believe that so mighty a building had been the conception of one man . . . and yet impossible, had it been otherwise, but that some early examples of approximate Gothic form must exist. There is not one . . . The fact is, that the Ducal Palace was the great work of Venice at this period, itself the principal effort of her imagination, employing her best architects in its masonry, and her best painters in its decoration, for a long series of years.

But the building, like so many Venetian buildings during the Austrian occupation, was in perilous state. So 'rent and worn' were the massive capitals of the lower arcade – one had already fragmented into more than thirty pieces – that Ruskin doubted whether it would survive another five years. A vast programme of restoration was embarked upon in 1876 and continued for the next thirteen years. In the course of it, thirteen out of the thirty-seven intricately carved capitals on the lower storey, and twenty-seven of the seventy-three on the upper level, were replaced by copies, each copy representing between eighteen months' and two years' work for the sculptor before being carefully stained and blackened to give it the appearance of age.★

It is probably just as well that Ruskin never saw the Palace in its final restored state; he would certainly have hated it. As he wrote in *The Seven Lamps of Architecture*:

> It is *impossible*, as impossible as to raise the dead, to restore anything that has ever been great and beautiful in architecture . . . That spirit which is given only by the hand and eye of the workman can never be recalled . . . Do not let us talk then of restoration. The thing is a lie from beginning to end.

The pictures were in even worse state than the buildings, but he felt about them in much the same way. Venetian paintings, he wrote, are

> almost universally neglected, whitewashed by custodes, shot at by soldiers, suffered to drop from the walls piecemeal in powder and rags by society in general; but which is an advantage more than counterbalancing all this evil, they are not often 'restored'. Whatever is left of them, however ruinous, however obscured and defiled, is almost always *the real thing*; there are no fresh readings: and therefore the greatest treasures of art which Europe at this moment possesses are pieces of old plaster on ruinous brick walls, where the lizards burrow and bask, and which few other living creatures ever approach: and torn sheets of dim canvas in waste corners of churches; and mildewed stains, in the shape of human figures, on the wall of dark chambers, which now and then an exploring traveller causes to be unlocked by their tottering custode, looks hastily round, and retreats from in a weary satisfaction at his accomplished duty.

★ The original damaged capitals were transferred to a ground-floor room within the Palace, where a few years ago they were carefully restored by the Venice in Peril Fund.

It was in June 1853, just after the publication of the last two volumes of *The Stones*, that Ruskin and Effie went on that fateful holiday at Glenfinlas in the Scottish Highlands, accompanied by John Everett Millais and his brother William. As everyone knows, Millais and Effie fell passionately in love, and the following year Effie left Ruskin for ever. After the marriage was annulled on the grounds of her husband's 'incurable impotency' she married Millais on 3 July 1855. Though her life with him had its ups and downs, she was to bear him no fewer than eight children.

Ruskin had never paid much attention to Effie, and after the pain and embarrassment was over his life continued much as before. The year 1856 saw the publication of Volumes III and IV of *Modern Painters*, Volume V following four years later in 1860. Looking at the great Venetians of the sixteenth century, he reverted to one of his favourite themes, the distinction in a painting between high moral feeling on the one hand and base sensuality on the other. But his opinions were by now rapidly changing:

> Perhaps when you see one of Titian's splendidly passionate subjects and find Veronese making the Marriage in Cana one blaze of worldly pomp, you imagine that Titian must have been a sensualist and Veronese an unbeliever.

In the old days he would certainly have thought so; but he had now himself set off on his own personal road to Damascus – or, more accurately, his road *from* Damascus, since he was in fact moving in the opposite direction. The great truth to which his eyes were finally opened was not that of Christianity but of art. That Old Testament wrath of his younger days was gone: he could now write:

> No Venetian painter ever worked with any aim beyond that of delighting the eye, or expressing fancies agreeable to himself or flattering to his nation. They could not be either, unless they were religious. But he did not desire the religion. He desired the delight. The Assumption is a noble picture, because Titian believed in the

Madonna. But he did not paint it to make anyone else believe in her. He painted it, because he enjoyed rich masses of red and blue, and faces flushed with sunshine . . . Other men used their effete faiths and mean faculties with a high moral purpose. The Venetian gave the most earnest faith, and the lordliest faculty, to gild the shadows of an antechamber, or heighten the splendours of a holiday.

It is impossible not to speculate on the degree to which this dramatic change of attitude might have been influenced by a new overriding passion in Ruskin's life, a passion which was soon to become an obsession. He had first met little Rose La Touche in 1858, when he was approaching forty and she was ten. Five years later he knew that he was in love with her, and in 1866, when she was eighteen, he proposed. She, after some hesitation, asked him to wait three years. By 1869, however, her parents were violently against the marriage, which seemed to them unhealthy; there were also worries, which seem to have been spread by Effie, that if it were to take place and Rose were to have any children, then the previous annulment would itself be nullified and those children would be illegitimate. Still besotted and emotionally highly unstable, Ruskin went off that summer to Verona, from which he made several short visits to Venice – his first for seventeen years. There he met the painter William Holman Hunt, and the two of them together studied Tintoretto's *Annunciation* at the Scuola di S. Rocco; but his greatest excitement was reserved for Carpaccio's great St Ursula cycle in the Accademia. He had known it, of course, all his life; but now it was transformed, because now, for him, St Ursula *was* Rose La Touche. Returning to Venice in May 1870 and again in June 1872, he found himself still more obsessed by what he believed to be the identity of the two young women.

But Rose was by this time gravely ill. The precise nature of her illness is unknown, though it seems to have been largely psychological. At all events she grew rapidly worse, and died in Dublin on 25 May 1875. 'That death,' wrote Ruskin, 'is very bad for me, *seal* of a great fountain of sorrow which can never now ebb away; a dark lake in the fields of life as one looks back.'

On Friday 8 September 1876 he arrived in Venice on his tenth and penultimate visit, staying this time at the Grand Hotel. By now his mental balance was growing ever more precarious. Carpaccio's St Ursula still haunted him: he even had the first painting of the cycle – depicting the saint in her bed, dreaming that she was being visited by an angel – taken down from the wall for copying, and would sit alone staring at it for hours at a time. Fortunately for him, however, he had work to do. At this time a young man of thirty-one, Count Alvise Zorzi, having campaigned successfully to save the baroque (and admittedly hideous) church of S. Moisè from demolition, was beginning a campaign against the insensitive restorations going on in the Basilica; Ruskin invited him to his hotel and made him read extracts from the furious polemic he had written; so impressed was he that he immediately offered to finance the publication of the book, promising in addition to write a long letter which would serve as an introduction and put his by now immense international reputation behind it. His efforts were gratifyingly successful: the restoration work was suspended, until in 1880 a commission of inquiry upheld the protesters' case.

In February 1877 Ruskin left the Grand Hotel for what is now the Pensione Calcina on the Zattere, principally to save money but also the better to concentrate on his last work on Venice, *St Mark's Rest*. The subtitle he first proposed for it was *The History of Venice Written for the Guidance of English Travellers While They Visit Her Ruins*; but this he soon changed to *Written for the Help of the Few Travellers Who Still Care for Her Monuments*. It is effectively a guide for pilgrims rather than for travellers, concentrating on religious shrines rather than works of art or architecture; a cry of protest against Murray's tourist guides, which stood for secularism and everything he hated. But it is also the work of a profoundly unbalanced mind, as when he addresses the reader:

VIVA SAN MARCO! You wretched little cast-iron gas-pipe of a cockney that you are, who insist that your soul's your own . . . as

if anybody else would ever care to have it! Is there yet life enough
in the molecules, and plasm, and general mess of the making of you,
to feel for an instant what that cry once meant, upon the lips
of men?

Insofar as *St Mark's Rest* is a history at all, it is – as always with
Ruskin's historical writing – selective, tendentious and muddled to
the point where he constantly contradicts himself. For those who
are fascinated by every aspect of the writer, it is a book that must
be read. But it is not to be trusted an inch.

Ruskin left Venice on 23 May 1877. Over the following ten
years – during which he was twice appointed Slade Professor of
Art at Oxford and twice resigned the professorship – he suffered a
series of mental breakdowns. Most of the time he lived quietly
at Brantwood, the house he had bought sight unseen in 1871,
on Coniston Water in the Lake District. Not till 1888 did he go
once again to Venice, this time in the company of the nineteen-
year-old future architect Detmar Blow. The visit was not a success:
what he called 'the elements of imagination which haunt me here'
were too much for him, and after a few miserable days Blow had
to take him away. In Paris, on the way home, Ruskin broke down
completely.

John Ruskin's long love–hate relationship with Venice was over;
and for him the future outlook for the city looked bleak indeed:

> I have said that the crowds of travellers of different nations, who
> have lately inundated Italy, have not yet deprived the city of Venice
> of much of its original character, although its change of government
> and withering state of prosperity had brought the shade of melan-
> choly upon its beauty which is rapidly increasing, and will increase,
> until the waves which have been the ministers of majesty become
> her sepulchre.

Herein, where Venice is concerned, lies the immense importance
of John Ruskin today. We cannot hope to agree with him in
everything that he said and wrote about the city. Historically, he

tended to see what he wished to see and ignore the rest; and even artistically, he was always so captivated by the surface detail – by the crockets and cusps and mouldings – that he failed, all too often, to see the wood for the trees. All his life, however, he was supremely conscious of the fact that Venice is far, far more than the sum of her buildings – that the ultimate miracle in this most miraculous of cities is not St Mark's or the Doge's Palace or the Frari or the Ca' d'Oro; it is the *ensemble*, Venice herself. And he was also well aware – at least after his third visit, when he had compared the rate of decay to 'that of a lump of sugar in hot tea' – that Venice was in mortal danger.

Nowadays this is common knowledge; the ever-increasing frequency of the so-called *acqua alta* – a hundred or more in a single year – alone gives more than sufficient proof. But in the nineteenth century this was not generally recognized; indeed it was not until after the great flood of November 1966 that the world awoke to the realization of what was happening to its most beautiful and irreplaceable city. It is astonishing to find, not once but again and again in Ruskin's work – some of it dating from a century and a half ago – warnings like the one above.

And he sees other dangers too – dangers which in his day were imperceptible, but which are beginning to assume dimensions almost as alarming as that of the waters themselves. 'The crowds of travellers of different nations, who have lately inundated Italy', he writes; if he could only see them today . . . The resident population of Venice – which has halved since the end of the last war – now stands at little over 60,000: small indeed when compared with the 14 million tourists who descend on the city every year, and who are, quite literally, wearing it away. The numbers that Ruskin saw and deplored must have been infinitesimal in comparison; but he, and he alone, recognized the thin end of the wedge.

Thus John Ruskin was not just the first to draw attention to the fact that Venice was in mortal peril; he was the only voice to do so for well over a century. And, of course, his was the most influential voice of all. No one has ever thought so long and hard about Venice as he did, just as no one has written of it so magically.

At the time of writing, while work has not yet begun on the only scheme – that of moveable gates across the three entrances to the lagoon – that can ensure the city's survival, we need him more than ever.

5. The Browns
(1833–1926)

Many a time hath banish'd Norfolk fought
For Jesu Christ in glorious Christian field,
Streaming the ensign of the Christian cross
Against black pagans, Turks, and Saracens,
And toil'd with works of war, retired himself
To Italy; and there at Venice gave
His body to that pleasant country's earth,
And his pure soul unto his captain Christ,
Under whose colours he had fought so long.

William Shakespeare, *Richard II*

When people asked Rawdon Brown why he had settled in Venice, he used to tell them that he had originally come to look for the tomb of Thomas Mowbray, Duke of Norfolk. Mowbray, banished by Richard II in 1398 after his quarrel with Henry Bolingbroke, had come to the city early the following year in the hopes of borrowing a galley in which to make a pilgrimage to the Holy Land; but he would hardly have had time to make the journey, since we know that he was in Venice when he died of the plague on 22 September 1399. He left instructions that his body should be brought back to England, but nothing seems to have been done about it until 1532, when Thomas Howard, third Duke of Norfolk – uncle of Anne Boleyn – made a formal application through the Venetian Ambassador in London for its return. His request was granted; the ornate tombstone, however, without inscription but bearing Mowbray's badge – with that of King Richard and, rather more surprisingly, Bolingbroke – was left behind in Venice and was subsequently set into the wall of the outer gallery of the Doge's

Palace, facing the island of S. Giorgio Maggiore, England's patron saint. There it remained until 1810, when the occupying French, recognizing the arms of their English enemy, ordered it to be defaced. Fortunately the poor mason detailed for the work – whose name, Domenico Spiera, deserves to be remembered by us all – could not bring himself to commit such vandalism and instead set the stone face downwards into the pavement.

All this we learn from Brown himself. 'On Christmas Eve 1839,' he records,

> the writer, in making inquiries for this monumental tablet, had the good fortune to discover the humble antiquary by whom it had been concealed, then the only person living acquainted with the transaction; by this man's assistance he was enabled to recover the stone. For its future safe custody he sent it to England, and presented it to one of Thomas Mowbray's descendants.*

This descendant was Mr Henry Howard of Corby Castle, near Carlisle; and the stone remains at the castle to this day.†

It was typical of Rawdon Brown that he should somehow have succeeded in finding what he was after, even though it had taken him over six years to do it. Born in 1806 and educated at Charterhouse, he seems to have had an unhappy youth, as a result of which he had broken off all family ties. He had fallen in love with Venice on his very first visit at the age of twenty-seven, and seems to have made his home there shortly thereafter. Where he first settled is uncertain; but we know that in 1838 he bought the exquisite little late-fifteenth-century Palazzo Dario for £480, leaving it only four years later for the Palazzo Businello, further along the Grand Canal

---

* Preface to Vol. I of Brown's *Calendar of State Papers and Manuscripts Relating to English Affairs Existing in the Archives and Collections of Venice and Other Libraries of North Italy* (London, 1864).

† A photograph will be found in Nikolaus Pevsner's *Cumberland and Westmorland*. The author writes in the Introduction: 'The heraldic slab . . . remains a mystery. It is said to have been brought from St Mark's, but it is neither Italian in design or workmanship nor English.'

near the Rialto.★ The story – repeated in the *Dictionary of National Biography*† – that he never left the city again is not strictly true, though the lamentable sonnet of his friend Robert Browning – telling of how one day, when he actually had his bags packed ready to leave, he glanced out of the window and changed his mind – may well be founded on fact.‡ What is certain is that for the next fifty years he was a fixture of the city, its best-known and best-respected foreign resident – much as Consul Joseph Smith had been during the previous century. Brown himself would have been happy with a consulship: he was not a rich man, and although, as Lord Acton noted, 'his modest income went a long way in the city of deserted palaces', the small salary would have been welcome. Alas, it never came; but he too, though in less spectacular fashion, earned his country's gratitude – in the Archives of Venice, which

---

★ The Dario is in Dorsoduro, almost immediately opposite what is now the Gritti Palace Hotel; it is immediately recognizable from the roundels of red and green marble inlaid in its façade. The Businello is on the same side of the Canal, on the corner of the Rio dei Meloni, next to the obelisked Palazzo Papadopoli. It dates from the middle of the thirteenth century, and despite many alterations has retained its original Byzantine arcading on the two upper floors.

† The *Dictionary* also gives Brown's date of birth as 1803; he was in fact born in 1806. It is hoped that both mistakes will be rectified in the *New D.N.B.*, currently in preparation.

‡   Sighed Rawdon Brown: 'Yes, I'm departing, Toni!
        I needs must, just this once before I die,
        Revisit England: *Anglus* Brown am I,
        Although my heart's Venetian. Yes, old crony –
        Venice and London – London's 'Death the bony'
        Compared with Life – that's Venice! What a sky,
        A sea, this morning! One last look! Good-bye.
        Ca' Pesaro! No lion – I'm a coney
           To weep – I'm dazzled; 'tis that sun I view
              Rippling the – the – *Cospetto*, Toni! Down
                 With carpet-bag, and off with valise-straps!
        Bella Venezia, non ti lascio piu!'
                 Nor did Brown ever leave her; well, perhaps
              Browning, next week, may find himself quite Brown!

have been kept since 1817 in a former Franciscan convent next to the Order's great church of the Frari.

No country in Europe – perhaps in the world – possesses a record of its successive administrations more comprehensive, more detailed or more revealing than that which was preserved, and left to posterity, by the Most Serene Republic. Venice virtually invented diplomacy. She was the first European state to maintain permanent embassies in foreign lands, and her ambassadors were required to make the fullest possible reports not only on the government, but on every aspect of life in the countries to which they were accredited. Not surprisingly, by the fifteenth century at the latest Venice's intelligence service was unparalleled anywhere else in the world – as was her diplomatic archive. A few cases of documents were removed by the French during their occupation, a few more by the Austrians; fires and other accidents raised the total a little higher. But, as Brown himself records, the surviving archives fill 'no less than 298 of [the convent's] spacious halls and chambers . . . the shelves occupy the whole of the space from floor to ceiling; the book-cases have a linear extent of 17,438 feet [nearly three and a half miles], and the volumes are stowed in double rows, so packed as to economize space to the utmost'. The number of volumes and bundles of papers, he tells us, has been estimated at 12 million.

To this formidable repository, or to the Marciana Library or to that of the Correr, Rawdon Brown would walk every morning for half a century, carrying with him his pen and a portable inkstand, and would settle down for four or five hours to seek out all the material he could find which had a bearing on the history of England. Historical research in Venice in his day could not have been easy, and Brown had had no academic training as a historian; he seems, however, to have had a remarkable grasp of the work of his predecessors, concerning both Venice in particular and Italy as a whole. In 1854 he published his most readable work, *Four Years at the Court of Henry VIII, a Selection of Dispatches Written by the Venetian Ambassador, Sebastian Giustinian, and Addressed to the Signory of Venice, January 12th 1515 to July 26th 1519.* The originals of these dispatches had been lost; it says much for Brown's scholarship and persistence that he found copies of 226 of them among the Contarini archives in the Marciana Library. They include this account – translated, it need hardly be said, by Brown himself – of the Ambassador's meeting with the 23-year-old King Henry in the country near Greenwich on 3 May 1515:

> After riding about a mile, we were met by a triumphal car, full of singers and musicians, drawn by griffins with human faces; then a little farther on, we found the King's guard, all dressed in green, in the German fashion, with certain slashed hoods on their heads, and bows and arrows in their hands, and having divided into two bands, they being in number three hundred, each man shot an arrow. We next met his Majesty the King on a bay Frieslander, which had been sent him as a present by the Marquis of Mantua; he was dressed entirely in green velvet, cap, doublet, hose, shoes, and everything, and directly we came in sight, he commenced making his horse curvet, and performed such feats, that I fancied myself looking at Mars. He was accompanied by a number of noblemen, most capitally mounted, and richly clad, with all of whom we entered a wood, where a sort of labyrinth had been prepared beforehand with boughs, within which were some places surrounded by ditches, like bastions, destined for company, according to their grade, and inside these bowers tables were laid, where we ate, and made what they call here a proper good breakfast.
>
> His Majesty came into our arbour, and, addressing me in French, said: 'Talk with me awhile! The King of France, is he as tall as I am?' I told him there was but little difference. He continued, 'Is he as stout?' I said he was not; and he then inquired, 'What sort of legs has he?' I replied, 'Spare.' Whereupon he opened the front of his doublet, and placing his hand on his thigh, said, 'Look here! and I also have a good calf to my leg . . .'
>
> After dinner, his Majesty and many others armed themselves *cap-à-pie*, and he chose us to see him joust, running upwards of thirty courses, in one of which he capsized his opponent (who is the finest jouster in the whole kingdom), horse and all. He then took off his helmet, and came under the windows where we were,

and talked and laughed with us to our very great honour, and to the surprise of all beholders.

It was indirectly as a result of the publication of the Giustinian dispatches that in 1862 Lord Palmerston's government decided to sponsor a calendar of all Venetian state papers and manuscripts relating to British affairs, engaging Brown to produce it at an annual salary of £200. On this he worked happily every morning for the next twenty-one years until his death. His routine never changed. A friend remembered how

> day after day, year after year, the Vice-Librarian Lorenzi having regularly breakfasted with him at 8 o'clock, Rawdon Brown's truly English head, with his shrewd, shaven face and close-cut hair, would be seen poring over some dull and dusty delicacy; and equally, day after day and year after year, did his tall, slim and well-knit figure, after his work was done, appear on the Grand Canal, rowing himself, gondolier fashion, to the Lido.

Here, in the summer months, he would bathe before returning home. The evenings he would devote to his friends, or to the countless visitors – largely but not exclusively English or American – who would seek him out the moment they arrived in Venice and whom he never tired of taking round the city he loved.

Among those visitors, in 1849, were John and Effie Ruskin. On 22 December Effie wrote to her mother:

> . . . We have found a most agreeable acquaintance in Mr Rawdon Brown who is a most agreeable, clever literary person and yet not at all grave. He knows and has seen everybody worth seeing of English [sic] and has lived in a beautiful Palace on the Grand Canal for the last 15 years.* He is exceedingly energetic . . . in telling stories and knowing about people, but he is not pushing and a gentleman. He is between forty & fifty and suits me very well and

---

* Palazzo Businello. See pp. 104–5.

also John. He has much influence here and has got John already some very precious books out of the Library of St Mark's regarding the old architecture of Venice which will be most useful to him, and is helping him in every possible way, and on the other hand he will take Charlotte & me into many places that we had no conception of before, and he knows and visits with all the best Society . . .

On 6 January 1850 she continued:

Mr Brown is also exceedingly kind to us. We went to see his house the other day and were quite delighted with it; it was furnished in such exquisite taste, and besides possessing a great many pictures illustrative of Venetian History or Costume which are most interesting, he has a very fine collection of manuscripts of the Doges and many curiosities of great value which could only be got by a long residence in Venice and watching continually whenever any rarity or other fell in his way . . . He is a curious person Mr Brown, extremely clever, and greatly occupied in research. He continually talks of people who living 4 or 5 hundred years ago seem to have been his particular friends or guests. 'Here,' he says, 'are some letters from Worcester, a very fine fellow indeed, Ambassador from Henry VIII to Rome, came to Venice such a day of such a month, lived in that house over there,' then he describes his dress & how many dinners were given him, what he said & how he looked. 'And here are his letters to his friends in England telling them how he was enjoying himself, etc,' and the same way he talks of Doges, Bishops, everybody. He showed me some very touching letters of a Doge Mocenigo to Mary Queen of Scots on the death of her first Husband the Dauphin . . .

Mr Brown wants us to take the two lower floors of his Palace which are unoccupied which would be delightful and economical as we would both have the same cook . . .

The Ruskins never availed themselves of this fine opportunity, though they did stay briefly with Brown at the Businello at the beginning of their next visit, in September 1851, while negotiating terms with Baroness Wetzlar for the accommodation that Brown had arranged for them.★ All too soon, however, their relations began to deteriorate. On 30 November we find Effie writing:

> I see Mr Cheney† and Mr Brown very seldom. I think they have got some idea about us that I can't make out. They always were satirical to John and laughed at him because they were in reality angry to find he knew much better about art here than themselves and now they have a very queer manner to me. Mr Brown never asks me to come and see him although I call regularly on both as politeness requires but there is something about them both that I can't make out at all. However it is not of much importance as we are quite independent of each other but Mr B. has been so kind that I am sorry to have any disagreeable feeling between us . . .

A fortnight later, on 14 December:

> I am good friends again with Mr Brown because I go to take tea with him sometimes without being invited. I never knew anybody so peculiar or so touchy or yet so agreeable when in good humour, but it is very troublesome to be so changeable – he says that I prefer bad company to his and how I can endure to know both he can't imagine. I say there is only one step between the sublime and the ridiculous and he probably considers himself belonging to the first. He says he does. I answer that, being a person of wonderfully staid taste, I also like the other and that I suppose he has nothing to say against their birth or manners. Oh no, he says, but they are all such idiots and fools &c, and so he rails against everybody whom he don't in the least know . . .

Matters finally came to a head early in 1852 when Brown came upon Effie sitting on the open loggia of the Doge's Palace and

★ See Chapter 4, p. 87.
† Colonel Edward Cheney, the only other permanent English resident of Venice at this time.

listening to the band playing in the Piazza below. He asked what she was doing and, when she told him,

> declared that he did not believe me, that he was convinced I came for some reason – that I walked with some one, or watched some one on the Place and that he would soon find out. I kept my temper and said that as he did not believe my word, nor walked, nor watched any one, that so neither could I walk with him and begged to bid him good morning.

Later Brown claimed to have been joking and the relationship was finally patched up, but the damage was done: the old warmth and cordiality never returned.

As Brown grew older his touchiness and tetchiness increased; by the end of his life he had lost nearly all his old friends. Conversations with him were made more difficult still by a number of curious theories that he had developed, and that he loved to expound to those around him. One of these theories was that Shakespeare had based his Othello not on a Moor but on a certain Cristofalo Moro, who had been Venetian Governor of Cyprus; the arms of the Moro family featured three mulberries – presumably owing to its early associations with the silk industry – which Brown identified with the strawberries on Desdemona's handkerchief. According to another, Cervantes had intended Don Quixote as a caricature of the Duke of Lerma, favourite of Philip III, and the entire novel was in fact a satire directed against him. While he was expatiating on subjects such as these, to allow one's attention to lapse was dangerous indeed; to disagree was fatal.

In 1852 Rawdon Brown moved into the Palazzo Gussoni-Grimani-della Vida;* it was to remain his home for the next thirty-one years until his death. The move was prompted by the need for additional space to accommodate his rapidly increasing art collection, by now the most extensive private collection in all Venice. The Italian historian Alfredo Reumont, in an appreciation

* Opposite Ca' Pesaro at the junction of the Rio di Noale and the Grand Canal.

written shortly after Brown's death, said that the palazzo was more
like a museum than a residence. As well as a superb library, 'which
grew daily in size' and in which historical and art-historical works
predominated, it contained portraits and genre pictures of Venetian
life by Longhi and others, porcelain and majolica, embroideries and
tapestries, *objets d'art* and curiosities of all kinds – including a
facsimile of Mowbray's famous tombstone. All this he liked nothing
better than to show to visitors – so long as they were properly
appreciative. The faintest breath of criticism was enough to arouse
his wrath. When the great German scholar Ferdinand Gregorovius
wrote slightingly in his life of Lucrezia Borgia of two pieces of
majolica belonging to Brown – he actually dared to cast doubt on
their owner's conviction that they bore portraits of Lucrezia and
were the personal work of Duke Alfonso of Naples – Brown never
spoke to him again.

As his social life grew increasingly restricted, Rawdon Brown
withdrew more and more into his work. In addition to his *Calendar
of State Papers and Manuscripts* – which, beginning at 1202, he
brought down to 1558 – he found time to edit the copious diaries
of the Venetian historian Marin Sanudo, whose importance he was
one of the first to recognize. These diaries – seldom personal, but
providing an astonishing record of events in Venice and throughout
Europe – run from 1496 to 1533, occupying no fewer than fifty-
eight folio volumes and some 40,000 pages. The originals had been
taken by the Austrians to Vienna; Brown had to work from a copy
which, with his usual serendipity, he had found in the Marciana.
The diaries, edited in their original Venetian, have vastly increased
our knowledge of the Republic in the first three decades of the
sixteenth century.★ Brown continued to work until he was well
into his seventies; but in 1880 his handwriting began to give way,
and in the following year, after a bad fall down a staircase which
injured his head, he gave up writing altogether, thenceforth dictat-

---

★ Brown was also responsible for the commemorative plaque which today marks
Sanudo's house on the Fondamenta del Megio (no. 1757, near the Fondaco dei
Turchi).

ing all his letters to a young assistant. He died on 25 August 1883, at the age of seventy-seven.

In his youth Rawdon Brown had held unashamedly reactionary views. He had little interest in Italian unity, which he believed could lead only to mob rule and the possible destruction of everything he valued most; and he had made no secret of his pro-Austrian sympathies – which, it must be said, were shared by most of his English friends, including the Ruskins. But after the incorporation of Venetia-Lombardy into the Kingdom of Italy in 1866 he had been obliged to accept the new dispensation, and – as time went on and the dangers he had foreseen did not come to pass – he had gradually become reconciled. A letter to *The Times* of 8 September, signed simply 'E.E.', ends with these words:

> His funeral took place on the 28th of August, and was attended by old friends, Italian and English. His beloved banner of St Mark, with the winged lion, was obtained from the Municipality by the Countess Pisani, an English lady and friend,★ and wrapped round him in the coffin. The service was held at the Protestant church at the SS. Apostoli, and a funeral discourse read over him in the name of the authorities of St Mark's Library by his friend Cecchetti, Director of the State Archives at the Frari, who set forth the pure and simple life of one whose zeal for the honour of Venice, knowledge of her history, and unostentatious charity to many of her humble citizens had converted from a stranger and foreigner to one whom they were proud, grateful and eager to claim as their own – *il nostro*.
>
> He now lies in that cemetery island against which the waters of the Adriatic perpetually break – a man of no common heart and head, crusty and odd occasionally it might be, but racy, humorous, generous, faithful and tender, the type of the bookworm, the old bachelor, the warm friend and the true gentleman. Venice will hardly be Venice without him.

★

★ See Chapter 8.

Although Horatio Robert Forbes Brown was no relation to Rawdon, he was in a very real sense his successor. He arrived in Venice with his mother at the age of twenty-five in 1879, and lived there for the next forty-seven years. Born in Nice — which was then still part of Italy — he was nevertheless a Scotsman through and through, the elder son of Hugh Horatio Brown of Newhall House and Carlops, Midlothian, by his wife, Guilelmina, daughter of Alexander Ranaldson Macdonell, last chief of Glengarry and 'the last specimen of the Highland chiefs of history'.* According to the *Dictionary of National Biography*, Macdonell 'killed a young subaltern, Norman Macleod (a grandson of Flora Macdonald) in a duel arising out of a fierce quarrel at a ball at Fort William. He was arraigned on a charge of murder before the high court of justiciary at Inverness, but was acquitted.' When he died a few years later in a shipwreck he had exhausted his once considerable fortune and most of his penniless family were obliged to emigrate to Australia. Guilelmina thus had little if any dowry to bring to her bridegroom — though he, fortunately, had means of his own.

After her husband's death, she took a house at Clifton for the education of her two sons. They were entered at Clifton College, where in 1869 young Horatio attended a series of lectures on the Greek poets by the man who was to be the most important influence in his life, John Addington Symonds. From Clifton he went on to Oxford, and eventually — after two failures to pass responsions — became a senior commoner of New College, 'a position which' — once again according to the *D.N.B.* — 'he used to say nothing but death or bankruptcy could take from him. He thought, however, that he would have made a good Fellow of All Souls. The few surviving among his contemporaries remember him as "pleasant and sociable . . . having artistic tastes which he could afford to

---

* A. Mackenzie, *History of the Macdonalds* [*sic*], Inverness, 1881. The author adds: 'When visiting his friends in Lochaber, he would march from Invergarry to Fort William in full Highland dress, with eagle feathers in his Glengarry bonnet, followed by his tail [a body of a dozen or more retainers similarly clad], while Ailean Dall, his family bard, in full professional costume, was prepared with a bardic oration at the end of the journey.'

indulge", and as "a fair-haired, breezy, outdoors person with a crisp Highland-Scottish speech".'

But his friend John Addington Symonds had his reservations. 'I am not very happy about him,' he wrote to a friend,

> He is 26, and he does not seem to get a grip on any vocation, though he has abundant good gifts, mental moral emotional and social. I wonder whether he will get into public life and make anything of it. Tom [T. H. Green] told him, it appears, that 'literature is only justified by success'. That is true of everything a man attempts – equally true and false, I mean, for all possible careers. What I doubt is, whether Brown has the quality of success. He cannot spell: he wrote 'sucess'. Will he make a secretary?

Throughout his years at Oxford Brown and Symonds continued to correspond, perhaps unusually for the time (since there was an age difference of fourteen years), on Christian name terms. Then in 1877 Symonds – the state of whose lungs was by now giving serious concern – went with his wife to Switzerland. They had originally planned to spend the winter in Egypt but, having accepted a fortuitous invitation from friends to make a diversion and join them in the little village of Davos Platz – at that time a small and rather unattractive town in the Grisons – Symonds had found the mountain air so beneficial that they had travelled no further. His wife hated it and made no secret of the fact; but even she could not deny its effect on her husband, and a year or two later they built themselves the large and rambling chalet-style house, Am Hof, which was to become their permanent home.

It seems to have been their example that decided Horatio Brown also to seek a more temperate climate. With his now widowed mother he moved first to Florence, where Mrs Brown had relatives; but they were not happy there, and in 1879 they transferred to Venice. Their first Venetian address was that of an apartment in the Palazzo Balbi-Valier – three palaces down from the Accademia towards the Salute – on which they took a five-year lease; but this still had a year to run when, determined now to spend the rest of his life in the city, Horatio bought a five-storey tenement house on the Zattere, just beyond the former orphanage of the Incurabili on the Rio delle Torreselle;★ it now bears the number 560. The Ca' Torresella, as he called it, was at the time of its acquisition by the Browns inhabited by a number of different tenants, not all of whom were initially willing to leave; but they were evicted at last, and Horatio moved with his mother into what was to be his home for nearly forty years, converting it by degrees into a moderately distinguished *palazzino* in which he could entertain his friends among the rapidly increasing Anglo-American colony.

This above all was to be his world: the world of the Cosmopolitan Hospital of which he became president, of the Sailors' Institute of which he served as treasurer, and of St George's English church on the Campo S. Vio of which he was a churchwarden. His upper-class Venetian friends were few, to some extent because his and his mother's command of Italian was never quite good enough for intellectual conversation. In any case he infinitely preferred the local gondoliers. Quite shortly after his arrival in Venice, his eye had fallen on the outstandingly handsome Antonio Salin; he had taken him into his service, and as soon as the Ca' Torresella was habitable had moved him and his family into an apartment of their own. The gondolier had in return introduced him to several of his friends, and all his life Horatio was never happier than when playing *tre sette* in the neighbourhood bars, a glass of the rough local wine at his elbow.

It was probably only in this sort of company – and when he was

★ The Incurabili was one of the four institutions in Venice – the other three were the Pietà, the Mendicanti and the Ospedaletto – which in the eighteenth century provided the city with all its best music. They had originally been founded at the time of the Crusades as hostels (*ospedali*) for pilgrims, but had later become orphanages for foundling girls, who received a thorough musical education. Best known of the four was the Pietà, where the *maestro di cappella* in the first half of the century was Antonio Vivaldi himself; but the Incurabili, presided over by Baldassare Galuppi – immortalized in Browning's poem – ran it a close second. The name Torresella commemorates the towers of an ancient palace of the Venier and Donà families, long since demolished.

with his few close English and Scottish friends – that he could really relax; and even then, the precise extent of that relaxation remains uncertain. There can be no doubt that Horatio Brown's tastes lay exclusively with his own sex; it was almost certainly this, even more than their mutual love of literature, that formed the true basis of his friendship with Symonds. But whereas Symonds, after fearful and prolonged agonizing, eventually took the plunge into the active homosexual underworld, with Brown it somehow seems unlikely. Pompous, self-important and – so far as one can see – not over-endowed with humour, conditioned by a puritanical Scottish background and by a formidably powerful mother, he would have been terrified of any disgrace or scandal that might have imperilled his position in Venetian society. His regular afternoon excursions with Antonio in his boat the *Fisole*, its orange sail was emblazoned with a fleur-de-lis, together with a number of overtly pederastic poems which he never published and a few others, more heavily disguised, which he did: such things as these sufficed him – these, and the long, passionate conversations with his friend Symonds that would continue far into the night.

Few men have ever been more tortured by their homosexuality than John Addington Symonds. In his youth, like any conscientious Victorian of the professional class, he had fought it manfully and with determination, marrying the ill-tempered Miss Catherine North in November 1864 and somehow managing to beget four daughters over the next nine years; but within a fortnight of the marriage he was confessing to his friend Henry Dakyns his passion for *both* the sons of Alfred Tennyson, Lionel and Hallam, and for the remainder of his life his raging libido gave him no rest. No sooner had he settled in Switzerland than he realized that he could not live there all the year round; his health might depend on the mountain air, but his sanity demanded that he go south for a few weeks every spring, to enjoy the warmth and sunshine of Italy and above all to escape the company of his gloomy, difficult and disapproving wife. Throughout the 1880s, therefore, he was a regular and frequent visitor to Venice. 'When you are in Venice,' he wrote, it is like being in a dream, and when you dream about Venice it is like being awake. I do not know how this should be, but Venice seems made to prove that *la vita è un sogno*. What the Venice dream is all the world knows. Motion that is almost imperceptible, colour too deep and gorgeous to strike the eye, gilding so massive and ancient as to wear a mist of amber brown upon its brightness, white cupolas that time has turned to pearls, marble that no longer looks like stone, but blocks cut from summer clouds, a smooth sea that is brighter and more infinite than the sky it reflects – these are some of the ingredients of the dream which are too familiar for description. Nothing can describe the elemental warmth of the days, the sea-kisses of the wind at evening, the atmosphere of breathless tepid moonlight in the night. Some people dislike this part of the dream. It just suits me – only I dream of myself in it dressed in almost nothing and very lazy.

Regarding his life in Venice, he wrote in a letter:

I cannot describe the curious mosaic of this Venetian existence . . . It is a jumble of palaces and pothouses, princesses and countesses, gondoliers and *facchini* [porters], hours and hours by day upon the lagoons, hours and hours by night in strange places of the most varied description . . . It is good for me, meanwhile, to be able to string all these things upon the thread of my dear old friend H. F. Brown, who is both sympathetic and wise . . .

Sometimes, though by no means always, he brought one or more of his daughters; but none of these, it need hardly be said, were in Venice when, on a May afternoon in 1881, he and Horatio Brown were sitting 'in a little backyard to the wineshop of Fighetti at S. Elisabetta on the Lido' – and he met the love of his life.

He was tall and sinewy but very slender . . . Black broad-brimmed hat thrown back upon his matted *zazzera* of dark hair. – Great fiery eyes, gazing intensely, with compulsive effluence of electricity – the wild glance of a Triton. – Short blond moustache; dazzling teeth; skin bronzed, but showing white and delicate through open front and sleeves of lilac shirt. – The dashing sparkle of this splendour, who looked to me as though the sea waves and the sun had made him in some hour of secret and unquiet rapture, was somehow emphasized by a curious dint dividing his square chin – a cleft that harmonized with smile on lips and steady fire in eyes . . . Angelo's eyes, as I met them, had the flame and vitreous intensity of opals, as though the quintessential colour of Venetian waters were vitalized in them and fed from inner founts of passion . . . He fixed and fascinated me.

That description of the 24-year-old Angelo Fusato is taken from *The Memoirs of John Addington Symonds*, the unpublished manuscript of which was entrusted to the London Library by Horatio Brown as his literary executor in December 1925, thirty-two years after the author's death. Essentially, it stands as his testament: being, however, a candid – though seldom entirely explicit – account of his sexual life, it remained for many years under embargo in the Library, first seeing the light as recently as 1984. Symonds goes on to tell us how, after a sleepless night, he tracked Angelo down and made an assignation with him on the Zattere.

True to time he came, swinging along with military step, head erect and eager, broad chest thrown out, the tall strong form and pliant limbs in action like a creature of the young world's prime. All day I had been wondering how it was that a man of this sort could yield himself so lightly to the solicitation of a stranger . . . I am now inclined, however, to imagine that the key to the riddle lay in a few simple facts. He was careless by nature, poor by circumstance, determined to have money, indifferent to how he got it. Besides, I know from what he has since told me that the gondoliers of Venice are so accustomed to these demands that they think little of gratifying the caprice of ephemeral lovers – within certain limits, accurately fixed according to a conventional but rigid code of honour in such matters . . .

Well: I took him back to Casa Alberti; and what followed shall be told in the ensuing sonnet, which is strictly accurate – for it was written with the first impression of the meeting strong upon me.

> I am not dreaming. He was surely here
>   And sat beside me on this hard low bed;
>   For we had wine before us, and I said –
> 'Take gold: 'twill furnish forth some better cheer.'
> He was all clothed in white; a gondolier;
>   White trousers, white straw hat upon his head,
>   A cream-white shirt loose-buttoned, a silk thread
> Slung with a charm about his throat so clear.
> Yes, he was here. Our four hands, laughing, made
>   Brief havoc of his belt, shirt, trousers, shoes:
> Till, mother-naked, white as lilies, laid
>   There on the counterpane, he bade me use
> Even as I willed his body. But Love forbade –
>   Love cried, 'Less than Love's best thou shalt refuse!'

The meaning of this last line is not entirely clear; at all events, Symonds was unable to stand the strain and left Venice the next morning. But he was back in the autumn with his passion still as consuming as ever, determined to consolidate the relationship.

We often met at night in my rooms; and I gradually strove to persuade him that I was no mere light-o-love, but a man on whom he could rely – whose honour, though rooted in dishonour, might be trusted . . . I discovered that he was living with a girl by whom he had two boys. They were too poor to marry. I told him that it was his duty to make her an honest woman, not being at that time fully aware how frequent and how binding such connections are in Venice. However, the pecuniary assistance I gave him enabled the couple to set up house; and little by little I had the satisfaction of perceiving that he was not only gaining confidence in me but also beginning to love me as an honest well-wisher.

Before long Angelo left his previous employer to become Symonds's personal gondolier; and when in 1888 Symonds took the lease of the mezzanine floor of the Ca' Torresella, he and his wife – who seemed perfectly ready to share her husband – moved in too. By then he had been the subject of at least fifty passionate sonnets. Soon he was visiting Symonds regularly at Davos; on one occasion Symonds even took him to London. When they travelled in Italy he accompanied his master everywhere, and he was to be with him in Rome on 19 April 1893 when he died.

Horatio Brown must have followed the whole affair with fascination – and, perhaps, with more than a little envy. But such shenanigans were not for him. Nor, he had regretfully decided, was poetry. All his life he had longed to be a poet, and virtually all the work of which he was proudest he had submitted to his friend and father-figure Symonds for an expert opinion. Symonds had been as kind as he could, but had never been able to work up much enthusiasm; and Brown, who for all his faults was far from stupid, had finally got the message. If he were ever to succeed in the world of letters, it would have to be as a writer of prose. His first work, a portrait of Venice entitled *Life on the Lagoons*, was published in 1884; in the last weeks of that same year, however, there came a development of far greater importance, both to his literary career and to that position in society for which he cared so much: he was appointed by the British government to succeed the recently deceased Rawdon Brown and to continue his work on the *Calendar*.

Rawdon Brown had, as we have seen, brought the work down to 1558 when in 1880 ill-health had obliged him to give up. His friend and literary executor, the Rt. Hon. George Cavendish-Bentinck, had briefly taken over and had somehow advanced it as far as 1580; volume 7 of the *Calendar* is credited to the two of them jointly. Assuming responsibility for the project in 1883, Horatio Brown laboured on it for the next twenty-two years, producing five more volumes – though he still progressed no further than 1613. He had had no academic training as a historian – until now he had thought of himself more as a man of letters – and he never seems to have flung himself into his task with quite the skill and enthusiasm shown by his predecessor; unquestionably, however, he was the right man for the job. Though his understanding of sixteenth- and seventeenth-century England may have been no greater than that of many another reasonably cultivated Englishman, his knowledge of Venice, Venetian history and the Venetian language was, since Rawdon's death, unrivalled among his compatriots.

But he never gave the *Calendar* all his time. *Life on the Lagoons* was followed in 1887 by *Venetian Studies*; in 1893 by *Venice, an Historical Sketch*;★ and in 1895 by *John Addington Symonds: a Biography*. As Symonds's literary executor, Brown had travelled to Davos in the summer of 1893, returning to Venice with a plethora of papers: 'Diaries, of the fullest and minutest; and autobiography ... quantities of unpublished verse; and bundles of letters.' All these, at Catherine Symonds's insistence, had to be somehow compounded to make a biography – but a biography, of course, of the conventional Victorian kind.

And here was the problem; for Symonds's life had been far from conventional. He himself had had no patience with what he had called, in a letter to the writer and critic Edmund Gosse, 'an unnatural disnaturing respect for middle-class prudery'; indeed, at the time of his death he had been collaborating with Havelock Ellis on a book on homosexuality.† There is no doubt that, all other things being equal, he would have preferred his friend to produce a truthful, fully rounded portrait, warts and all. On the other hand, there were his wife and daughters to be considered, and he himself had no doubts where his duty lay. Of the all-important *Memoirs* he had written to Brown:

It is doubtful when or whether anyone who has shown as much to the world in ordinary ways as I have done, will be found to speak so frankly about his inner self. I want to save it from destruction

★ Later abridged as *The Venetian Republic*, 1902.
† His contributions were later to be suppressed on Catherine Symonds's insistence. All that remains is Case XVII in the chapter 'Sexual Inversion' of Ellis's *Studies in the Psychology of Sex*.

after my death, and yet to reserve its publication for a period when it will not be injurious to my family.

All this put poor Horatio Brown in a quandary. In January 1894 he himself wrote to Gosse:

> The composition of the life and letters will not prove an easy task to me, I imagine. I see how important you think it will be as regards the reputation of our friend, and I also gather that you, and I suppose most of his friends, consider that no allusion should be made, at least directly, to that question which occupied so much of his life and thoughts. I think that if he had lived he would certainly, sooner or later, have opened the whole question in public. But ought I? . . .
>
> I think it will be my duty, even at the cost of veracity, to dwell as much as possible upon the student, the philosopher, the brilliant talker, the almost sophistical dialectician, the genial companion, the religious strain in his nature, rather than upon the actualities of his friendships and his strong desire to be an innovator, even a martyr.★

And so he did. The two thick volumes of the *Biography*, which he produced little more than two years after his friend's death, strike the modern reader, like the other biographies of their time, as little more than extended funeral orations. He lays much stress – rightly – on Symonds's remarkable scholarship and on his published works; but of his true character and of the unhappiness of his domestic life, to say nothing of the sexual orientation which was so essential a factor in any understanding of the man himself, not a suggestion is to be found. It was to be another generation before Lytton Strachey could finally free biography from its age-old bonds and allow it to flourish as an art form in its own right; and Horatio Brown was no Strachey. In any case his hands were tied. He had undertaken to publish nothing without the consent of the widow; and that widow, who had made her husband's life a misery for

★ Gosse Papers, Brotherton Collection, University of Leeds; quoted in Pemble, *Venice Rediscovered*.

nearly thirty years, proved an adamantine guardian of his reputation after his death. So, later, did their daughter Madge, who in 1923, when the moral climate was considerably more enlightened and Brown published a heavily edited volume of her father's letters, objected even to a mild editorial reference to his interest in psychoanalysis. John Addington Symonds was to wait seventy-one years for a biography that did him justice, and another twenty years after that before his own *Memoirs* were finally published.★

The death of John Addington Symonds and the subsequent problems over his biography involved only a temporary disturbance in the life of Horatio Brown. Well before the end of 1895 he had resumed his old routine, working all morning in the archives, cruising the lagoon with Antonio in the afternoons, spending the evenings with his friends. In 1900 he published a slim volume of verses, *Drift*. They were not very good, and he knew it;† he always claimed to prefer minor poets to major ones, because they were 'more like us'. He also found time to write a chapter on Venice for the *Cambridge Modern History* and two for the *Cambridge Medieval History*, as well as two volumes of *Studies in the History of Venice*, which appeared in 1907. His labours were to earn him an honorary doctorate from the University of Edinburgh and to give him much pleasure besides (he soon tired, however, of the *Calendar*, passing on the torch to a certain Allen B. Hinds, whose principal scholarly achievements until that time had been a book about the Age of Elizabeth and a modest contribution to the official history of Northumberland). Meanwhile his social life continued as active as ever. On Mondays he and his mother – described by F. W. Rolfe as 'a wonderful tottering dame of ninety in black satin and lace and diamonds'‡ – were unfailingly 'at home' to members of the

---

★ The biography is by Phyllis Grosskurth. A fuller – and fascinating – account of the later history of Symonds's papers will be found in Chapter III of *Venice Rediscovered* by John Pemble.

† One of the poems, entitled 'Awake! Awake!', contains the immortal lines:

> Love's Bank is large, fear not an overdraft,
> While youth is Cashier and the Banker daft.

‡ *The Desire and Pursuit of the Whole*, Chapter XXI.

Anglo-American colony in Venice, together with any visitors whom they cared to bring with them. But unlike his namesake Rawdon – who, as we know, was famous for hardly ever leaving the city – Horatio remained at heart a Scotsman, returning every summer to the small estate at Newhall, near Penicuik in Midlothian, which he had somehow managed to retain.

Guilelmina Brown died in 1909, and was duly buried in the island cemetery of S. Michele; and five years later came the First World War. Horatio, now sixty, decided to stay on in Venice, even after Italy entered the war on the Allied side in 1915, when he announced that in the case of any Austrian bombardment the Ca' Torresella would be open as a refuge to all the poor of the quarter. 'My duty,' he wrote, 'is to appear at the top of the stairs and say *calma, calma, calma.*' In May 1916, however, that calm was seriously threatened when the Austrian army crossed the river Tagliamento and swept into the province of Venezia Giulia: to many Venetians it looked very much as though, after exactly half a century, their city was once again to fall under Habsburg rule. Having no wish to spend the rest of the war in an Austrian prison or to be what he called 'an idle mouth', Horatio departed first to Florence and then – with some difficulty – to Scotland where, Newhall being closed up, he divided his time between the New Club in Edinburgh and the village pub at Penicuik.

When he returned to Venice in 1919 he found himself a poor man. He was obliged to sell the Ca' Torresella, his home for thirty-six years, renting back the mezzanine which long ago he had let to Symonds; and by August 1920 he was facing a still greater tragedy. From Niederdorf in the Italian Tyrol he wrote to his friend Lord Rosebery:

> . . . that awful document my half-yearly account settled the [? matter]. I could not afford it, so I came up here to this quiet, cheap little village which I have known for long and always liked, and set myself down to contemplate the inevitable (I fear) – the parting with Newhall. Most of my mother's family, the Glengarrys, died without a roof of their own over their heads, and I doubt whether

the blood of 'those beastly Browns' as she called them will save me from a like fate. I am getting over it though, and don't take it too tragically.

Soon, too, his sight began to fail and he had to give up his writing; nor, in his present circumstances, could he any longer afford to entertain on the lavish scale of pre-war years. Those Monday evenings at the Ca' Torresella were now only distant memories. He was sick, he was lonely, and he had to a large extent lost the will to live. In March 1925 he suffered a major heart attack, and a year and a half later another, severer still. This second he did not survive. He died on Thursday 19 August 1926, not in the Venice he loved and had made his own, but in his doctor's house at Belluno, some seventy miles to the north, where he had gone to escape the heat.

★

Neither Rawdon nor Horatio Brown was a great man, in the sense that Napoleon, Byron and Ruskin were great men. They did not change the face of Europe, or write deathless poetry or prose, nor did they profoundly affect our approach to art and architecture. Horatio was a genuine if uninspired historian, Rawdon essentially no more than an archivist, though a brilliant one. But they were great Venetians. Each, at the time of his death, probably knew more about Venice, her people and her history not just than any other foreigner but than anyone alive, including Italians born in the city. This is no reflection on the great Venetian scholars of their day; but native-born Venetians inevitably tend, to some degree at least, to take their city for granted. Only the outsider, discovering Venice for himself, falling in love with it and resolving to devote his life to its study, can at the same time stand back from it and view it objectively. And only he, perhaps, can harbour that last, vital spark of enthusiasm that drives him on towards ever new discoveries.

Rawdon Brown arrived in Venice in 1833, just twelve years after the death of Napoleon; Horatio Brown died in 1926, when the Ca'

Rezzonico was being rented by the Cole Porters. Together – and with a four-year overlap – they covered only seven years short of a century, for the vast majority of which they formed the centre of the British community in Venice. For most of that time it would have been unthinkable for any self-respecting visitors from England not to have come armed with a letter of introduction to one or the other. In Rawdon's day they would almost certainly have been taken by him on a tour of the city or, in later years, invited to see his celebrated collection; in Horatio's, they would have presented themselves at the Ca' Torresella on the first Monday evening after their arrival, where, over refreshments served by a smiling Antonio, they would have been introduced to virtually all the leading members of local society, Venetian and foreign. These two very different men were thus part of the fabric of Venice, in a way that Napoleon the conqueror, Byron the brilliant but embarrassing guest and Ruskin the scholar could never have been. That is why they deserve to be remembered, and that is why they have a place in this book.

6. Revolution
(1848–9)

We are free, and we have a double right to be proud since we
have freed ourselves without shedding a drop of blood, either
our own or that of our brothers – for me, all men are brothers.
But it is not enough to have overthrown the former government; we must replace it with another. In my opinion, the
right answer is the Republic.

Daniele Manin, 22 March 1848

Of all the distinguished men and women whose Venetian lives are
traced in this book, only Rawdon Brown lived through the great
Revolution of 1848–9; and since no portrait of nineteenth-century
Venice can be complete without at least a brief account of that
Revolution, this seems the most suitable place to attempt it.

The first blast of the trumpet was sounded four years earlier, by
three young Venetian officers at the Naval Academy. (Although
Trieste was now Austria's most important port, all those in search
of a naval commission were sent to Venice for their training.)
Unlike the army, the imperial navy was officered largely by Italians
and Croats; and when the two brothers Attilio and Emilio Bandiera,
together with their friend Domenico Moro, founded a secret
society with the object of bringing out the whole Austrian fleet
in mutiny, there was no lack of support among their colleagues.
Unfortunately their society did not remain secret for long. In
1844, threatened with arrest by the Austrian authorities, the three
conspirators fled to Corfu, which was at that time under British
protection. From there, on the night of 12 June 1844, they sailed
with a handful of others who shared their ideals in a small boat
across the Adriatic and landed four days later on the coast of

Calabria, hoping to start an insurrection against the tyrannical Bourbon Kingdom of Naples. The whole enterprise was quixotic in the extreme: Calabria was certainly ripe for revolution, but there were no organized resistance groups – or, if there were, they knew nothing of them – and they were almost immediately arrested by the Bourbon police. After a brief appearance before a military tribunal, they and six of their companions were executed at Cosenza on 25 July.★

Although their expedition had ended in abject failure, the news of their deaths had an immense impact on public opinion in Italy. If three Venetians – to say nothing of their fellow martyrs from Perugia, Rimini and several other towns – were prepared to die for Naples, then Italian unity must after all be something more than an empty dream. In Venice, the tension increased day by day; it seemed unthinkable that the three heroes should have perished in vain. The time for secret societies was over. The moment had now come when the whole population of the city must speak out with a single voice; and the voice with which it spoke was that of Daniele Manin.

He was born on 13 May 1804 in the parish of S. Agostino. His Jewish father had converted to Christianity in his youth, and had adopted the family name of Pietro Manin – brother of Lodovico Manin, the last Doge of Venice – who had stood godfather to him at his baptism.† With the fall of the Republic, however, the stigma of bearing the same name as the man he believed to be the betrayer of the Venetian cause was almost too much for him, and after the birth of his son he would repeatedly urge him to wipe out the stain. Daniele himself was something of a prodigy. Determined to be a lawyer like his father, he was only twelve when he published his

★ They are commemorated by the former *campo* of S. Giovanni in Bragora, which has been renamed in their honour, and also in the collection of nine plaques depicting the leaders of the Revolution in Calle Larga dell' Ascension, at the western entrance to the Piazza.

† In the parish church, which was unforgivably demolished (with its fine campanile) by the Venetian Municipality in 1873. In the adjoining *campo* stood the so-called Column of Infamy – now in the Correr Museum – recording the rebellion by Bajamonte Tiepolo in 1310.

first work, a legal treatise on wills. At twenty-one he graduated as Doctor of Law at Padua University, by which time, as well as Italian and his native Venetian dialect, he had a good working knowledge of Latin, Greek, Hebrew, French and German.

Brought up by his father to share his own republican and liberal ideals, Daniele Manin had already been politically active for some sixteen years when in 1847, with nationalist feeling growing throughout Italy, he launched what he called his *lotta legale* – legal struggle – against Austrian despotism, principally on the grounds that Austria had never observed the constitution that she had herself granted in 1815. He was not at this stage openly calling for full independence – to do so would have been suicidal; instead, as a tactical measure, he advocated home rule under the Empire. Only when this had been refused (as he knew full well that it would be) would he call his fellow citizens to arms.

The first moment of open defiance came on 30 December 1847, when the distinguished Dalmatian scholar and academic Niccolò Tommaseo gave a lecture in the Ateneo Veneto. Its subject was announced as 'The State of Italian Literature', but it proved to be an open attack on Austrian censorship which, he maintained, was in breach of the Austrian press law, passed in 1815. At the end of the lecture Tommaseo circulated a petition. It was signed, over the next few days, by over 600 leading names in Venice and the Veneto. Early in January 1848 the British Consul-General Clinton Dakins reported that

> there is hardly a Venetian house to which an Austrian is admitted
> . . . Persons supposed to have a leaning towards the Government
> are held up to public execration, and their names are written upon
> the walls as traitors to their country.

As a further sign of their anger all the Venetians gave up smoking. The moment the Austrian band struck up in the Piazza, they turned on their heels and left.★

★ Since the start of the Austrian occupation they had always refused to applaud.

Only a week or so later, Daniele Manin followed up with a sixteen-point charter, demanding *inter alia* vastly increased rights for all Italians under Austrian rule; a separate North Italian government answerable to the Emperor alone; the army in Italy and the navy in Italian waters to be entirely Italian; and finally the complete abolition of censorship, and of arbitrary action by police. This, for the imperial authorities, was the last straw. On 18 January Manin and Tommaseo were arrested and marched to the old prisons opposite the Doge's Palace. Since they were on remand, they were given the most comfortable cells available: Manin's was even frescoed, with two windows looking out on to Riva degli Schiavoni and one over the Rio di Palazzo. Tommaseo was next door. Once the Venetians had discovered where they were, crowds collected daily to stand in respect, bareheaded and silent, on the Riva below.

The tribunal before which the two men appeared sat in private, without a jury. In early March, to everyone's surprise, they were acquitted; but the Austrian chief of police insisted none the less that they should remain in prison. It was a disastrous mistake. As popular indignation grew, Manin's fellow lawyers took over all his work without pay. The annual Carnival was cancelled. Even the two working-class factions, the Castellani and the Nicolotti, who had been at each other's throats for centuries, buried the hatchet: their two chiefs met one morning for early mass at the Salute and formally intertwined their respectively red and black sashes. '*La patria*,' they later explained, '*vuol un sacrificio.*'★

The first Italian Revolution broke out in Sicily on 12 January, and within the next few weeks constitutions were granted to Naples, Piedmont, Tuscany and the Papal States. In Venice and Milan, however, people remained outwardly calm, knowing that Austria had gradually gathered in Venetia-Lombardy a highly trained army of 75,000, under the command of the celebrated Marshal Josef Radetzky. Radetzky was now eighty-one. He had been chief of staff at the Battle of Leipzig thirty-five years before and had been in command in Italy since 1831, but he had lost none

★ 'The motherland requires a sacrifice.'

of his energy or efficiency. (He had fathered his most recent
illegitimate child only two years earlier, at the age of seventy-nine.)
Had the Venetians and the Milanese decided to take up arms, he
would have made short work of them. But then, on 17 March, the
regular postal steamer from Trieste brought the news that Vienna
itself was in revolt, that the rebels had triumphed and that the hated
Prince Metternich had fled for his life. Overnight, the situation was
transformed. As the word spread through the city, an immense
crowd flocked to the Piazza and collected in front of the Governor's
Palace in the Procuratie Nuove (where Napoleon had stayed in
1807), shouting '*Fuori Manin e Tommaseo!*'★ The Venetians, it was
clear, would no longer be gainsaid.

    The Hungarian Governor, Count Pàlffy, and the Military Gov-
ernor, Lieutenant-Marshal Zichy, found themselves in a quandary.
What would the government in Vienna wish them to do? And
what, for that matter, was the government in Vienna anyway?
Eventually Pàlffy appeared at the window and protested that even
if he had wished to release the prisoners, he had no power to do
so. Not surprisingly, the crowd refused to accept this for an answer
and, led by Manin's sixteen-year-old son Giorgio, streamed across
the Piazzetta to the prison and began hammering at the doors,
which were finally opened. It was typical of Daniele Manin that he
should have refused to leave the building until he had an official
order to do so – an order which Pàlffy, at the urgings of his
near-hysterical wife, hastily signed. Only then did the two men
emerge, to be carried shoulder-high to the Governor's Palace. The
crowds made as if to break down the doors, but Manin restrained
them. 'Do not forget,' he told them, 'that there can be no true
liberty, and that liberty cannot last, where there is no order.' Only
when they had calmed down did he allow them to bear him off up
the Merceria to his house in S. Paternian.†

★ 'Release Manin and Tommaseo!'
† The Campo S. Paternian was remodelled and enlarged in the 1870s to become
the present Campo Manin. Alas, the few remains of the old church, suppressed
by Napoleon, that used to close the square to the east, and – more tragic still –
its leaning pentagonal campanile, erected in 999, were demolished in the process,

1. Andrea Appiani:
Napoleon as King of Italy

2. T. Phillips: *Lord Byron
in Albanian dress*

3. John Everett Millais: *John Ruskin*, at Glenfinlas

4. Vittore Carpaccio: *The Dream of St Ursula*

5. V. Giancomelli: *The Proclamation of the Republic of Venice in 1848*

6. Pierre Auguste Renoir: *Richard Wagner*

7. John Singer Sargent: *Henry James*

8. John Singer Sargent: *The Curtis family in the Palazzo Barbaro*

9. John Singer Sargent: *Isabella Stewart Gardner*

10. L. Passini: *Sir Austen Henry Layard at his desk in the Ca' Cappello*

11.Vicente Palmaroli Gonzalez: *Lady Layard looking out over the Grand Canal*

12. John Singer Sargent:
Self-portrait

13. John Singer Sargent:
The Grand Canal (watercolour)

The next day found Venice still in chaos, to the point where Pàlffy was obliged to seek Manin's help. Manin replied that he could indeed restore order, but only if he were allowed to form a Civic Guard. The Governor reluctantly agreed, so long as its numbers did not exceed 200; by midnight Manin had recruited 2,000, wearing as their uniform a simple white sash. He himself, with characteristic modesty, would accept no rank senior to that of captain; the command of the whole force he entrusted to none other than that same Angelo Mengaldo who had raced Byron across the lagoon thirty years before.

★

That evening's steamer carried the announcement that the Emperor had agreed to the principle of constitutional government for Venetia-Lombardy. Tommaseo was inclined to accept, but for Manin the offer had come too late; he now demanded nothing less than the expulsion of all Austrians from Venetian territory. This, he knew, could not be achieved without bloodshed; but he had his Civic Guard, the Austrians were in a state of confusion, and he now put all his faith in a single, dramatic coup: to capture the Arsenal. It contained vast quantities of arms and ammunition, and even a few warships; it was the obvious place from which the Austrians would bombard the city, if they decided to do so; moreover the 2,000-odd workers there, the so-called *arsenalotti*, were a proud, tough body of men with strong republican sympathies. He knew he could count on their support.

On the morning of 22 March – a date now commemorated in one of Venice's principal shopping streets – the highly unpopular Deputy Commander of the Arsenal, a Croat named Marinovich, was murdered by the mob. Manin hurried there at once, keeping

---

a piece of gratuitous vandalism that Manin himself would never have forgiven. His family house still stands at the western end and is marked by a plaque; in the centre is his statue, a magnificently winged lion at its foot; and at the eastern end the hideous new seat of the Cassa del Risparmio, on which he is very properly turning his back.

to the back streets through S. Giovanni in Bragora and S. Martino; there were too many Austrians along the Riva. On leaving his house he was accompanied only by Giorgio, but as they walked they were joined by more and more members of the Civic Guard: by the time they arrived, their party was about a hundred strong. They found the Commander cowering in his office by the main gateway, terrified that he was going to suffer the same fate as his colleague. When Manin announced that he and his men intended to search the building to satisfy himself that there were no preparations for bombardment, he unhesitatingly agreed.

By this time Austrian reinforcements had arrived, but were held back by the Civic Guard; meanwhile the many Italians among them immediately joined the revolt. Manin, now in undisputed control, ordered the opening of the armouries, whose contents were distributed among the Civic Guard and the *arsenalotti*. When this had been done, at around three o'clock in the afternoon, he was utterly exhausted – he had not slept for three nights – and in considerable pain from a stomach disorder. Only after an hour's rest in a neighbouring tavern was he able to lead the triumphal procession to the Piazza, where Pàlffy and Zichy, blockaded in the Palace by a jubilant crowd, soon gave themselves up. There, with what little strength remained to him, Manin climbed on to a table and proclaimed the Republic, ending his speech with the words '*Viva San Marco!*', now heard in public for the first time for over half a century. Then he returned home and fell exhausted on his bed. Pàlffy and Zichy meanwhile signed a formal act of capitulation, leaving effective power in the hands of 'the Provisional Government which is to be formed' and undertaking that all Austrian troops were to be evacuated – without their arms – to Trieste. One unit only objected: the Kinsky Regiment, based on the Zattere. Under their General, Culoz, they held out another three days, surrendering only when they heard of the fall of Milan.

Venice was once more a republic; but it was plain, from its earliest days, that that republic was in mortal danger. The Austrians had retreated: they were by no means beaten. The Revolution had been confined to the major towns. Radetzky's army, though somewhat reduced because of Italian defections, was still in control of most of the countryside, and after the fall of Vicenza on 10 June the whole of the Venetian *terra firma* was back in Austrian hands. Meanwhile Naples had made a separate peace; Rome had capitulated; France, in the person of her Foreign Secretary, the poet Alphonse de Lamartine, had published a republican 'Manifesto' but had offered no active or material help. King Charles Albert of Piedmont, encouraged by Count Camillo Cavour to take up arms, had declared war on Austria on 22 March, and had even scored a minor victory on 30 May at Goito, near Mantua; but Austrian reinforcements were already pouring into Italy and he had been obliged to retreat. Less than four months after the proclamation of the Republic, the forces of the counter-revolution were triumphant across mainland Italy.

And so, on 4 July, the newly elected Venetian Assembly reluctantly voted for fusion with Piedmont, where Cavour was calling ever more insistently for the unification of Italy. It was a tragic day for Daniele Manin, who at once handed over to an interim ministry and retired from public life. (A few days later he was spotted in the uniform of a private in the Civic Guard, on sentry-go in the Piazzetta.) Meanwhile 3,000 Piedmontese troops were billeted in the city; for many Venetians, it was almost as bad as having the Austrians back again. But this new state of affairs was not to last for long. On the 25th the Piedmontese army was routed by the Austrians at Custoza and obliged to fall back on Milan, Radetzky in hot pursuit. Charles Albert was ready to defend the city to the last, but a new humiliation awaited him. The largely republican Milanese stormed the palace in which he was staying, while the town council negotiated a peace. The King, with what was left of his shattered army, was allowed to return to Piedmont, and on 6 August Radetzky re-entered the city. Three days later an armistice was concluded, by the terms of which the Piedmontese escaped Austrian occupation only by agreeing to evacuate Venetia-Lombardy.

Once again, Venice stood alone. Her only hope was Manin, who cast aside his private's uniform and addressed a furious crowd

on the Piazza. 'The day after tomorrow,' he told them, 'the Deputies will meet and elect a new government. For the next forty-eight
hours, *governo io*.' That same night he drafted a letter to Lamartine's
successor as French Minister for Foreign Affairs, Jules Bastide,
appealing for military intervention – without which, he emphasized, the restored Republic was doomed. The letter was entrusted
to Niccolò Tommaseo, who at once – though with considerable
reluctance – left for Paris as Manin's personal ambassador; but it is
unlikely that either of them had very much hope. Meanwhile the
Assembly duly met on 13 August and invited Manin to assume
dictatorial powers. He declined, on the grounds that he knew
nothing of military matters; but eventually agreed to accept membership of a triumvirate, together with Colonel Giovanni Battista
Cavedalis and Admiral Leone Graziani.

Under this new dispensation Venice fought desperately on.
Hopes revived briefly in October, when there was a second revolution in Vienna and a second flight of the Emperor from Schön-
brunn, together with a Hungarian rising under Lajos Kossuth; but
with Russian help this was soon crushed, and with sinking hearts
the Venetians settled down to a winter – and, as it turned out, a
spring – of intermittent Austrian blockade. This at least gave them
an opportunity to try to organize an effective army – a task which
was entrusted to Cavedalis and to a gigantic Calabrian general
named Guglielmo Pepe,★ who, like him, had fought with Bonaparte and now cheerfully proclaimed his readiness to give his life
for Italy and the Republic. He proved able to recruit a large number of officers and men formerly in the Neapolitan army to join
what had been the Civic Guard but which was now conscripted
for service. The result by the beginning of April was a reasonably disciplined fighting force some 20,000 strong, enabling the
Assembly, meeting in the Sala del Maggior Consiglio of the Doge's
Palace, to publish the heroic decree: 'Venice will resist Austria at all

★ The house in which Pepe lived during his stormy stay in Venice bears a
memorial plaque. It is by the Sottoportico dei Dai, no. 167a, just behind the
north side of the Piazza. Pepe also figures among the relief plaques in the Calle
Larga dell' Ascension. (See p. 129n.)

costs. President Manin is invested, for that purpose, with unlimited powers.'

The blockade continued until May 1849, when the Austrian general commanding, Lieutenant-Marshal Julius von Haynau, finally accepted that, even with an army of 30,000, a lagoon ninety miles in circumference could never be completely cordoned off, and a city of some 200,000 inhabitants would take a long time to starve. There was nothing for it but a full military siege. The first target was the fort at Malghera (now Marghera), at the mainland end of the railway bridge. After three weeks' bombardment it finally gave in; but the bridge itself, with several other makeshift forts along its length, somehow held. Early in July the Austrians had the extraordinary idea of trying to drop bombs on Venice from a fleet of large balloons; the experiment proved a fiasco and gave the Venetians at least something to laugh about – but they had very little else. Already there was a serious shortage of food, and as the month wore on they were on the brink of famine. Even fish – the Venetian staple – was in short supply, since the amount furnished by the lagoon was hopelessly inadequate for the city's population; a government decree restricted its sale to the *pescheria* at the foot of the Rialto Bridge and the two other markets at Burano and Chioggia. Bread had long been rising as rapidly in price as it was declining in quality; on 16 July one of the leading clerics addressed a *cri de coeur* to the Military Commission:

> For God's sake, there is no bread left! Yesterday it was the people of Castello who were furious; today the fury is everywhere. This morning there was a lamentable scene in Campo SS. Giovanni e Paolo. The women who had gathered to buy bread were swearing and praying, and tearing the earrings from their ears and the wedding rings from their fingers . . . We must not wait until the people take matters into their own hands.★

Bread rationing was introduced immediately, but the situation

★ Quoted by P. Ginsborg, *Daniele Manin and the Venetian Revolution of 1848–49*.

continued to deteriorate. At a meeting of the Assembly on 28 July, Manin asked whether it was possible for Venice to resist any longer; his hearers, however, voted to fight to the last.

Then, on the night of the 29th, the bombardment began. It was confined to the western half of the city, since the Austrian guns, even when raised to their highest elevation, could lob their cannon balls no further; the Piazza was fortunately just out of range. It was also fortunate that the vast majority of the projectiles were merely balls, and not shells that exploded on impact; and since they had lost all momentum by the time they were over the city they had only the force of gravity to propel them and seldom penetrated below the top floors.* In an attempt to make them more effective, the Austrians frequently made them red-hot before firing; but there were not enough furnaces to heat them all, and the occasional small fire that resulted could usually be dealt with by the fire brigade – which now included Daniele Manin as one of its members.

Nevertheless, the sheer intensity of the bombardment over the next three and a half weeks – some thousand projectiles every twenty-four hours – could not fail to take its toll on Venetian morale; and by now Venice had fallen victim to the greatest scourge of all – cholera. The first cases had been reported in early July, and by the end of the month the disease was raging in every quarter of the city. In the heat of August it grew worse still, especially in the hideously overcrowded easternmost region of Castello, to which most of the people from the westernmost areas had fled. The gravediggers could not hope to keep pace – burial is anyway a difficult process in Venice – and the corpses were being piled up in the *campo* of Venice's old cathedral, S. Pietro di Castello; the smell, we are told, was asphyxiating. In one single day – the 17th – no fewer than 247 deaths were reported, and ten days later the total number had reached 2,788.

It was plain that the end was near. On 19 August Cavedalis and two other members of the Assembly set off for Mestre in two

---

* One of them – as the French Consul gleefully reported – landed on the bed of his British colleague, Clinton Dakins, but did no serious damage.

gondolas flying white flags; three days later, agreement was reached. The Austrian terms were surprisingly generous. All officers and all Italian soldiers who were subjects of the Empire and had fought against it must leave Venice; forty leading Venetians were also to be expelled. There would be no reprisals, though Cavedalis was to remain a hostage until the Austrians reoccupied the city – which, on 27 August, they did. That same afternoon the French ship *Pluton* sailed from Venice. On board were, with thirty-seven others, Guglielmo Pepe, Niccolò Tommaseo and Daniele Manin.

★

Manin and his family were bound for France, but hardly had they disembarked at Marseilles than his beloved wife died of cholera. He, his son Giorgio and his daughter Emilia continued their journey to Paris, where he lived for the rest of his life, supporting himself by giving Italian lessons and nursing Emilia through a long and distressing illness until she died in 1854. He also wrote articles for the French papers in the hope of rallying French liberals to the Italian cause. When in March 1854 the British Prime Minister Lord John Russell said in Parliament that if the Italians had been less aggressive they might have persuaded the Austrians to rule more liberally, he retorted in *La Presse*: 'We don't want the Austrians humane and liberal; we want them *out!*' But by now he had given up his republican ideals; his sights were set on Italian unification. 'I am convinced,' he wrote, 'that our first task is to make Italy a reality . . . the republican party declares to the House of Savoy: "If you create Italy, we are with you; if not, not."' He died in Paris on 22 September 1857, aged fifty-three. Eleven years later his remains were brought back to Venice and placed in a specially designed sarcophagus against the north wall of the Basilica.

There remained only Giorgio, who had distinguished himself as a sixteen-year-old during the Revolution and who, despite serious wounds sustained with Garibaldi's army at Calatafimi, lived on to see Venice join the Kingdom of Italy in 1866. He spent the last years of his life in his native city, universally respected as his father's son.

7. Wagner
(1858–83)

Venice was a happy choice . . . I am greatly attracted by the
place, which is so unique and melancholy: I desire the most
absolute privacy, and I can certainly find this better here than
anywhere else. And so I am hoping for a calm and undisturbed
frame of mind with which to resume my work.

Richard Wagner to Hans von Bülow,
27 September 1858

In the early afternoon of Thursday 19 April 1883, a slow procession
of boats left the Riva degli Schiavoni. It was led by the state barges
of the Municipality of Venice, together carrying the members of
a full-sized symphony orchestra. Behind these followed a cluster
of six gondolas, linked together in the Venetian manner, in which
sat some of the greatest German singers of their day; behind them
again, hundreds of other gondolas, *sandoli* and smaller craft, all
jostling for position. Slowly the cortège wound its way up the
Grand Canal in the warm spring sunshine, passing under the Rialto
Bridge and continuing to a vast early Renaissance palazzo on the
right-hand side of the Canal, at the corner of the Rio di San
Marcuola.

There the orchestra prepared itself while the singers disembarked,
appearing a minute or two later on the balconies of the *piano nobile*;
the conductor, Wagner's friend and protégé Anton Seidl, raised
his baton; and the first familiar bars of the Funeral March from
Götterdämmerung echoed across the water. The artists on the balconies bared their heads, while the crowds below – in boats and on
the quays, even on the roofs of the neighbouring houses – mutely
followed their example. There was no clapping when the music

stopped; everyone stood in silence. Then the orchestra moved on to the Overture from *Tannhäuser*, after which all the pent-up emotion exploded into a frenzy of applause. The ceremony was over, and to the strains of the *Marcia Reale* the procession set off once more in the direction from which it had come.

Just nine weeks before, on the mezzanine floor of this palace, the Vendramin-Calergi – today occupied by the Municipal Casino – Richard Wagner had died of a massive heart attack. For him, death in Venice was not inappropriate. On his first visit to the city, in 1858, he had found it beautiful but dull. Apart from the theatre – which he later denied having ever attended – 'there was little else that attracted my attention in the oppressed and degenerate life of the Venetian people, and the only impression I derived from the exquisite ruin of this wonderful city as far as human interest was concerned was that of a watering-place kept up for the benefit of visitors'. But over the next quarter-century he was to return five times and grew to love it more and more; he would hardly otherwise have decided, in 1882, to spend his last winter there, with his wife Cosima, their three children and a numerous retinue.

He loved it for its quietness and its peace: those same attractions which had drawn him there in the first place, in 1858. By then his first marriage had become unbearable. His actress wife Minna – nearly four years his senior – was insanely jealous (though she herself had had an illegitimate daughter, Natalie, when she was barely seventeen and had briefly eloped with a rich local merchant only six months after her marriage to Wagner). Although he was to continue to write her affectionate letters until her death, his absences grew longer and more frequent. He always maintained that she never really loved him, and he was probably right: her spirit, practical and earthbound, made no attempt to follow his into the worlds of poetry, music and legend. It rebelled, too, against the poverty in which they were forced to live, and the humiliation of continued borrowings. She longed to return to the stage, but she was fast losing her looks and she knew it.

Yet somehow the marriage might have endured if her husband

had not, in the spring of 1852, encountered Mathilde Wesendonk,★ the much younger wife of a prosperous silk merchant. Although the business of her husband Otto was based in New York, he and Mathilde spent most of their time in Zurich; and it was there that she attended a performance of the Overture to *Tannhäuser*, which she later described as the overwhelming experience of her life. From that moment on she was captivated, and by autumn she and Wagner were seriously in love – to the point where he suspended his work on *The Ring* and began *Tristan und Isolde*, inspired by Mathilde and a celebration of his passion for her. Strangely enough, the precise nature of their relationship remains unclear: the affair was certainly not platonic, but there is evidence to suggest that neither was it fully consummated.

Perhaps for just this reason, Mathilde's husband seems not to have been particularly troubled. In 1853 Otto had given Wagner enough financial help to allow him to present and conduct three concerts of his works and to take a trip to Italy; and in September 1854 he offered to settle all the composer's debts in return for a percentage of future profits from his concerts and operatic perform-ances. Meanwhile he was building for himself and his wife a magnificent house just outside Zurich, and when the work was finished in 1857 he offered the Wagners a small cottage on the estate, to be at their disposal for life at a nominal rent. The offer was generous, but ill-advised: with Minna and Mathilde so close to each other the sparks were bound to fly. On 3 April 1858 Wagner dispatched Act I of *Tristan* to his publisher Breitkopf for engraving, and a few days later sent Mathilde his original sketch for the Prelude. His wife, however, intercepted the package and found, with the music, an eight-page letter. It was not really a love letter, covering as it did any number of other subjects; but for Minna it was the last straw. She was by now approaching fifty; heart trouble was giving her increasing cause for worry; and she found it hard to accept that her youth and beauty were gone. She faced both her husband and

★ For many years her husband's family had been uncertain whether or not to spell its name with a penultimate 'c', but had eventually decided against it.

Mathilde with the letter; and the next four months were, in Wagner's own words, 'a veritable hell'. At last in August he could bear it no longer. In such an atmosphere creative work was impossible, and on 17 August he left for Venice, picking up his young friend Karl Ritter on the way in Lausanne.

★

The railway bridge connecting Venice with the mainland, seriously damaged during the 1848 Revolution, had now been rebuilt; once again it was possible to enter the city by train. Wagner wrote in his autobiography: 'As we were looking from the railway dike at Venice rising before us from the mirror of water, Karl lost his hat out of the carriage owing to an enthusiastic movement of delight; I thought that I must follow suit, so I too threw my hat out; consequently we arrived in Venice bareheaded.' Their delight, however, proved short-lived.

> The weather had suddenly become gloomy, and the aspect of the gondolas quite shocked me; for, in spite of what I had heard about these peculiar vessels draped in black, the sight of one was an unpleasant surprise: when I had to go under the black awning . . . I felt I was taking part in a funeral procession during a pestilence.

Their boat entered the Grand Canal, but

> the impression that everything made on me here did not tend to dispel my melancholy frame of mind . . . At last I became silent, and allowed myself to be put down at the world-famous Piazzetta and to be shown the Palace of the Doges – though I reserved to myself the right of admiring it until I had freed myself from the extremely melancholy mood into which my arrival in Venice had thrown me.

They had booked rooms at the Danieli, 'where', he wrote, 'we found only a gloomy lodging'; they did not stay there for long. Ritter soon settled cheerfully into a small apartment on the Riva, 'which, being in a sunny position, required no artificial heating';

but Wagner was more ambitious. He eventually decided on 'spacious and imposing' apartments in the second of the three Giustiniani palaces just before the first bend of the Grand Canal, between Ca' Rezzonico and Ca' Foscari. The entrance was in what he called Campiello Squillini – properly Campiello degli Squellini (named after the majolica bowls which were once made there), no. 3228. 'On the evening of 30 August,' he wrote, 'I said to myself "At last I am living in Venice." ' Two days later he reported to Minna:

> I am of course in furnished accommodation: there is no other kind. My landlord, who is Austrian, was delighted to house such a famous name. All such apartments here are in large palaces that have been abandoned by their former aristocratic owners; speculators have now turned them into apartments for foreigners . . . This town is exceedingly interesting, and the actual stillness – one never hears a carriage – is indispensable for me. I receive no visitors, and hope to live here totally withdrawn into myself.

Mein Leben takes up the story:

> My leading idea was that I could work here undisturbed. I immedi-ately wrote to Zurich asking for my Erard grand piano and my bed to be sent on to me, as with regard to the latter, I felt that I should find out what cold meant in Venice. In addition to this, the grey-washed walls of my large room soon annoyed me, as they were so little suited to the ceiling, which was covered with a fresco which I liked. I decided to have the walls of the large room covered with hangings of a dark red colour, even if they were of quite common quality.★ This immediately caused much trouble; but it seemed to me that it was well worth while when I gazed down from my balcony with growing satisfaction on the wonderful canal, and said to myself that here I would complete *Tristan*.

★ Ernest Newman suggests that 'the real explanation no doubt was that, as usual when he had a composition in hand, he wished to give himself the illusion of being insulated from the outer world'.

Venice in the mid nineteenth century was by no means the healthy city that it is today, and Wagner had hardly settled in when he was stricken with a serious attack of dysentery. But the Erard arrived in mid-October and for the next five months he was hard at work. Soon, too, he 'learned to appreciate the matchless beauty of Venice'. He would work every day until 2 p.m., then take his gondola – 'which was always in waiting' – to the Piazzetta, 'the peculiar charm of which always had a cheerful effect on me'. There he would meet Ritter, and the two would lunch together at the Albergo S. Marco before strolling up the Riva to the Public Gardens. At nightfall he would return to Palazzo Giustinian and a little more work, after which Karl would turn up around eight o'clock 'for a few hours' chat over our tea'. Sometimes, instead of the walk, they would take the gondola to the Lido, while in bad weather they normally went – despite Wagner's later denials – to a matinée at the Teatro Malibran. 'The audiences were excellent, the majority being in their shirt-sleeves, and the plays were usually passionate melodramas.'

Apart from Karl Ritter, Wagner's two closest friends in Venice were a local piano teacher named Tessarin – he gives no indication of his Christian name – and a Russian nobleman, Prince Dolgorukov. Tessarin 'was a typical handsome Venetian, with a peculiar impediment in his speech; he had a passion for German music, and was well acquainted both with Liszt's new compositions and with my own operas. He admitted that in his present milieu he was a "white raven" where music was concerned.' Tessarin was Wagner's only Venetian friend and, after the Master himself, was the principal performer at the occasional musical evenings held in the Giustinian. As for the Prince, he had accosted Wagner on one of his daily walks along the Riva to offer him his congratulations on *Lohengrin*, of which he had seen the first performance in Vienna only a week or two before. As was to be expected, he showed a good deal more sophistication than Tessarin. 'He had an earnest and extremely expressive face (he prided himself on being of direct Caucasian descent) and showed remarkable culture in every respect, a wide knowledge of the world, and above all a taste for music, in the literature of which he was also so well versed that it amounted to a passion.' Wagner at first tried to keep his distance but, as Dolgoru-kov was actually staying at the Albergo S. Marco where he and Ritter took their daily lunch, they were often thrown on each other's company and finally became close friends.

A less welcome presence was that of another pianist, a German named Winterberger, 'who felt it incumbent on him on certain occasions to behave eccentrically . . . He declared that he was provided by a brother with money enough to enjoy Italy – an experience which he declared necessary for his recreation and recovery, from what disease I do not know.' He also claimed to be a friend not only of Ritter but also of Liszt himself and, to Wagner's horror, rented an apartment in the same palazzo. The composer – never one to mince matters – demanded that he leave at once, pointing out that the rooms there were extremely expensive, and that he had accepted the additional cost simply because it was essential that he should not be disturbed, have no neighbours, and above all hear no piano. A compromise was finally reached when Winterberger agreed to move to the far end of the building, safely out of earshot. 'In this way I put up with his proximity, although it was a long time before I allowed Ritter to bring him to me of an evening.'

Musical performances, on the whole, he avoided. Venetian music had been in steady decline since the death of Vivaldi more than a century before. Already in October 1816, the German composer Ludwig Spohr had written:

There are two series of dilettanti-concerts here. One, under the direction of Count Tomasini, offers a concert every two weeks at the Fenice Theatre. At the one which I attended, Teresa Sessi, formerly engaged at Vienna, sang . . . in her old style, which is neither better nor worse. There was also an amateur who sang a number of buffo pieces in the authentic, rather exaggerated Italian manner. Everything else, particularly the composition and perform-ance of the overture was, as is usual in Italy, most wretched. The other is a mere rehearsal series under Signor Contin. The orchestra, with the exception of the basses and a few wind instruments, consists exclusively of amateurs and devotes itself principally to German symphonies and overtures. But a proper study of these works is quite out of the question: just getting through without breaking down is reckoned quite a success . . .

For the finale I was asked to conduct Beethoven's Symphony No. 2 in D major, which I could not very well refuse. It was an ordeal. The orchestra was used to tempi very different from mine, and seemed unaware of the distinction between *forte* and *piano*. Everyone scraped and blew for all he was worth. The noise was such that my ears ached all night.

The following half-century had shown little improvement. Nineteenth-century Italy was simply not interested in instrumental music. It thought only of opera, and Italian opera at that, which represented everything that Wagner despised. Even Giuseppe Verdi, in age his almost exact contemporary – there were only five months between them – receives not a single mention in his autobiography. During his stay in Venice he found only one sort of music tolerable:

It was the thoroughly German element of good military music, to which so much attention is paid in the Austrian army, that brought me in touch with public life in Venice. Both Austrian regiments stationed there had military bands, which played on alternate nights in the Piazza, and usually included the *Rienzi* or the *Tannhäuser* Overture in the programme. I was often startled towards the end of my meal by the sound of my own overtures; then, as I sat at the restaurant window giving myself up to impressions of the music, I did not know which dazzled me most, the incomparable piazza magnificently illuminated and filled with countless numbers of moving people, or the music that seemed to be borne away in rustling glory to the winds. Only one thing was wanting that might certainly have been expected from an Italian audience: the people were gathered round the band in thousands listening most intently, but no two hands ever forgot themselves so far as to applaud, as the least sign of approbation of Austrian military music would have been looked upon as treason to the Italian fatherland . . .

During one sleepless night, when I felt impelled to go out on to my balcony in the small hours, I heard for the first time the famous old song of the *gondolieri*. I seemed to hear the first call, in the stillness of the night, proceeding from the Rialto about a mile away like a rough lament, and answered in the same tone from a yet further distance in another direction. This melancholy dialogue, which was repeated at longer intervals, affected me so much that I could not fix the very simple musical component parts in my memory. But on a subsequent occasion another special experience revealed to me all the poetry of this simple song. As I was returning home late one night on the gloomy canal, the moon appeared suddenly and illuminated the marvellous palaces and the tall figure of my gondolier towering above the stern of the gondola, slowly moving his huge sweep. Suddenly he uttered a deep wail, not unlike the cry of an animal; the cry gradually gained in strength, and formed itself, after a long-drawn 'Oh!' into the simple musical exclamation 'Venezia!' This was followed by other sounds of which I have no distinct recollection, as I was so much moved at the time. Such were the impressions that appeared to me the most characteristic of Venice during my stay there; they remained with me until the completion of the second act of Tristan, and possibly even suggested to me the long-drawn wail of the shepherd's horn at the beginning of the third act.

At about this time Wagner developed an agonizing carbuncle on his leg, which kept him indoors – and largely bedridden – for nearly four weeks; and it was while he was thus incapacitated that he received a visit from Angelo Crespi, the Venetian Chief of Police. Crespi told him that his superior in Vienna, Baron von Kempen, was seriously concerned about his presence in Venice. His revolutionary activities at Dresden in 1848–9 had made him a wanted man in Saxony, and von Kempen had already given full particulars of him to the Saxon authorities who – despite the fact that he now carried a perfectly legitimate Swiss passport – had called for his expulsion. Von Kempen had accordingly ordered that he be kept under close surveillance, and that as soon as his health was sufficiently improved he must leave imperial territory.

Crespi had protested that Wagner was devoting himself exclusively to his art, 'in which his genius as a composer, musical essayist and critic has enabled him to open out a new path: as the creator of the so-called music of the future he stands at the head of the musical and aesthetic movement of today'. Von Kempen, however, remained adamant, and on 3 February 1859 Crespi called at Palazzo Giustinian to say that his efforts on Wagner's behalf had failed, and that he was now obliged to inform him, with the deepest possible regret, that he must leave Venice at his earliest convenience. If he wished to stay, one course only was open to him: he must appeal personally – with a doctor's certificate – to the Governor-General, the Emperor's younger brother Archduke Maximilian. Wagner did so, and was finally given permission to remain in Venice; but by now he himself had realized that the time had come to go. He felt unable to face the heat of another Venetian summer, and he yearned to be back in Switzerland where he could take the long mountain walks he loved. Moreover the political situation in Italy was deteriorating fast. On 10 December 1858 the Chief Minister of Savoy, Camillo Cavour, had formally enlisted the help of Napoleon III for a war of liberation. That war was indeed to break out the following spring; and already, Wagner noted, 'day by day the Riva was so crowded with newly disembarked troops that it became impossible to walk along it'. On 9 March he completed the orchestration of Act II of *Tristan*; back went his piano over the St Gotthard; and on the 23rd he left Venice for Lucerne.

★

It was two and a half years later, in the autumn of 1861, that Wagner wrote one of his all-too-frequent letters to Otto Wesendonk confessing that his 'affairs were in a bad way'. In his reply Otto – at whose patience one can only marvel – made no promises, but mentioned that he and Mathilde were shortly leaving on a pleasure trip to Venice, and suggested that Wagner might like to join them

there. Fortunately, Wagner had by then received a substantial
payment of royalties for a recent performance in Brunswick
of *Tannhäuser*; with this money he was able to take the train
from Vienna to Trieste and thence a boat – 'which did not agree
with me at all' – to Venice, where on 11 November he moved
into a small room at the Danieli. The journey seemed to him a
good investment. When he had last appealed to Otto six months
earlier, the Wesendonk business in New York was going
through something of a financial crisis and he had been sent
empty away; but now all was well and he clearly hoped for better
luck. Alas, once again he was in for a disappointment: Otto was
kindness itself, but his chequebook remained closed. 'They
seemed,' Wagner wrote ruefully, 'to have no desire to realise my
position in Vienna . . . I had learned to recognise, among most of
my friends, a tacitly submissive abandonment of all hope for my
future success.'

Meanwhile Otto and Mathilde did everything else they could to
cheer him up – and perhaps, to broaden his mind:

> Wesendonk, who never moved without an enormous pair of field-
> glasses and was always ready for some sight-seeing, once took me
> with him to the Academy of Arts, a building which on my former
> visit to Venice I had known only from the outside. In spite of all
> my indifference, I must confess that the *Assumption of the Virgin* by
> Titian★ exercised a most sublime influence over me so that, as soon
> as I realised its conception, my old powers revived within me as
> though by a sudden flash of inspiration. I determined at once on
> the composition of the *Meistersinger*.†

There seemed no longer any reason to stay:

★ Now back in the Frari, where – having first been hung there on 19 March
1518 – it belongs.
† It is in fact clear from his letters that he had taken this decision the previous
August, on a day's visit to Nuremberg; but perhaps the *Assumption* strengthened
his resolve.

After a frugal dinner with my old acquaintances Tessarin and the Wesendonks, whom I invited to the Albergo San Marco, and once more exchanging friendly greetings with Luigia, my former attendant at the Palazzo Giustiniani, to the astonishment of my friends I suddenly left Venice. I had spent four dreary days there, and now started by train on my dull journey to Vienna, following the roundabout overland route. It was during this journey that the music of the *Meistersinger* first dawned on my mind, in which I still retained the libretto as I had originally conceived it. With the utmost distinctness I at once composed the principal part of the Overture in C major.

It was fifteen years before he saw Venice again, on this third visit being accompanied by his second wife, Cosima, the daughter of Franz Liszt. They had married in August 1870, barely a month after her divorce from Wagner's friend and colleague, the conductor Hans von Bülow; but they had already lived together for six years, during which time she had borne him three children – on whom they had bestowed the appropriately Wagnerian names of Isolde, Eva and Siegfried. In the summer of 1876 they had embarked on a long Italian journey, in the course of which they also stayed in Verona, Bologna, Naples, Sorrento and Rome. They were in Venice for a week in late September, but *Mein Leben* stops in 1864 so we have all too little information about what went on.

By 1879, under the stresses of life at Bayreuth, Wagner's health was causing grave concern and his doctors advised a long period of rest in a warm climate. To him this could mean only Italy; he took the unfortunately named Villa Angri at Posilipo near Naples for six months, and on 3 January 1880 the whole family set off once again across the Alps, to find Naples suffering the coldest winter in living memory. Perhaps the most important event for Wagner during this protracted Italian journey – they were actually away for almost a year – was his meeting with a young Russian painter named Paul Zhukovsky. Fluent in German, he had long been an enthusiastic Wagnerian and had attended the Bayreuth Festival of 1876. The two took to each other at once. 'No one,' wrote Zhukovsky,

who has not known Wagner in the intimacy of his home can have
any idea of the goodness of his nature, his childlike lovableness.
Frau Wagner was right when she compared him to the child with
the orb whom St Christopher carries across the stream: he was a
child in spirit, with a whole world within him.

Wagner's views on Russia, as outlined to his new friend, were
however not so much childlike as infantile:

> I know how Russia can be helped, but no one asks me for my
> opinion. The Tsar should set fire to St Petersburg with his own
> hand, transfer his residence first of all to Odessa, and then go to
> Constantinople. That is the only way to show what there is in the
> Slav race. But to do that would need a stout fellow, and that sort
> isn't made any more.

Zhukovsky's reaction to this grotesque proposal is not recorded;
but his friendship with Wagner continued, and it was he who
would design the sets for *Parsifal*, which was to have its first public
performance two years later in July 1882.

Naples and Posilipo, meanwhile, had utterly failed to improve
Wagner's health. In August, to escape the worst of the summer
heat, he moved with Cosima and the children to the Villa Torre
Fiorentina just outside Siena; and from there, at the beginning of
October, they went on to Venice, where they remained till the
end of the month. They took rooms first at the Danieli and then at
one of the Contarini palaces; but the bad weather that they had
experienced since their arrival in Italy seemed to follow them
wherever they went. October in Venice is usually the most beautiful
month of the year, but 1880 proved an exception: the city was
unseasonably cold, and the rain never stopped. The one bright spot
on an otherwise murky scene was the writer and retired diplomat
Count⋆ Joseph-Arthur de Gobineau. Wagner had met him before

⋆ Or so, at least, he called himself; but the *Dictionnaire de biographie française*
maintains that he had no right to the title.

and had been intrigued; but it was only now in Venice that the two really got to know each other. Gobineau was clearly a fascinating man. Thanks to his diplomatic background he had travelled the world over and had served in capitals as widely dispersed as Tehran, Rio de Janeiro and Stockholm; among his books were a history of Persia, an inquiry into the philosophies of central Asia, a study of the Renaissance, a long novel (*Les Pléiades*) and a biography of the Norwegian pirate from whom he claimed to be descended; but perhaps his most challenging and controversial work was his thousand-page *Essai sur l'inégalité des races humaines*, in which Wagner believed that he had found the ultimate confirmation of his own hideously racialist ideas.

★

Of the Wagners' last two Venetian visits, one was little more than a preparation for the other. Both were in 1882, the year of *Parsifal*. The composer, now in his seventieth year, was obviously a sick man; and he and Cosima, knowing full well that the strain of the coming production must seriously threaten what little remained of his strength, resolved to leave for Venice at the earliest possible moment after the final curtain had fallen. Despite the fact that the opera was already in rehearsal, they therefore slipped away for a fortnight in April to seek a suitable lodging. They looked first at one of the Loredan palaces, but failed to reach agreement with the owners; and so on 28 April they decided to take, for 6,000 francs, the fully furnished mezzanine floor of Palazzo Vendramin-Calergi.

The remainder of the building was occupied by members of the family of King Charles X of France, who had been deposed half a century before. It is not perhaps one of the most immediately endearing of Venetian palaces, but it must surely be one of the most impressive. Designed and partly built by one of the greatest of early Renaissance Venetian architects, Mauro Coducci, it was completed by the equally distinguished Lombardi family. Beneath the ground-floor windows – a curious place for an inscription – are incised the words of the psalmist NON NOBIS DOMINE (Not unto us, O Lord) for reasons not entirely clear.★ It is conceived on a huge scale: even the mezzanine, with nearly twenty rooms, was big enough – as it had to be – to accommodate all five Wagners, Cosima's daughter Daniela von Bülow, a Sicilian governess for Isolde and Eva and a German tutor for Siegfried, together with a cook, maid and man-servant also from Germany, to say nothing of an old porter (who came with the palace) and two gondoliers.

After the last performance of his opera on 29 August, Wagner thought only of getting to Venice. His health was failing fast and his heart was giving serious cause for concern. He had also fallen into a profound depression, and told Cosima that he longed for death. Obviously the family could not get away immediately – there was too much to be done – but they managed to leave Bayreuth on 14 September and two days later arrived in Venice where, after a brief stay at the Hotel Europa, they finally installed themselves in their palazzo. Wagner immediately redecorated his study as he had at the Giustinian – and indeed as he always did if he expected to be somewhere for any length of time – transforming it into what was described as a 'blue grotto'. As always, too, he sprinkled the furniture with the most powerful perfumes he could find – another attempt, we can only assume, to insulate himself from the outside world.

But for Richard Wagner insulation was impossible. He was soon besieged by old friends, among them his father-in-law, Liszt, the composers Joseph Rubinstein and Engelbert Humperdinck and, of course, his faithful friend Paul Zhukovsky. The party was not altogether happy. Zhukovsky wrote:

> As they grew older, each of these two great men and unique friends gradually lost the capacity to understand the other's way of life. Liszt loved to have a numerous company about him; Wagner could endure only a small band of intimates. When they talked together, neither paid attention to what the other was saying: both spoke at

★ Although, since the words leap out at everyone entering the Municipal Casino, which it now accommodates, they may not be thought altogether inappropriate.

the same time, and this often led to the strangest quiproquos [*sic*]. Each was so accustomed to being the sole centre of attention that there was always a certain amount of awkwardness when they were together.

Another visitor was Anton Seidl, who had acted as Wagner's general secretary and amanuensis for six years during the 1870s. He hero-worshipped his master, and would willingly have remained with him for the rest of his life; but Wagner believed that he was destined for better things and in 1879 had recommended him to his friend the impresario Angelo Neumann, begging him to take on 'this young musician, in whom I have more confidence than in any other'.★ Seidl too now arrived in Venice, with exciting news: the long-lost instrumental parts of Wagner's early C major symphony – composed in the late spring of 1832 – had recently been found in Dresden, and with the help of these he had been able to put together a full orchestral score. Wagner, despite his steadily deteriorating health, decided to conduct a performance of it at the Fenice as a birthday present for Cosima, entrusting the task to the orchestra of the Liceo Benedetto Marcello, founded just a few years before. During the final rehearsal on 22 December he suffered a minor heart attack after the first movement and had to ask Seidl to take over; but somehow he recovered enough to conduct the full symphony on Christmas Eve. It was in no sense a public performance; the audience consisted only of Cosima herself and the children, with Liszt (who brought two of his friends), Zhukovsky, Humperdinck and Count Contini, founder-president of the Liceo.

On Shrove Tuesday, 6 February 1883, Wagner went out with his children to watch the celebrations of the last night of the Carnival – looking, it was thought, better than he had for some time. The next morning, however, he was found to have developed

★Two years after Wagner's death Seidl moved to New York, where he took US citizenship and lived until his death in 1898. Principal Conductor at the Metropolitan Opera (1885–91) and of the New York Philharmonic (1891–8), he set new standards in American orchestral playing and became the foremost American musical celebrity of his day.

a feverish cold; he had no choice but to cancel the trip to Verona or Bologna that he had been planning with his son Siegfried, now thirteen. By the afternoon of the 12th he was sufficiently recovered to take a short walk with his daughter Eva and, the same evening, to play on his piano the final song of the Rhine Maidens from *Rheingold*; but on the morning of the 13th he was clearly very ill. 'I shall have to look after myself today,' he remarked to his valet on waking. He dressed, and went into his study to work on an article, but at two o'clock, when the family normally lunched, he sent word that they should start without him. An anxious Cosima went at once to the study. Hunched over his desk, he waved her away; then, a short time afterwards, his bell rang twice and he ordered the maid to bring 'the doctor and my wife'. The doctor arrived at three, but it was too late: another heart attack had burst a blood vessel and he was dead. Just before he died, Cosima was trying to move him to a more comfortable position, and his watch – a present from her – slipped from his pocket to the ground. '*Meine Uhr*', he murmured, 'My watch'. Then his head fell forward. Throughout the night Cosima kept vigil by the body; not until four o'clock on the afternoon of the 14th – more than twenty-four hours later – did she allow herself to be helped away. Later she cut off the gloriously thick hair that her husband had always loved, and laid it on his breast.★

A heavy oak coffin was ordered by telegraph from Vienna and arrived only two days later. Then, on the 16th, the body was rowed in a twelve-oared funeral gondola the short distance to the station to begin its long journey to Bayreuth. Cosima alone accompanied it in a private *coupé*; the children, with Zhukovsky and the con- ductor Hans Richter – who on hearing the news had taken the next train to Venice – were in a separate coach behind. With them also were two other friends of the Wagners, Adolf von Gross and

---

★ This account of Wagner's death is taken almost entirely from pp. 680–83 in Vol. 4 of Ernest Newman's magisterial biography. Some of the less important details have been omitted, but there is nothing to add: Newman remains the greatest Wagnerian of them all.

his wife, who were to give Cosima much valuable support in the sad months to come.

★

The mezzanine floor of Palazzo Vendramin-Calergi remains much as the Wagners left it; one can still see – and indeed sit in – the chair in which the great man died. The façade of the palace and its little garden are also largely unchanged. The principal difference is the large plaque, clearly visible from the passing *vaporetti*, bearing a relief portrait by the Venetian sculptor Ettore Cadorin and a characteristically flowery inscription by Gabriele d'Annunzio; and even this is passed unnoticed by the vast majority of the patrons flocking to the Casino Municipale. Yet the Venetians still show a certain proprietorial feeling towards Richard Wagner: until the tragic destruction of the Fenice by fire on the night of 29 January 1996, his works were performed there more frequently than in any other Italian opera house; and many of us well remember how in the 1950s, when the municipal orchestra used to give alfresco performances in the Piazza on summer nights, the overtures to *Rienzi*, *Tannhäuser*, *Lohengrin* and *Meistersinger* were regular favourites, just as they had been when Wagner had heard them played by the Austrian military band while he sat with Karl Ritter in the Albergo San Marco, almost a century before.

8. Henry James
(1869–1907)

'Well,' said I, 'what has Venice done for you?'
   'Many things. Tired me a little, saddened me, charmed me.'
   'How have you spent your time?'
   'As people spend it . . . You must have learned already how sweet it is to lean back under the awning, to feel beneath you that steady, liquid lapse, to look out at all this bright, sad elegance of ruin.'

Henry James, 'Travelling Companions'

Henry James first arrived in Italy on foot from Switzerland. There were no tunnels through the Alps in 1869; sending his luggage in advance to Milan, he set forth from Brig early in September and trudged the thirty-three miles over the Simplon Pass to Iselle, on the Italian frontier. A few days later, from the Hotel Barbesi at S. Samuele, he wrote to his brother William of 'that mighty summer's day upon the Simplon, when I communed with immensity and sniffed Italy from afar. This Italian tone of things which I then detected lies richly on my soul and gathers increasing weight.' By the middle of the month he reached Venice – where, like many another diligent American tourist of the day, he would spend the next fortnight in a gondola, being paddled through the countless canals of the city with Murray in one pocket and Ruskin in the other, springing ashore whenever some glorious church or picture claimed his attention. In the evenings he would wander down to the Piazza and sit at Florian or Quadri, writing countless letters and quietly meditating on all that he had seen.

   Only three or four years earlier, the atmosphere in the great Square would have been very different. While Venetia-Lombardy was still part of the Habsburg Empire, no self-respecting Italian would have been seen dead at Quadri, which teemed with the white-and-red uniforms of the Austrian army; unhesitatingly he would have headed for Florian, where for half a century his compatriots had planned and plotted the overthrow of the hated occupiers. Now at last Venice was part of a united Italy, her citizens jubilant at their newfound freedom. Henry James, for his part, does not seem to have noticed. Nowhere in his copious writings on the city is there any mention of the momentous political events of the late 1860s. But there: he was not interested in politics – nor, perhaps more surprisingly, was he really interested in the Venetians. No one better understood the motivations of the human heart, so long as that heart remained part of the world that he had made his own – the world of the leisured and usually wealthy English or American upper class. In London or New York he felt at home; in Venice he was always an outsider – on this first visit, indeed, almost painfully so. On 25 September he wrote to his brother William:

> I can't for my life frankly surrender myself to the Genius of Italy, or the Spirit of the South – or whatever one may call the confounded thing; but I nevertheless *feel* it in all my pulses . . . Ruskin recommends the traveller to frequent and linger in a certain glorious room at the Ducal Palace, where Paolo Veronese revels on the ceilings and Tintoret rages on the walls, because 'nowhere else will he enter so deeply into the heart of Venice.' But I feel as if I might sit there forever (as I sat there for a long time this morning) and only feel more and more my inexorable Yankeehood.

Back in America in 1870, however, the spell of Venice continued to work on him; scarcely otherwise could he have written the exquisite short story 'Travelling Companions', which was published in the *Atlantic Monthly* at the end of that same year. The first-person narrator, alone in Italy on a cultural tour, meets in Milan a fellow American from New Jersey and his beautiful and highly intelligent daughter. A few days later, now in Venice, he wanders into St Mark's, where, 'in the gorgeous composite darkness', he sees the girl again. The three renew their acquaintance and spend a week together sightseeing – about which, fortunately for him, the daughter is considerably more enthusiastic than her father; he manages thus to spend a fair amount of time alone with her, and one evening on the Lido he declares his love, which she gently but firmly brushes aside. Shortly afterwards, after what should have been a day trip to Padua, they miss the last train back to Venice and are obliged to stay in a local hotel. This clearly creates a compromising situation, and they return the following morning to find her father not best pleased. To protect her honour, the narrator is only too happy to propose marriage, but she refuses and he leaves Venice at once. It is only some weeks later, in Rome, that he finds her once more, this time in St Peter's, where she tells him that her father has died of a sudden stroke. On the following day he renews his offer – and is accepted.

Summarized as baldly as this, 'Travelling Companions' sounds both improbable and inconsequential. Already, however, the 27-year-old author has developed a brilliant narrative style, and the delicacy and sensitivity with which he tells his story make it both moving and completely convincing. There is, too, a description of the interior of St Mark's of which John Ruskin himself might have been proud:

> From those rude concavities of dome and semi-dome, where the multitudinous facets of pictorial mosaic shimmer and twinkle in their own dull brightness; from the vast antiquity of innumerable marbles, incrusting the walls in roughly mated slabs, cracked and polished and triple-tinted with eternal service; from the wavy carpet of compacted stone, where a thousand once-bright fragments glimmer through the long attrition of idle feet and devoted knees; from sombre gold and mellow alabaster, from porphyry and malachite, from long dead crystal and the sparkle of undying lamps, – there proceeds a dense rich atmosphere of splendor and sanctity which transports the half-stupefied traveller to the age of a simpler and more awful faith. I wandered for half an hour beneath those reverted cups of scintillating darkness, stumbling on the great stony swells of

the pavement as I gazed upward at the long mosaic saints who curve gigantically with the curves of dome and ceiling. I had left Europe; I was in the East.

At the beginning of September 1872 Henry James was back in Venice – this time with his sister Alice and his Aunt Kate (Mrs Catherine Temple). He wrote to his parents:

We gave ourselves four full days . . . Most delightful days they were, for it was only the [mosquito-ridden] nights that were obnoxious. We left nothing unseen that we wished to see, lived in our gondola, and found abundant coolness on the water and in the darksome churches. We went to Torcello – an ever memorable excursion; to Murano; twice to the Lido (which has been sadly 'improved' since I was there last) but where we dined most breezily on a platform where bathers and diners were strewn in true Italian promiscuity; spent much time in St Mark's, and had ample leisure to see all the desirable pictures. The weather was perfect, we ate innumerable figs, ices every night at Florian's and bought a few very beautiful photographs (all of pictures, many of which you have not seen) so that our four days were a great success and seemed more like a fortnight.

In short, the entirely predictable letter home from the cultivated tourist. His soul, clearly, still remained unmoved. Even Torcello – memorable or not – failed to enthral:

Torcello was the mother-city of Venice, and she lies there now, a mere mouldering vestige, like a group of weather-bleached parental bones left impiously unburied.

Nine years were to pass until he saw Venice again – years that saw the publication of *Roderick Hudson*, *The American* and *Daisy Miller*. All these novels are concerned, to a greater or lesser degree, with the impact of European civilization on American life. Then, in 1881, his writing begins to concentrate on Europe, and particularly on England. That year was, arguably, the year in which he became a true European; and it was also the year in which he returned to Venice. He arrived on 25 March and stayed – with short excursions to the mainland – till 1 July. On 12 June he wrote to his friend Mrs Charles Eliot Norton:

> The simplest thing to tell you of Venice is that I adore it – have fallen deeply and desperately in love with it; in spite of their having just begun to run an infamous *vaporino* on the Grand Canal. I had been there twice before but each time only for a few days. This time I have drunk deep, and the magic potion has entered into my blood . . .
>
> Tell Charles, whom I salute *caramente*, that I can tell him little good of St Mark's. I know nothing of the necessities of what they are doing to the poor dear old beautiful building; but the effect produced is that of witnessing the forcible *maquillage* of one's grand-mother! In a word, if it be a necessity, it is an abominable necessity, and the side of the church toward the Piazzetta, where the *maquillage* is now complete, is a sight to make the angels howl.★

He found what he described as 'dirty apartments, meagrely and hideously furnished, with a lovely view' on the fourth floor of a house on the Riva degli Schiavoni (no. 4161, now the Albergo Paganelli), looking straight out over the lagoon to S. Giorgio Maggiore, where he confessed to spending hours with a pair of binoculars looking at the ships and – especially – the gondoliers, whose motions, he wrote, had 'the boldness of a plunging bird and the regularity of a pendulum'.

> The view from my windows was *una bellezza*; the far-shining lagoon, the pink walls of San Giorgio, the downward curve of the Riva, the distant islands, the movement of the quay, the gondolas

★ This, it should be noted, was four years after Count Alvise Zorzi, with the support of John Ruskin, had stopped the restoration work, not a moment too soon, in 1877. See p. 99.

in profile. Here I wrote diligently every day and finished, or virtually finished, my novel.★

At last, as it were, he had entered into possession of the city. After an early breakfast at Florian's he would go – weather permitting – to the Stabilimento Chitarin for a salt-water bath, then spend the morning strolling through the city until it was time for lunch, usually at Quadri. Afterwards he would return to his rooms and work through the afternoon, occasionally wandering to the window to see whether 'out in the blue channel, the ship of some right suggestion, of some better phrase, of the next happy twist of my subject, the next true touch for my canvas, mightn't come into sight'. How often such a vessel appeared he does not say, but the trips to the window seem to have been fairly frequent: as he himself was later to point out in *Italian Hours*, 'Venice isn't in fair weather a place for concentration of mind. The effort required for sitting down to a writing-table is heroic, and the brightest page of MS looks dull beside the brilliancy of your *milieu*.' The day's work done, he would spend a couple of hours drifting gently in a gondola before taking another stroll, sitting at Florian's listening to the music in the Piazza or, two or three times a week, calling on his friend Mrs Katharine de Kay Bronson.

★

James had first met Mrs Bronson in October 1875, on a particularly rough crossing from New York. (Also on board had been Anthony Trollope, who had greatly impressed him by his ability, while all the other passengers were groaning in their cabins, to work regardless for four hours a day.) In 1876, with her husband and daughter Edith, she had taken a small house directly opposite the Salute. In 1880 Mr Bronson had left for Paris – the victim, according to Lady Layard, of 'a softening of the brain brought on by dissipation'; thenceforth the two ladies lived there alone. Though the house was also known as Palazzo Gaggia, it somehow seemed too

★ *Portrait of a Lady.*

modest to deserve so grand a title: to the Bronsons and their guests it was always simply the Ca' Alvisi. James wrote of his new friend:

> She sat for twenty years at the wide mouth, as it were, of the Grand Canal, holding out her hand, with endless good-nature, patience, charity, to all decently accredited petitioners, the incessant troop of those either bewilderedly making or fondly renewing acquaintance with the dazzling city . . .
>
> The house, in a city of palaces, was small, but the tenant clung to her perfect, her inclusive position – the one right place that gave her a better command, as it were, than a better house obtained by a harder compromise; not being fond, moreover, of spacious halls and massive treasures, but of compact and familiar rooms, in which her remarkable accumulation of minute and delicate Venetian objects could show. She adored – in the way of the Venetian, to which all her taste addressed itself – the small, the domestic and the exquisite; so that she would have given a Tintoretto or two, I think, without difficulty, for a cabinet of tiny gilded glasses or a dinner-service of the right old silver.

She and her daughter were endlessly hospitable. Though her own house was small, she had managed to acquire part of the old Palazzo Giustinian which stood immediately behind it, and here she delighted to put up her friends – always giving them their own cook-gondolier, so that they could feel independent and join their hosts only when they wished. Moreover, unlike all the other British and American residents except Horatio Brown, she flung herself with enthusiasm into the life of the Venetians themselves:

> She cultivated their dialect, she renewed their boats, she piously relighted – at the top of the tide-washed *pali* of traghetto or lagoon – the neglected lamp of the tutelary Madonetta; she took cognizance of the wives, the children, the accidents, the troubles, as to which she became, perceptibly, the most prompt, the established remedy . . . She put together in dialect many short comedies, dramatic proverbs, which, with one of her drawing-rooms permanently

arranged as a charming diminutive theatre, she caused to be performed by the young persons of her circle – often, when the case lent itself, by the wonderful small offspring of humbler friends, children of the Venetian lower class, whose aptitude, teachability, drollery were her constant delight.

It was somehow inevitable that on Henry James's next visit to Venice, from February to April 1887, Mrs Bronson would insist that he should be her guest. Despite her efforts, however, the visit was not a complete success. The cold was extreme by Venetian standards – there was a blizzard and heavy snowfall in March; he complained, too, of the 'glutinous malodorous damp', and of the Bronsons' milieu which he condemned as 'too American'. On the other hand he met the Curtises, who were also to become firm friends.

Daniel Curtis and his English-born wife Ariana were rich Bostonians who might never have left their native city but for an unfortunate incident some years before, which was later to be reported in two different versions. The story assiduously spread round Venice by Mrs Curtis was that her husband had knocked down a policeman who had insulted her; in fact the altercation had occurred in a Boston tramcar, and the victim had been a judge called Churchill, who had later testified that Curtis had attacked him, twisted his nose and broken his spectacles; the only policeman involved had been the one who made the inevitable arrest. The consequence – and here both versions were in agreement – had been a two-month prison sentence, after which Curtis had indignantly shaken the dust of America off his feet and settled with his wife in Europe. In July 1881 and for the next four years they rented Palazzo Barbaro on the Grand Canal – Henry James wrote inquiring about their 'palatial experiment' – and on 3 December 1885, at half past two in the afternoon, they acquired it as their permanent home. It was to remain in their family for well over a century.

Venice is, as everyone knows, awash with palaces; but few of them are more genuinely palatial than the Barbaro. The second one down from the Accademia Bridge on the S. Marco side, with a magnificent early fifteenth-century Gothic façade, it had been built around 1460 by Zaccaria Barbaro – though it suffered import-ant alterations at the end of the seventeenth century – and had remained the property of the family until the nineteenth. The Barbaros had not, on the other hand, always lived in it themselves. In 1499 it had served as the French Embassy; later it was occupied by the celebrated patron of the arts Isabella d'Este, widow of the Marquis of Mantua, Francesco Gonzaga.* It was, wrote James, 'all marble and frescos and portraits of the Doges'. The Tiepolo frescoes are alas gone, though several others remain; and there are still many fine pictures, together with some superb furniture and plaster-work.† Here Mr and Mrs Curtis, with their painter son Ralph and a cat named Caterina Cornaro, lived a life of unashamed luxury, waited on by innumerable servants and a whole company of gondo-liers. James was to grow very fond of them – despite Mr Curtis 'doing his best to make the Grand Canal seem like Beacon Street' and his appalling jokes‡ – but would return to the more modest attractions of Ca' Alvisi with more than a touch of relief.

He was still there early in April 1887, when he suffered an attack of jaundice and was laid up for a fortnight; he then fled to Florence, to convalesce with his cousin Constance Fenimore Woolson. Miss Woolson – 'Fenimore', he always called her – was the great-niece of James Fenimore Cooper. Like the rest of her family she hailed from Cooperstown, in the lake country of upstate New York; but later, during the Reconstruction, she had spent much time in the

---

* Her portrait by Titian hangs in the Gemäldegalerie in Vienna.

† As for the plasterwork, the great Salone degli Stucchi was at one moment almost sold to the Victoria and Albert Museum. It was saved only because its transportation was found to be practically impossible. It is clearly visible in the superb painting of the Curtis family by their distant relative and constant guest John Singer Sargent, now in the Royal Academy, London – which, incidentally, Henry James 'absolutely adored'. 'I've seen few things of Sargent's,' he wrote, 'that I've craved more to possess.' See p. 230.

‡ 'One calculates the time when one shall have worked through his anecdotes and come out the other side. Perhaps one never does – it is an unboreable – or unbearable – St Gothard.'

South. When she first came to Europe in the winter of 1879–80 at the age of thirty-nine, she was already an established author: her first major novel, *Anne*, had sold 57,600 copies, and she had followed it with two volumes of short stories and two more novels. She had first met Henry James in 1880 in Florence. 'She is amiable but deaf,' he wrote, 'and asks me questions about my works to which she can't hear the answers'; but he was struck, nevertheless, by her intelligence and charm and he genuinely admired her writing, on which he had contributed an article to *Harper's Weekly*.* The two became firm friends, he being a good deal more at ease with her than he was with most women; she – in her prim, spinsterish way and perhaps for the first and last time in her life – seems to have been more than a little in love with him. Now, after seven years' acquaintance, the two were staying together in the Villa Brichieri-Colombi under the same roof – a fact which occasioned some comment in Anglo-American Florentine society,† even though there can be little doubt but that the strictest proprieties were observed. It was while staying with Miss Woolson that he began – and very nearly completed – one of the greatest of his shorter novels, *The Aspern Papers*.

When in Tuscany the previous January, James had visited 'the most intelligent person in Florence', his old friend Violet Paget, who had already lived thirty years in Italy and – under the name of Vernon Lee – had written an impressive number of books on Italian art and architecture. With her he had met the Contessa Gamba, who had married the nephew of Byron's Teresa Guiccioli and who told him that she had a number of 'shocking and unprintable' letters from Byron, one of which she had decided to burn. After she had left, Miss Paget's half-brother Eugene Lee-Hamilton, now confined to a sofa with partial paralysis,

* In the issue of 12 February 1887. A revised version of this article was included in his *Partial Portraits* – in which Miss Woolson, now rubbing shoulders with George Eliot, Maupassant and Turgenev, might be thought a little out of her league.
† Memorably described by James in a letter: 'The queer polyglot promiscuous society struck me as a vain agitation of insignificant principles.'

told me a curious thing of Capt. Silsbee – the Boston art-critic and
Shelley-worshipper; that is of a curious adventure of his. Miss
Claremont, Byron's *ci-devant* mistress (the mother of Allegra) was
living, until lately, here in Florence, at a great age, 80 or thereabouts,
and with her lived her niece, a younger Miss Claremont, of about
50. Silsbee knew that they had interesting papers – letters of Shelley's
and Byron's – he had known it for a long time and cherished the
idea of getting hold of them. To this end he laid the plan of going
to lodge with the Misses Claremont – hoping that the old lady in
view of her great age and failing condition would die while he was
there, so that he might then put his hand upon the documents,
which she hugged close in life. He carried out this scheme – and
things *se passèrent* [turned out] as he had expected. The old woman
did die – and then he approached the younger one – the old maid
of 50 – on the subject of his desires. Her answer was – 'I will give
you all the letters if you marry me!' H. says that Silsbee *court encore*
[is still running]. Certainly there is a little subject there – the picture
of the two faded, queer, poor, discredited old English women –
living on into a strange generation, in their musty corner of a foreign
town with these illustrious letters their most precious possession . . .

For *The Aspern Papers*, James transferred the action to Venice,
setting it in the house of another American literary friend, the writer
Constance Fletcher: this was the late-sixteenth-century Palazzo
Soranzo-Cappello on the Rio Manin (no. 770, just behind
S. Simeone Piccolo).

It is the old faded pink-faced battered-looking and quite homely
and plain (as things go in Venice) old Palazzino on the right side of
the small Canal, a little way along, as you enter it by the end of the
Canal towards the Station. It has a garden behind it, and I think,
though I am not sure, some bit of garden-wall beside it; it doesn't
moreover bathe its steps, if I remember right, directly in the Canal,
but has a small paved Riva or footway in front of it, and *then*
water-steps down from this little quay. As to that, however, the
time since I have seen it may muddle me . . .

It seems fairly clear that 'Miss Tita' – to give her her original name before James changed it to 'Tina' – the middle-aged niece of Juliana Bordereau, she is clearly a portrait of Constance Fenimore Woolson herself.

★

In May 1887 James was back in Venice, intending to spend only ten days with the Curtises in Palazzo Barbaro; but his health was restored, spring was in the air, he had been given a suite of delightfully cool rooms at the back looking over the garden, and he could not bring himself to leave. 'If,' he wrote,

> in the absence of its masters you have happened to have it to yourself for twenty-four hours you will never forget the charm of its haunted stillness, late on a summer afternoon for instance, when the call of playing children comes in behind from the campo, nor the way the old ghosts seemed to pass on tiptoe on the marble floors.

Yielding to Mrs Curtis's repeated invitations to stay on, he did so for five weeks – the longest visit he had ever paid to the city – during which he made an interesting new friend. The name of the Contessa Pisani has already once been mentioned in these pages, when she provided the Venetian banner, representing the winged Lion of St Mark, which was wrapped around the dead body of Rawdon Brown in his coffin.★ Born Evelyn van Millingen, she was the daughter of Dr Julius van Millingen, who had attended Byron during his last illness at Missolonghi. Later, while serving as a surgeon in the Greek army, he had been taken prisoner by Ibrahim Pasha and had been released only on the urgent representations of Sir Stratford Canning, then British Ambassador to the Porte. In 1827 he had settled permanently in Constantinople, where he was court physician to no fewer than five successive Sultans – Mahmoud II, Abdul Mejid, Abdul Aziz, Murad V and Abdul Hamid. According to the *Dictionary of National Biography*, 'He was married three

★ See Chapter 5, p. 113.

times, having separated from his first wife, a Roman Catholic who thereupon embraced Islam and entered a harem. Her son, Frederick Millingen, became Osman Bey in the Turkish army, and afterwards turned Greek under the name Alexis Andrejevitch.' (An odd name, it might be thought, for a Greek.)

Evelyn was the daughter of that first wife. Sent by her father to Rome for her education, she had then rejoined him in Constantinople; but it was not long before he brought her back to Italy, where in Venice she is said to have captivated everybody by appearing at the Fenice, on the very evening of her arrival, in exotic oriental dress. Later she married Almorò III Pisani, thus becoming a member of one of the oldest and most distinguished of all the old noble families of Venice. After his death she moved her principal home to the family's great seventeenth-century country villa at Vescovana, between Este and Rovigo, where she worked tirelessly to improve the condition of the 400 *contadini* on the estate. Meanwhile she maintained an apartment in Venice, next to the Palazzo Barbaro. 'Widowed, childless, palaced, villaed, pictured, jewelled and modified by Venetian society', she fascinated Henry James, who was at least once her guest at Vescovana. She was, he wrote, 'a most remarkable woman – a lady who vaguely suggests Caterina Cornaro and makes one believe in the romantic heroines of D'Israeli and Bulwer'. Many years later he was to write to Mrs Curtis:

> I bless your house and all it contains – not least the ghost of what prevails there of the presence of the noble Pisani. There ought, for her, to be no decline, but a kind of swift immersion – into the Adriatic, say, of Almorò and his Doges . . .

By now the idea of a permanent *pied-à-terre* in Venice has become a recurrent theme in James's letters. It was an ambition, however, never to be fulfilled; and he was back in London when, on the evening of 12 December 1889, Robert Browning died in the Ca' Rezzonico. He had known Browning well, and had certainly heard him giving readings of his poems, both at Ca' Alvisi and at the Palazzo Barbaro. 'It seems to me,' he wrote, 'that on the whole he is the writer of our times of whom, in the face of the rest of the world, the English tongue may be most proud, for he has touched every thing and with such a breadth! I put him very high – higher than anyone . . .' As a man, on the other hand, he found Browning quite unrevealing of his genius as a poet, and James had never 'seized the link between the two'. However that might be, there could be no doubt that his death was an immeasurable loss to English letters, and James duly attended the memorial service at Westminster Abbey on 31 December, which was held before Browning's burial in Poets' Corner.

He was back in the Barbaro in July 1892; this time, however, as the guest of the formidable Mrs Isabella Stewart Gardner, who made a point of renting the palace from the Curtises whenever she came to Venice. Today she is remembered above all for the superb museum at Fenway Court, Boston, which she created after her husband's death and which bears her name; but this was still in the future. Thanks to her passion for art, her immaculate taste and the advice that she sought from experts such as the young Bernard Berenson – to whom her husband had given considerable financial help in his early days – she was now, at the age of fifty-two, making her name as one of the leading collectors of her time: awaiting her when she arrived in Venice that summer were seven armchairs, gilded and painted, that she had acquired at the Borghese sale a month or two before and that were said to have been a present from the Doge to Pope Paul V. James wrote to Mrs Curtis in Asolo that 'her seven glorious chairs' were 'the loveliest I ever saw, but they are not a symbol of her attitude – she never sits down'. To Mrs Gardner herself, after his departure, he wrote:

Dear Donna Isabella, I don't know where this will find you, but I hope it will find you with your hair not quite 'up' – neither up nor down, as it were, in a gauze dressing-gown on a sea-green (so different from pea-green) chair, beneath a glorious gilded ceiling, receiving the matutinal tea from a Venetian slave.

The house was – as usual during Mrs Gardner's occupancy – full to bursting with her guests, and he was particularly pleased to find that she had put up a bed for him in the library where, like his future heroine Milly Theale, he would awake every morning to find himself tracing the arabesque decorations of the ceiling. He had always had a taste for the rich and palatial; here at the Barbaro, waited on hand and foot, he could indulge it to the full.

★

Until now, all Henry James's visits to Venice had been for pleasure and relaxation. His next provided neither, occasioned as it was by a tragedy: the suicide of Constance Fenimore Woolson. Miss Woolson had been living in Venice since May 1893, admitting herself to be 'depressed in spirits'. She had at first taken rooms in Casa Biondetti★ but was soon driven out by overcrowding – there were four other American ladies in the same building – and in September had moved into the top two floors of Palazzo Semitecolo,† renting them on an eight-month lease at $40 a month.

It was there at the Semitecolo, soon after midnight on Wednesday 24 January 1894, that Miss Woolson, aged fifty-three, threw herself from her bedroom window. A moment later two passing men saw a heap of white lying on the cobbles and prodded it with a stick; it gave a low moan, and they immediately raised the alarm. Miss Woolson's servants ran out and carried her back upstairs, but it was too late: three-quarters of an hour later she was dead. She had taken to her bed ten days before with a high fever – probably influenza – and at the instigation of Edith Bronson had engaged a lady named Marie Holas as secretary-companion for the duration of her illness. Unfortunately Miss Holas did not live in the palazzo, which she had left at about nine o'clock the previous evening; but

---

★ On the Dorsoduro side, next to the Palazzo Venier dei Leoni (the Peggy Guggenheim Collection) towards the Accademia. No. 715 at S. Vio, it was formerly the home of the pastel portraitist Rosalba Carriera, and bears a plaque in her memory.

† This is the small fifteenth-century Gothic palazzo, with a row of six arches along the *piano nobile* and a little dormer window, almost directly opposite the Giglio *vaporetto* stop across the Grand Canal.

she subsequently wrote a full account of Miss Woolson's last days.★
At first, it seemed, her employer had been in quite good spirits; but
on the 17th she had suddenly asked to make her will. 'She told me
also, that in case of her death I must not let her be buried in the
cemetery of Venice, as she hated the place, & the only place where
she could rest in peace was the cemetery in Rome.'

On the following day Miss Woolson's condition deteriorated
alarmingly and a trained nurse was called – a nun. She in her turn
testified that at a quarter past twelve Miss Woolson asked for some
milk, but refused to drink it from the cup she was given and sent
her down to the dining room to fetch another one, of pink china.
The nun went, and on her return found the window open, the
curtains flung wide and the bed empty. She shouted for Angelo,
the gondolier who slept in the house, and as he dashed downstairs
the doorbell rang. It was the two men, with the motionless body
of Miss Woolson in their arms. At first light the American Consul
was informed of her death, and a telegram was sent to her sister,
Clara Benedict, in New York; Mrs Benedict in turn cabled a cousin,
Grace Carter, who was in Munich and thus within fairly easy reach.
She arrived in Venice on the evening of the 25th and took over
the situation at once. She it was who accompanied the body to
Rome, where – thanks in large measure to John Hay, an old friend
of the family who chanced to be in the city at the time – the burial
took place as Miss Woolson had wished.

Henry James received the news in a cable from Mrs Benedict,
which was followed almost at once by another from John Hay,
informing him of the plans for the funeral. He went straight to
Cook's to arrange his journey to Rome, but on returning home
that evening found a note from Constance Fletcher in Venice,
enclosing a cutting from a Venetian newspaper. Now for the first
time he read of the manner of Miss Woolson's death, and the truth
was borne in upon him that she had killed herself. The realization
affected him profoundly. He wrote to John Hay:

★ This is printed in full on pp. 267–70 of *A Private Life of Henry James*, by Lyndall
Gordon.

I have utterly collapsed. I have let everything go, and last night I wired to Miss Carter that my dismal journey was impossible to me. I have, this morning, looked it more in the face, but I can't attempt it . . . Miss Woolson was so valued and close a friend of mine and had been for so many years that I feel an intense nearness of participation in every circumstance of her tragic end and in every detail of the sequel. But it is just this nearness of emotion that has made – since yesterday – the immediate horrified rush to personally *meet* these things impossible to me.

And to Mrs Bronson:

> . . . I can't, while the freshness of such a misery as it all must have been, is in the air, feel anything but that Venice is not a place I want immediately to see. I had known Miss Woolson for many years and was extremely attached to her – she was the gentlest and tenderest of women, and full of intelligence and sympathy.

In neither letter does he give any reason, other than his own emotional state, for the cancellation of a journey which he would unquestionably have made if, as he had first believed, Miss Woolson had died of natural causes; and it seems likely that, quite apart from the horror that anyone would feel on learning of the suicide of a friend, there was also a feeling of guilt. She had loved him and he knew it. Perhaps indeed he was the only man she had ever taken to her heart. She had written him countless letters of enormous length – 5,000 to 7,000 words, occasionally even more – but she had never imposed upon him; and he, for all his protestations, had made little attempt to see her, or to do anything to relieve the appalling loneliness of her life – a loneliness made more unbearable still by the fact that in recent years she had been virtually stone deaf. Had he written to her rather more often than he did, had he come out to Venice at any time during the last seven terrible months of her life, she might be living yet. But he had done neither; and the suspicion that he might have been at least partially responsible for her death must have weighed heavily on his shoulders.

There was another anxiety too: Miss Woolson never threw anything away. She had lived surrounded by boxes and trunks, all of them overflowing with letters, records, manuscripts, notebooks, commonplace books and diaries. How many of his own letters were among them? What secrets, what confidences, might they conceal? Soon after the tragedy he had written to his friend Margaret Brooke, Ranee of Sarawak, that he had been 'extremely intimate' with the dead woman; and though we can hardly believe this intimacy to have been remotely sexual, he may well have shared confidences, even confessions, with her of which he – the most private of men – could not contemplate exposure to the public gaze. It was perhaps with some such thoughts in mind that he now wrote to Mrs Benedict, offering to meet her when she came to Italy and help her sort through her sister's belongings. He knew that she would welcome his offer, the more so since she spoke no Italian; he for his part could then discharge some of the obligation he felt, while at the same time being in a position to look through the papers of his friend and to remove any that threatened to be compromising.

On learning that his offer had been accepted he wrote at once to Mrs Bronson, telling her that it was 'absolutely necessary' that he should be in Venice from the first of April. Since this coming visit would be in no sense a holiday he preferred not to stay with her, asking her instead to reserve accommodation if possible in the same suite of rooms in Casa Biondetti that Miss Woolson had occupied before moving to the Semitecolo. This was done, and on 29 March he was on the pier in the port of Genoa to greet Mrs Benedict, who was accompanied by her daughter Clare. The two ladies left immediately for Rome to see the grave, but James himself went straight to Venice to make the necessary preparations. They returned a day or two later, and on the morning after their arrival the seals of the apartment doors and windows were broken and, for the first time in more than two months, the light came flooding in.

The three of them worked for five weeks: it was not till early May that the twenty-seven boxes containing Miss Woolson's possessions, literary and otherwise, were shipped off to America. It had been, James confessed to his brother, 'a most devouring, almost a fatal, job'. In later life he would tell the macabre story of the day he had himself rowed to one of the most remote regions of the lagoon, there – at Miss Woolson's express request – to consign her entire wardrobe to the waters. Despite all his efforts, however, her clothes refused to sink; every time he prodded them down, up they rose to the surface 'like vast black balloons'. They were still floating when, deeply upset and acutely embarrassed, he ordered his gondolier to return to Venice.

But Venice was changing fast. A regular steamship line had recently been opened between Italy and the United States, and the city had become 'if I may be allowed the expression, the mere *vomitorium* of Boston'. He wrote to his friend Morton Fullerton:

> They are all 'our' people, yours and mine, and they dis-Italianize this dear patient old Italy till one asks oneself what is at last left of its sweet essence to come to, or for. The accent of Massachusetts rings up and down the Grand Canal and the bark of Chicago disturbs the siesta.

He left Venice feeling like 'Apollo fleeing the furies' and after a day or two in Florence at last found himself in the comparative tranquillity of Rome.

And there, in the Protestant Cemetery, he stood at last beside the grave of Constance Fenimore Woolson, close to those in which Shelley and Trelawny lie side by side, and not far from those of John Keats and his friend the painter Joseph Severn, who had closed his eyes in death and, over half a century later, was buried beside him.

★

It was five years before Henry James could bring himself to return to Venice; not till the spring of 1899 did he accept an invitation from the Curtises. He found them increasingly difficult as hosts; old Daniel's jokes, in particular, irritated him to the point of desperation, and he hated the way 'they can't keep their hands off their native land, which they loathe; and their perpetual digs at it fanned (if a dig can fan) my patriotism to a fever'. He bore it all for two reasons. First, his friend Mrs Bronson – now old, lonely and depressed – had removed to Asolo; James called on her one day and found her 'with a great deal of rheumatism, an enormous appetite, not a scrap of possible action'. Second and more important was the fact that he had long been turning over in his mind an outline for what was arguably to be the greatest novel he ever wrote – a novel in which Palazzo Barbaro was to play an all-important part:

> . . . the warmth of the southern summer was still in the high florid rooms, palatial chambers where hard cool pavements took reflexions in their life-long polish, and where the sun on the stirred sea-water, flickering up through open windows, played over the painted subjects in the splendid ceilings – medallions of purple and brown, of brave old melancholy colour, medals as of old reddened gold, embossed and beribboned, all toned with time . . .

Venetian guides love to tell their clients that James wrote *The Wings of the Dove* while staying at the Barbaro. In fact, although he had sketched out the basic idea of the story in a notebook as early as 1894, he did not begin the actual writing until 1900; the work took him less than a year, and the book was published early in 1902. Virtually every word of it was written at Lamb House, Rye, which he had acquired on a twenty-one-year lease in September 1897 and was now his permanent home. But after two prolonged visits to the Curtises and one to Mrs Gardner he knew every corner of the venerable old palace, and there is no question but that it was the model for the 'Palazzo Leporelli' in the novel, in which the poor, doomed heroine Milly Theale lives and dies. The character of Milly herself is modelled on James's adored young cousin Minny Temple, who had wasted away with tuberculosis in March 1870, aged twenty-five; thirty years later, his memories of her were still green. She had in fact died in Pelham, Massachusetts; but for the last tragic act of *The Wings of the Dove* Venice was the perfect – perhaps the only possible – setting. Besides, since 1894 it had been, to Henry James, a city of death.

He was to see it only once more: in 1907, at the conclusion of an extended Italian tour which took him to Rome, Naples and south Italy and then back through Florence to Venice. Mrs Bronson and most of his other old friends were dead; the Curtises were still there at the Barbaro, hospitable as ever; but this time he lost patience with what he described as 'their terror of the vulgar'. They made him feel, he wrote, that 'they discriminated so invidiously against anyone I might meekly wish to see, of my little other promiscuous acquaintance in Venice, that I felt I could never again face the irritation and the inconvenience of it'. With Venice itself, however, he seemed to fall in love all over again: 'never has the whole place seemed to me sweeter, clearer, diviner'.

Over the thirty-eight years that he had known the city it had taught him much – indeed, it might be said to have completed his cultural education. It was there, perhaps more than in either London or Paris, that he had learned to appreciate great painting and to understand great architecture. Leaning on the balcony of the Ca' Alvisi with Katharine or Edith Bronson, smoking a cigarette and watching the endless traffic of the Grand Canal, he had known complete contentment; sorting through the papers of poor Constance Fenimore Woolson, then struggling – vainly and somehow ridiculously – to sink her clothes in the waters of the lagoon, he had also known despair. Venice had inspired some of his greatest work; at other times, the city had enabled him to enjoy those opportunities for sublime relaxation that only a gondola can offer. It had given him many friends, and no enemies; and gradually, as visit succeeded visit, it had worked itself deep into his heart. 'I don't care, frankly,' he confessed, soon after his return, to his newest and greatest friend Edith Wharton, 'if I never see the vulgarised Rome or Florence again – but Venice never seemed to me more lovable'.

9. Robert Browning
(1838–89)

STRAFFORD: Too many dreams! That song's for Venice, William:
You know how Venice looks upon the map –
Isles that the mainland hardly can let go?
WILLIAM: You've been to Venice, father?
STRAFFORD: I was young then.
WILLIAM: A city with no King; that's why I like
Even a song that comes from Venice . . .
But I'll see Venice for myself one day.

Robert Browning, *Strafford*, V. ii

With some of us, it is love at first sight. With others – Edward Gibbon, for example, or Mark Twain – it is immediate, instinctive revulsion. Yet others, such as Napoleon or Charles Dickens, are unable to shake off their prejudices and preconceptions and so see the city, as it were, through a distorting glass. As for Robert Browning, like Richard Wagner – whom he in no other way resembled – Venice grew on him. When he first saw it, aged twenty-six, at 7 a.m. on Friday 1 June 1838 on the steamboat from Trieste, he gave no sign of being enraptured; and although after a month's stay at Casa Stefani, Calle Giacomuzzi, San Moisè 1139,★ he could write of 'fabrics of enchantment piled to heaven', there is somehow a suggestion that this sprang more from a young man's poetic fancy than from any deep emotional commitment. On this first Italian visit, the town with which he fell in love was unquestionably Asolo, which by his own admission was to haunt his dreams for half a century. He was later to describe it to Mrs Katharine de Kay Bronson:

★ The house, alas, no longer exists.

I am travelling with a friend, sometimes with one person, sometimes with another, oftenest with one I do not recognize. Suddenly I see the town I love sparkling in the sun on the hillside. I cry to my companion, 'Look! look! there is Asolo! Oh do let us go there.' The friend invariably answers, 'Impossible; we cannot stop.' 'Pray, pray let us go there', I entreat. 'No,' persists the friend, 'we cannot; we must go on and leave Asolo for another day,' and so I am hurried away, and wake to know that I have been dreaming it all, both pleasure and disappointment.

Thirteen years later, early in May 1851, he returned to Venice, coming this time from Florence, with his wife Elizabeth and their two-year-old baby Robert Wiedemann Barrett Browning, known throughout his life as 'Pen'. Surprisingly, perhaps, they did not go to Asolo; instead, they stayed five weeks in rented accommodation near the gigantic Palazzo Grimani, looking out on to the Grand Canal. They admired St Mark's; they went twice to the opera, seeing *Ernani* and *Attila*; they even sailed across the lagoon to the Armenian monastery on the island of S. Lazzaro and talked to Fr. Pasquale Aucher, who had tried in vain to teach Byron Armenian some thirty-five years before.★ Elizabeth loved every moment; but he himself was ill at ease, tetchy and unable to sleep, plagued (as they all were) by ravenous mosquitos. When they left on 13 June for Padua and home, it was – for him at least – not a moment too soon.

Perhaps as a result of this experience, he and Elizabeth – though living permanently in Italy – never returned to Venice; and it was only after his wife had been seventeen years in her grave (at the protestant cemetery in Florence) that Robert Browning saw the city again. He now had as his constant companion his younger sister Sarah Anna, known always as Sarianna. Coming by train through France and Switzerland he finally satisfied his age-old longing for Asolo, arriving there towards the end of September 1878 and staying a fortnight at the Stella d'Oro, 'the

★ See Chapter 3, pp. 43–5.

most unsophisticated of inns'. From here the pair made a brief excursion to the birthplace of Antonio Canova at Possagno, where they attended an exhibition of the sculptor's watercolours – 'a wonder of detestability', sniffed Robert – before travelling on to Venice.

They arrived on 4 October, and it was now that the long love affair with the city began – an affair that was to bring brother and sister almost annually to Venice until the poet's death in 1889. On this occasion, as on their two subsequent visits in 1880 and 1881, they put up at the Albergo Universo, which occupied part of what was then the Palazzo Brandolin-Rota on the Dorsoduro side of the Grand Canal, looking on to the Accademia Bridge – at that time still the hideous cast-iron affair constructed in 1854 by the English engineer Alfred Neville.★ All this changed, however, in 1880 when their close friend the American writer and sculptor William Wetmore Story introduced them to Mrs Bronson. Thereafter they were honoured guests at Ca' Alvisi or its effective annex the Giustinian-Recanati, and quickly found their niche in Anglo-American society. On 13 October of the same year, after a visit to Mrs Bronson, they went on to the Teatro Rossini for a performance of Paisiello's *Barbiere di Siviglia*, only to find, sitting just a few places away, Richard Wagner.† The next evening they dined with the Layards, being shown round Ca' Cappello by Sir Henry himself.

There was no visit in 1882, freak flooding having rendered Venice virtually inaccessible; but they were there again in 1883, arriving on 4 October and going straight to Mrs Bronson, who welcomed them to the Giustinian-Recanati. By this time a Venetian regime had been established: every morning they would take a long walk, of three hours or more – often to the Public Gardens, on which occasions they always took food for the caged

★ He built it at his own expense, in exchange for the right to collect tolls from all who used it. It lasted until 1934, when the present wooden structure was built – as a 'temporary measure' – to allow the newly introduced *vaporetti* to pass underneath.

† Browning later described him to Mrs Bronson as 'a great genius but greater curmudgeon . . . a monster of peacock-like vanity'.

elephant, the poet bidding good morning to all the animals as he passed them. They would then return for lunch and, in the afternoon, cruise through the city or lagoon in a gondola. On one of those morning walks they went further still, beyond the gardens to Sant' Elena, at Venice's easternmost tip; and Browning was horrified by what he saw. 'The exquisite little island of St Helena,' he wrote, 'all but one garden with a solitary church two years ago, is now a treeless yard built over by an iron foundry – the most hideous object imaginable.'

A happier experience was in store for him, however: the unveiling, soon afterwards on the island of Burano, of a commemorative plaque to the memory of its most distinguished son, the composer Baldassare Galuppi. Galuppi's fame has in recent years been somewhat overshadowed by that of his contemporary Antonio Vivaldi; but during their lives he was if anything still more celebrated than his rival. In the eighteenth century all the best music in Venice was performed in the four women's 'orphanages' (*ospedali*) and he was for many years *maestro di cappella* both of the Mendicanti at SS. Giovanni e Paolo and the Incurabili on the Zattere, while Vivaldi concentrated on the Pietà. He could turn his hand with equal facility to comic or serious operas as well as to church music, travelling, to produce them, as far afield as London and Moscow.★

By the 1880s, on the other hand, at least to the English-speaking world, he was best known for having been the subject – and indeed the addressee – of one of Browning's loveliest lyrics. 'A Toccata of Galuppi's' – though technically a misnomer, since the composer never wrote a toccata in his life – reflects the mood of the Venice of Casanova and Canaletto more brilliantly than any other poem in the language. It was written not in Venice but in Florence, on 15 January 1853; and yet, curiously enough, the title seems already to have been in existence for some time. As early as 1838 we find Florence Nightingale, who had arrived in Italy with her family that spring, writing of a song which was being sung or whistled all over

★ For some reason, no comic operas were allowed on the St Petersburg stage till 1779.

Florence 'it is all to the tune of the Toccata of Galuppi'. Could this, one wonders, be the same tune as that mentioned – and actually transcribed – by Browning in a letter of April 1839 to his friend Fanny Haworth, describing it as 'what the children were singing last year in Venice, arm over neck'? It seems more than likely. The complete text is given in the Appendix, together with the tune – still unidentified – transcribed in Browning's letter.

Thanks to the bottomless hospitality of Mrs Bronson – 'Nothing,' wrote Henry James, 'in all her beneficent life, had probably made her happier than to have found herself able to minister, each year with the returning autumn, to his pleasure and comfort' – the Brownings stayed on in Venice till 8 December, leaving some ten days after the writing of the appalling sonnet to Rawdon Brown quoted in Chapter 5.★ As a parting present Mrs Bronson seems to have given the poet a coin of the Republic of 1848, since he writes to her soon afterwards that he has hung it on his watch-chain, 'the only other token of love there being my wife's ring'. He loves the coin, he writes, as she would have loved it: 'You know what she felt about a united Italy.'

★

In 1884 an outbreak of cholera and the consequent absence of Mrs Bronson kept the Brownings away from Venice; but by the end of September 1885 they were back in their old rooms at the Giustinian-Recanati, where they were joined by Robert's son Pen, now thirty-five. In the Browning family Pen had always been something of a problem. He enjoyed painting and played the piano passably well, as did his father; academically, however, he was a disaster. Again and again he tried to pass into Balliol College, Oxford – whose master was the great Benjamin Jowett – and though he did manage eventually to get a place at Christ Church, repeated failures in his examinations soon obliged him to give it up. To make matters worse, he was irresponsible – he is said to have got two Breton peasant women with child before he was

★ See p. 105. The poem was published in the *Century Magazine*, February 1884.

nineteen – and recklessly extravagant. 'All I can do – except give money – is *done* and done in vain', wrote his father, and, in another letter, 'I am merely the manger at which he feeds, and nothing is more certain than that I could do him no greater good than by dying tonight and leaving him just enough to keep him from starving.' A good marriage might have helped; unfortunately Pen was, in the opinion of two women who knew him well, 'a veritable curly ball, grotesquely ugly', with 'a beef-red face, baldness and a fawnish smirk'.

And yet, despite everything, father and son loved each other. 'If the thing were possible,' wrote Robert, 'I would renounce all personal ambition and would destroy every line I ever wrote, if by so doing I could see fame and honour heaped on [my son's] head'; and during his last years, it was clear to those around him that Pen was constantly in his thoughts. He talked of him all the time: 'How I wish Pen could see this', he would say, or 'I wonder how soon Pen will be here'. And when, at the age of twenty-five, his son announced his intention of becoming a professional painter he was overjoyed. Here again, Pen was his own worst enemy. He was in fact a good enough portrait painter to win medals in international exhibitions, but his many nudes tended to shock people. His sculptures too – he studied under Rodin – were more than competent; alas, those from his studio were hammered to bits by Freya Stark's mother in the 1920s.

In 1885 life with Mrs Bronson was rather quieter than in previous years. Her husband had died in March, and though she had hardly seen him for the past five years the ritual of mourning had to be observed. But the paucity of dinner parties left more time for the theatre, and Browning spent many evenings watching the plays of Goldoni and his followers, almost invariably in the Venetian dialect – which differs enough from classical Italian as to be almost another language. He followed it, he wrote, 'with a foreigner's difficulty – though I can read Venetian with tolerable ease'. He had also begun to give readings of his poetry to private circles of friends; there was one on 18 October at Ca' Alvisi, and another on 4 November at the Barbaro. 'A Toccata of Galuppi's' – not surprisingly, the universal favourite – was included in both. One of those present wrote:

His reading of his own poems was a never-to-be-forgotten delight – simple, direct and virile as was the nature of the man. The graver portions he read in a quiet, almost introspective way, as if he were thinking it all out again. I remember once that when finishing the grand profession of faith at the end of *Saul*, his voice failed him a very little, and when it was ended he turned his back to us, who were gathered about him in reverent silence, and laying the book quietly on the table, stood so for a moment . . . He seemed as full of dramatic interest in reading 'In a Balcony' as if he had just written it for our benefit.

That autumn Browning had come to an important decision. He and his son were falling increasingly in love with Venice, and both were eager to spend more and more time there; at the same time he did not want to trespass too far on the hospitality of Mrs Bronson (though she herself would have been only too pleased). He would therefore buy himself a palazzo of his own, in which Pen would live more or less permanently and paint. He himself would not give up London altogether; but the palazzo would provide, he wrote, 'a capital retreat' for his declining years. Soon after his arrival his eye had fallen on Palazzo Contarini del Zaffo – later the property of the Manzoni family and nowadays of the Duc Decazes – next to Palazzo Brandolin-Rota where he had formerly stayed, two buildings down from the Accademia. It is one of the loveliest palaces in all Venice, built at that magical moment in the last quarter of the fifteenth century when Venetian Renaissance architects adorned the outside of their buildings with slabs of coloured marble. Inside, there were friezes by Domenico Tiepolo and – in Browning's day – a glorious ceiling with an allegorical painting by the same hand.★ At that time it was owned by a certain Count Montecuccoli who, Browning heard, was anxious to sell. By early November the negotiations were virtually completed, and father and son were excitedly making plans for the future: 'I buy it solely for Pen,

★ This, alas, was later taken to Cologne, where it was destroyed during the Second World War.

who is in love with this city . . . Pen will have sunshine and beauty about him . . . I and my sister have secured a shelter when the fogs of life grow too troublesome.'

But then, at the very last moment, Montecuccoli reneged. Certain legal problems had arisen, he explained, as a result of which his title to the property was not as clear-cut as he had thought; other members of his family also had an interest, and they were no longer in Venice. The Brownings' disappointment can well be imagined; though it may have been somewhat diminished by Pen's subsequent discovery that there were serious structural faults in the building – which, he maintained, Montecuccoli had deliberately not revealed. (The dispute was eventually to end with a lawsuit.) For a moment Robert toyed with the idea of buying a still unfinished house on the Lido, from which he could watch the 'divine sunsets'; but a horrified Pen would have no part in it, and finally, when the Venetian friends to whom he mentioned it also showed a marked lack of enthusiasm, he gave it up. On 23 November he and his sister left disconsolately for London.

By the following summer Sarianna's health was giving cause for concern, and plans for the usual Venetian visit were cancelled. In 1887, however, there came a new excitement. Pen, now thirty-eight and long considered unmarriageable, had somehow got himself engaged – and engaged, what was more, to a very considerable heiress. He had first proposed to Fannie Coddington in 1873. On that occasion she had turned him down flat; but fourteen years later, when she was still unmarried and no longer in her first youth, he had proposed again, and – perhaps *faute de mieux* – she had accepted. His father's letter of congratulation that August – after Fannie and he had met – shows clearly enough the way his mind was working. 'She has every requisite to make you happy and successful,' he wrote, '[and has] spoken to me with the greatest frankness and generosity of the means she will have in contributing to your support.' He himself was prepared none the less to contribute £300 a year, and there might perhaps be an additional sum from the sales – if any – of Pen's pictures.

After a quiet country wedding in England on 4 October, the

happy pair went to Venice for their honeymoon; and it was then that Pen, still smarting from his disappointment over the lost palazzo, learned of the possibility of a yet greater prize: Ca' Rezzonico. This vast pile, begun by Baldassare Longhena (architect of the Salute) in the seventeenth century and completed by Giorgio Massari in the eighteenth, had once belonged to the family of Pope Clement XIII.* It was now for sale but in appalling condition, having been empty since Austrian days when the occupying soldiery had used it as a barracks: in one of the principal rooms on the *piano nobile* were the remains of a stove on which they had baked their bread. For this reason the price was probably moderate enough; to render it habitable, on the other hand, would clearly cost a fortune, and it says much for the couple's courage – and for the depth of Fannie's purse – that they decided to take it on.

When Robert and Sarianna arrived in Venice on 12 September 1888 – staying once more with Mrs Bronson, but this time in the Ca' Alvisi itself – they were astonished by what they saw. The long work of restoration had begun and Pen was in his element, showing a degree of energy and enthusiasm which no one had known he possessed. Every morning he would leave the Ca' Dario,† where he and Fannie were renting temporary accommodation, to oversee the workmen and to make a thousand daily decisions on design and decoration. As a first priority he had resolved to restore the ruined chapel in memory of his mother, 'whom Fannie from her girlhood has all but worshipped'. Here in particular was a project after Robert's own heart. He too threw himself enthusiastically into the task. When he was not at the Rezzonico he was usually out walking on the Lido. Though he was now seventy-six, his energy was undiminished: he prided himself on still being able to walk for hours without fatigue.

A year later, the palace was ready. The elder Brownings did not

---

* He was elected in 1758, and died – 'not without suspicion of poisoning', says the *Encyclopaedia Britannica* darkly – in 1769.

† One of the most enchanting early Renaissance palaces in Venice, but also the most accursed. The last eight occupants have come to violent ends – though Pen and Fannie do not seem to have suffered, at least in the short term.

go at once to Venice, preferring to spend the autumn with Mrs Bronson who, though now crippled with rheumatism, had recently bought La Mura, a small but romantic house at Asolo set in one of the eighteen towers of the town ramparts. There was no room for them to stay with her, so they rented a house nearby. Robert would always take his long walk in the morning, while most afternoons he and his sister would drive out with Mrs Bronson, and dine with her every evening. After dinner he would sometimes play to the two ladies on his hostess's old spinet; sometimes he would read aloud, usually from Shelley, Keats, Coleridge and his friend Tennyson. His own work he read only if specially asked.

It seems more than likely that during these weeks – his mind being as creative as ever – he was not only polishing his most recent poems but also writing new ones; for it was only on 15 October that he sent the final version of his new collection, *Asolando*★ – dedicated, it need hardly be said, to Mrs Bronson – to Smith, Elder, his publishers since 1867. By then, too, he had opened negotiations to buy a plot of land, once part of the palace grounds of Queen Caterina Cornaro,† with the object of transforming a roofless building on it into 'Pippa's Tower'; these were still in progress when at the end of the month he and Sarianna went on to Venice, where Pen had prepared a flat on the mezzanine floor of Ca' Rezzonico.

★

'I am really surprised,' Browning wrote of his son soon after their arrival, 'at his developing so much ability without any sort of experience. What I left, last year, as a dingy cavern is now bright and comfortable in all its quantity of rooms.' Certainly he was prejudiced; but no less an arbiter than Henry James said much the same thing. 'What Pen Browning has done here,' he wrote to his sister, 'transcends description for the beauty, and, as Ruskin would say, "wisdom and rightness" of it. It is altogether royal and imperial

★ The invented gerund of an invented word, taken from the town itself: *asolare*: 'to disport in the open air, amuse oneself at random'.
† The Venetian-born Queen of Cyprus, who abdicated in 1489 and settled with a little court at Asolo, where she died in 1510.

16. James Abbott McNeill Whistler: *Self-portrait*

17. J. A. M. Whistler: *Nocturne Palaces*

18. J. A. M. Whistler: *The Doorway*

19. Frederick Rolfe

20. (*above right*) After the fall of the Campanile, 14 July 1902

21. (*below right*) The Riva degli Schiavoni, western end

22. The Basin of St Mark

23. A canal

24. The Zattere: in the foreground, S. Maria della Visitazione; beyond, the Gesuati

25. Castello: Canale di S. Pietro

26. Doge's Palace – Scala dei Giganti

– but Pen isn't kingly and the *train de vie* remains to be seen. Gondoliers ushering in friends from pensions won't fill it out.' More than once, Robert had warned his son, 'Don't be the little man in the big house'; but that is exactly what Pen proved to be. A great palace like the Rezzonico needs a formidable figure to occupy it; and although Pen worked hard to impress what little personality he had on his grandiose surroundings by hanging his own paintings in the main reception room, neither he nor his wife, sadly enough, came up to scratch.

For the first three weeks of November 1889 all was well; Browning would work happily in a room known as 'the Pope's room'. In front of him was the Grand Canal, behind him a cage in which lived a parrot named Jacko whom he loved, taking delight in giving him cake and fruit after every meal. It was at about this time that Hiram Corson, Professor of English Literature at Cornell University and founder of the first known Browning Club, came to Venice on a visit. The two saw a lot of each other, the poet leading the professor on long walks through the city pointing out the palaces and churches of interest; Corson, though sixteen years younger, later reported that he found it difficult to keep up with him. On the 18th, Browning read from his work at Palazzo Barbaro for two hours, standing throughout; and at much the same time he quoted to Pen and Fannie those lines from the Epilogue to *Asolando*:

> One who never turned his back but marched breast forward,
> Never doubted clouds would break . . .

remarking that 'it almost looks like bragging to say this, and as if I ought to cancel it; but it's the simple truth; and as it's true, it shall stand'.

Three days later, however, he developed a bad cough, which soon turned to bronchitis. On 28 November he insisted on going to a performance of *Carmen*, but fainted on his return and had to be helped to his room. For two more days he struggled on; then, on 1 December, he retired reluctantly to his bed, protesting to his family that 'I so much dislike the quality of an invalid'. From then on, his condition deteriorated fast. After a few days Pen and Fannie vacated their own master bedroom, which faced the rising sun, and moved him into it. *Asolando* was published on Thursday 12th – less than two months after he had dispatched the final manuscript – and that evening Pen read him a telegram which had just arrived from George Smith, his publisher: '*Reviews in all this day's papers most favourable, edition nearly exhausted.*' 'More than satisfied,' he whispered. 'I am dying. My dear boy. My dear boy.' These were his last intelligible words. At eight o'clock he lost consciousness; and two hours later he died, as the bell of St Mark's was striking ten.

Pen's original intention had been to bury his father by his mother's side in the protestant cemetery in Florence; he was distressed to learn that this had now been closed and that – even for Robert Browning – it would need an Act of Parliament to open it again. But only two days later there arrived another telegram from Smith with exciting news: he had been in touch with the Dean of Westminster, who had offered a place in Poets' Corner. The following day there was a service in the *portego* of the Rezzonico, where the coffin rested, surrounded by wreaths and flowers; Mrs Bronson was there, and the Curtises and the Layards, and the British and French Consuls, together with a number of officials from the Municipality; then, as they watched, it was loaded on to an elaborate black-and-gold barge. A fleet of gondolas followed it to the cemetery island of S. Michele, where it remained until arrangements could be made for its journey to London. On the last day of the year, Robert Browning was buried, next to Geoffrey Chaucer and Edmund Spenser, in Westminster Abbey. The pallbearers included Benjamin Jowett, Frederic Leighton, Hallam Tennyson and George Smith.

It was as well, perhaps, that he died when he did, for even before his death relations between Pen and Fannie were steadily deteriorating. After at least two miscarriages it was clear that the wedding was to be childless; all too soon Pen lost interest in his wife, while she for her part relapsed into crotchety invalidism. She disapproved of the extravagance with which he spent her money; she hated the animals with which he surrounded himself – barking dogs, shrieking parrots and even a number of large snakes, of which he was particularly fond; and she became frenziedly jealous when he persuaded her companion-nurse Ginevra to model for him. In 1893 they separated, Pen removing himself to Asolo, where he finally completed the purchase of the land in which his father had been interested four years earlier and where he himself was to die, at the age of sixty-three, in 1912. 'Poor grotesque little Pen,' wrote Henry James,

and poor sacrificed little Mrs P. There seems but one way to be sane in this queer world – but there are so many ways of being mad. And a Palazzo-madness is almost as alarming – or as convulsive – as an earthquake – which indeed it essentially resembles.

In the service at Westminster Abbey, James had naturally been given an honoured place. Soon after his return, he was heard to comment on his old friend:

A good many oddities and a good many great writers have been entombed in the Abbey; but none of the odd ones have been so great, and none of the great ones so odd.

10. The Layards
(1874–1912)

Venice as a residence has many attractions for me, but one misses the society of one's superiors.

A. H. Layard

Austen Henry Layard first saw Venice in August 1839, when he was twenty-two. He fell in love with the city at once, spending two days in assiduous sightseeing, but all too soon he had to move on; there was a long journey ahead. With his friend Edward Mitford, his senior by some ten years, he was travelling to Ceylon. The normal route would have involved a crossing of the Mediterranean to Alexandria, up the Nile to Cairo, then across the desert to Suez, whence another ship would take them to their destination; but Mitford, who hated the sea, had decided on the overland route, and young Layard – whose favourite childhood reading had been *The Arabian Nights* – had jumped at the opportunity. It changed his life.

The two rounded the head of the Adriatic via Trieste – avoiding Venice – then rode south down the Dalmatian coast, through Montenegro and the Balkans, arriving on 20 September at Constantinople. 'In the hands of any other European Power,' wrote Layard, 'it would have been the strongest city in the world; in the hands of the Turks it is the most picturesque.' For him it was also – very nearly – the end of the journey: just as he and Mitford were about to continue across Anatolia to Syria he was stricken by malaria and for some days, despite the ministrations of Dr van Millingen,★ lay at the point of death. Fortunately he possessed an iron constitution

★ See Chapter 8, p. 169.

– it was to serve him in good stead in the years to come – and he and Mitford were on the road again by mid-October. Travelling conditions in Asia proved a good deal more difficult, and more dangerous, than in Europe; but Layard was in his element, visiting every Greek and Roman site that he could find. Already a considerable art historian – his childhood had been spent in Florence, where he had first acted as a guide to visitors at the age of eight – he was also fascinated by the frescoes in the early Byzantine churches along the way, to which few of his contemporaries would have given a second look. 'It was curious,' he wrote to his mother, 'to see in these places, deserted for centuries, the figures of saints & martyrs resembling those which exist in the paintings of Giotto and Masaccio.'

On they rode, through Antioch, Aleppo, Beirut and Acre, arriving on 10 February 1840 in Jerusalem; and it was here that, for the first time, the two quarrelled. Layard longed to explore the Dead Sea and the ancient cities of Jerash and Petra; Mitford, who had little interest in ruins – he preferred to study the local bird life – was anxious to get to Ceylon and did his utmost, with the help of the British Vice-Consul, to discourage his friend. These, he pointed out, were wild and lawless regions, in which bandits would demand vast quantities of protection money and would certainly not hesitate to murder him if this were not forthcoming. But Layard refused to listen: if Mitford would not accompany him, he was perfectly happy to travel alone. Somehow he found a young Arab who, having been brought up in an Italian monastery in Jerusalem, spoke passable Italian and was prepared to act as interpreter; and a few days later the two of them headed south.

All was well until they reached Petra. There, however, they were immediately surrounded by hostile bedouin, all armed to the teeth, who refused to allow them to enter the *Siq* – the narrow passage through the rocks leading to the ancient city – without extortionate payment. 'Swords,' wrote Layard,

> were drawn on both sides. An attempt was made to seize my effects, and I was told that I should not be allowed to leave the place until I had paid the sum demanded of me. As I still absolutely refused to

do so, one, more bold and insolent than the rest, advanced towards me with his drawn sword, which he flourished in my face. I raised my gun, determined to sell my life dearly if there was an intention to murder me.

But for the timely arrival of the local sheikh, one suspects, the present chapter would never have been written.

Once inside the city, Layard could hardly fail to be impressed:

> The gigantic flights of steps cut in the rocks leading to the tombs; the absence of all vegetation to relieve the monotony of the brown, barren soil; the mountains rising abruptly on all sides; the silence and solitude scarcely disturbed by the wild tribes lurking among the fragments of pediments, fallen cornices and architraves which encumber the narrow valley, render the ruins of Petra unlike those of any other ancient city in the world.

The architecture of the tombs themselves, however, proved a disappointment. It was, he reported, 'debased and wanting in both elegance and grandeur . . . a bad period and a corrupt style.'*

Returning by way of Amman, Jerash and Damascus he finally reached Aleppo, where Mitford was waiting. On they rode to Mosul, where they crossed the Tigris and almost at once found themselves among the huge tumuli marking what was then believed to have been Nineveh, capital of ancient Assyria. There was little enough to be seen on the surface; yet Layard was instantly fascinated, far more than by any other of the innumerable monuments he had so far visited. Much to Mitford's irritation, he insisted on staying there for more than a fortnight before riding the thirty-odd miles to Nimrud.

> As the sun went down, I saw for the first time the great conical mound of Nimrud rising against the clear evening sky . . . the impression it made upon me was one never to be forgotten . . . my

---

* One is reminded of the late Sir Charles Johnston's immortal lines:
> We flashed by Petra in a wink;
> It looked like Eaton Square, but pink.

thoughts ran constantly upon the possibility of thoroughly exploring with a spade those great ruins.

Although he did not yet know it, his new path was set.

★

In Mosul he and Mitford hired a raft, on which they floated for 300 miles down the Tigris to Baghdad. They spent two months in the city, during which Layard had plenty of opportunity to visit Ctesiphon, Babylon and several other sites before riding on with his friend into Persia; and it was near Hamadan, towards the end of August 1840, that they finally parted company. Mitford was anxious to complete his journey to Ceylon. For Layard, clearly, the island no longer figured in his plans; he could not tear himself away from the region which he now felt to be his spiritual home. But there was no rancour: each respected the other's point of view, and after fourteen months' companionship they separated with genuine regret.

Layard was to spend the next eleven years in the Middle East, years in which, while technically employed by the British Ambassador in Constantinople Stratford Canning (later Lord Stratford de Redcliffe), he worked – first under the French architect-archaeologist Emil Botta, later on his own account and for the British Museum – at Nimrud, where he identified at least six imperial palaces and sent back the great bas-reliefs which form the nucleus of the Museum's Assyrian collection. In 1848–9 he published his account of the excavations under the title *Nineveh and Its Remains*, and in 1853 a sequel, *Nineveh and Babylon*. It was unfortunate that both these titles were misnomers, Nimrud and Nineveh being later proved to be two separate places; none the less, they brought their author fame and fortune. Hailed as 'the man who made the Bible true', he was named a Freeman of the City of London and remained a celebrity for the rest of his life.

In 1851, still aged only thirty-four, Layard returned to England to embark on a political career; in 1852 he was elected Liberal Member of Parliament for Aylesbury, and never returned to

Mesopotamia. The next fifteen years saw him serving twice as Under-Secretary of State for Foreign Affairs – in which capacity, in 1862, he was responsible for the government's decision to sponsor Rawdon Brown's *Calendar*.★ In 1869 he was appointed British Minister in Madrid, and in 1877 – by Benjamin Disraeli – Ambassador in Constantinople; but in 1880, with the return to power of Gladstone – who saw in him the antithesis of his own Turkophobe opinions – he was removed. He had hoped for the Embassy in Rome, but it was bestowed elsewhere. His political and diplomatic career was at an end, and just three years later he and his wife decided to make Venice their principal home.

★

The city had long been part of their lives. Layard had been there in September 1860, and had reported:

> One hears on all sides that the city is deserted; that no Italian takes part in any public amusement; and that there is a general discontent and agitation which may lead to an outbreak whenever an opportunity may offer. An Austrian regimental band played last night in the Square of St Mark; there were a good many people present, but I could distinguish no respectable Italians. The prevailing language seems to be English, and the greater part of the crowd seemed to be made up of English and American travellers. Everywhere one hears the same story. It is impossible that the present state of things can continue. The country is getting daily more impoverished, and the expense of keeping it will be greater than even a Government far richer than Austria could afford. Nevertheless, I hope Garibaldi and his friends will not risk the whole Italian cause, hitherto so triumphant, by any wanton attack on Austria. The time will come when Venetia must be united to Italy; by endeavouring to hasten the union before the time, the whole cause of Italian independence may be jeopardised.

★ See Chapter 5, p. 108.

Six years later he had returned, this time with the Foreign Secretary Lord John Russell, to see the Austrians hand over the Province.

I am very glad to be able to spend a few weeks here, to see the last of Venice under the old rule, and the first of her under the new. Great preparations are being made, and, the moment the Austrians turn their backs, the city will be lined inside and out with the tricolor. The entry of the King will be a splendid sight; the enthusiasm after the pent-up feelings of two-thirds of a century will be boundless. At present the city is in a mournful condition. There is great poverty and suffering, and a complete stagnation of all trade. To add to the misery, the thousands who were employed in the Arsenal and other public establishments have been dismissed, and are starving. The Austrians, as usual, are doing every manner of mean and petty thing to humiliate and irritate the people they are leaving, instead of parting company with them generously and gracefully, they have stripped the Palace of every article of furniture, down to the gas and water pipes, tearing up all the parquet floors to make packing-cases; so that there is no place for the King to go to. They have carried away all the Venetian relics from the Arsenal, and such parts of the public archives as relate to Germany and Austria, and they have gutted the public buildings. Fortunately, they have spared the pictures in the Academy and in the Churches.

King Victor Emmanuel of Savoy arrived early in November, and once again Layard reported the scene:

The entry of the King was a very magnificent pageant, although the weather was unfortunately misty, and there was no sun during the day. The barges and gondolas decked with silk hangings and rich stuffs, and canopies and sculptures, rowed by gondoliers dressed in the costumes of the 15th and 16th centuries, gave a singularly rich and unique appearance to the Grand Canal. Magnificent as the sight was, it was less interesting to me than the departure of the last Austrian; the raising of the Italian standards in the Square of St Mark, and the entry of the Italian troops. Then enthusiasm was more spontaneous and more touching, and the weather was then magnificent. Last night the King went to the Fenice Theatre, and for the first time in this century all the nobility of Venice and the Venetian provinces was assembled. His reception was very cordial, and the sight was certainly a very grand one. There is to be a masked ball tomorrow night at the Fenice, and a regatta on Sunday – the entertainments for which Venice in the old days used to be celebrated.

It may have been during this visit that Layard began to put his own imprint on the city. He had recently been approached by a certain Dr Antonio Salviati, who believed that the traditional Venetian skills of glass manufacture and mosaic-working were in danger of being forgotten and was determined to revive them before it was too late. Layard, whose passion for Italian art burned as strongly as ever, had responded with enthusiasm; and the result was the foundation, on 2 January 1867, of the firm of Salviati and Co., which in October 1868 had changed its name to the Venice and Murano Glass and Mosaic Co. Ltd, with Layard heading the list of shareholders. Unfortunately, just two months later, Gladstone appointed him Chief Commissioner of Works and Buildings; and on 26 July 1869 this led Mr Cecil Raikes MP to put down a motion for inquiry into a contract formed with Salviati to supply mosaics for the decoration of the Central Hall of the Palace of Westminster. 'He was sure the House would conclude that it was very desirable that the right hon. Gentleman should be put in a position to assure the public that in the irregularity that took place in giving the company that contract for the decoration of the Central Hall, he was not influenced by the desire to benefit the company', and he proposed the appointment of a Select Committee to investigate the matter.

Layard replied with an indignation he made no effort to conceal:

Some years ago I made the acquaintance of Dr Salviati, a lawyer of Venice, and a man of great enterprise and ability. This gentleman, with the assistance of a common workman named Radi – one of those men of extraordinary artistic genius who are so frequently met with in Italy – had succeeded in restoring the art of working in enamel mosaic, which had been abandoned, if not entirely lost, for more than a century . . .

I saw in his discoveries a source of employment for a number of poor artists of Venice, and of future wealth for their city. Moreover, I was convinced that if the art were brought to perfection it might be introduced with the greatest advantage into England. In Venice it had already been successfully employed in restoring the magnificent mosaics of St Mark's . . . At the time of the Great Exhibition of 1862,★ Dr Salviati came to England, in the hope of being able to introduce his mosaic into this country. The first person in England who perceived the value and importance of Dr Salviati's discovery was the Queen, . . . who employed [him] to decorate the groined roof and the walls of the Wolsey Chapel at Windsor, and subsequently Her Majesty approved of his mosaics for decorating the spandrels and pediments of the Memorial to the Prince Consort in Hyde Park. Dr Salviati undertook these important commissions, and, in order to carry them out, established a school of young artists at Venice, bringing skilled workers in Roman mosaic from Rome to instruct them.

Three years ago I found that Dr Salviati, although a man of genius, was, like most men of the same class, without the pecuniary means necessary to carry out his discoveries . . . and was completely unable to carry out the commissions with which he had been entrusted . . . I would willingly have assisted [him] with my purse, but my means were too limited to be of any real use to him in his difficulties; so I wrote to some friends in England who, like myself, loved Art and Italy . . . and appealed to them not to allow Dr Salviati's remarkable undertaking to fall through for want of a small sum of money . . . With their assistance the necessary funds were subscribed, and the good work was carried on.

★ This was the Second Great International Exhibition, which opened at the Crystal Palace in London on 1 May 1862.

I need scarcely tell the House that these funds were furnished not with any prospect of or desire for gain, but out of a love of Art and for the sake of Venice and Italy. Owing to the assistance which he thus received Dr Salviati was enabled to execute his commission, with what result those who have seen the Wolsey Chapel, the mosaics of the Albert Memorial, and the beautiful reredos of Westminster Abbey, will be able to judge.

Since the undertaking has thus been carried on, I have taken a very lively interest in it. Every year I have myself spent two or three months in Venice, encouraging and directing the artists employed as far as I was able, furnishing them with books, drawings and models, and endeavouring to bring this important art to the perfection which it once attained in that illustrious city. But although feeling that, whether in Office or out, I might fairly and without exposing myself to attack, take a direct interest in an undertaking of a purely artistic character, yet I know also, from bitter experience, how ready men are, in order to injure a political opponent, to make use of any little tittle-tattle, and of any calumny, even in the House of Commons. I accordingly thought it best, as soon as I came into Office, to divest myself of every direct interest in the Salviati undertaking . . .*

Raikes, to give him his due, replied gracefully enough that he was sorry if he had used any expression which was offensive or unfair, and that he was quite satisfied with Layard's explanation. The matter was closed; and we are reminded of it only when we pass the palazzo immediately opposite the S. Maria del Giglio *vaporetto* stop, with its perfectly hideous mosaic façade that bears, in bold black letters a foot high, the single word SALVIATI.

★

Since his return to England from the East, Layard had been accustomed to spend much of his time at Canford Manor, the Dorset

---

* The speech as given here has been drastically abridged. Readers desirous of the full text of the debate − if such there be − will find it in Hansard, Third Series, Vol. 198, 26 July 1869, cols. 708−20.

home of his first cousin Lady Charlotte Guest, who had married the multimillionaire ironmaster John Guest in 1833. At the time English society had been scandalized by the marriage of the Earl of Lindsey's daughter to a mere tradesman, however successful; she and her husband had begun to receive invitations only after he was made a baronet five years later. But to Charlotte this scarcely mattered. She was attractive, highly intelligent and frighteningly well-read in English, French, Italian, Greek and Latin, with a fair knowledge of both Persian and Hebrew. After her marriage she decided to tackle Welsh – her husband being Member of Parliament for Merthyr Tydfil – and spent eight years translating the *Mabinogion*, a collection of medieval Welsh stories that inspired Alfred Lord Tennyson to write *The Idylls of the King*. She seems also to have been an excellent administrator: when Sir John died in 1852 she took over the management of his ironworks at Dowlais, which she ran for some years with extreme efficiency.★

It was hardly surprising in the circumstances that she should have been fascinated by her cousin, and he by her. Canford was formerly a medieval ruin – it still preserves a vast fifteenth-century kitchen – but Guest, as a wedding present to his wife, had had it converted by Charles Barry into a spectacular Victorian mansion. This was further embellished in 1851 with a so-called 'Nineveh Court', essentially a small museum built to accommodate the Assyrian sculptures presented by Layard to the house.† It was at Canford in 1848 that he had written the two volumes of *Nineveh and Its Remains*

★ In 1855 she married Charles Schreiber, fifteen years her junior, whom she had engaged at £400 a year as tutor to her son Merthyr. Layard never forgave her.

† The winged bull and winged lion that flanked its entrance are the twins of those in the British Museum. After the sale of Canford in 1914 they were acquired by the Metropolitan Museum of Art in New York, where they may still be seen. The house is now a school. In 1956 Sir Leonard Woolley spotted in the tuck shop (formerly the Nineveh Court), hidden behind the shelves, seven bas-reliefs from the Palace of Sennacherib at Nineveh. These were sold in 1959 for £14,000. In 1992 Dr J. M. Russell of Columbia University discovered in the same room another major sculpture which did rather better: in 1994 it fetched $12 million – according to Dr Russell, by far the highest price ever paid for an antiquity.

– the first of his several books on the subject – and there, on
2 January 1869, that he proposed to Enid Guest, the eighth of Lady
Charlotte's ten children. The wedding took place just two months
later. Despite her parents' opposition, which seems chiefly to have
been due to the difference in their ages – she was twenty-five, he
fifty-two – their marriage was to prove an idyllically happy one.

Enid too soon fell in love with Venice, and in 1871 the pair
asked Rawdon Brown to find them a suitable house. Three years
later he came up with Ca' Cappello, a fine Renaissance palazzo of
the sixteenth century on the corner of the Grand Canal and the Rio
di S. Polo. Its façade had originally boasted frescoes by Veronese, but
these had alas perished in a disastrous fire in 1627. The Layards
bought it at once, though it was only after their recall from Constantinople in 1880 that they could consider making it their permanent
home. They finally moved in in 1883, and quickly became the
leaders of smart Anglo-Venetian society.

Layard was by now sixty-six, though had it not been for his thick
white hair and beard he would have looked a good deal younger;
ten years later a guest in Ca' Cappello★ noted that 'he gave one a
sense of power, but the twinkle in his eye and kindly manner
invited friendship'. He spent much of his time at his desk. There
was one book of autobiography, *Early Adventures in Persia, Susiana
and Babylonia*, published by John Murray in 1887; but he was now
able to concentrate on his earliest love, Italian art, and in the same
year he brought out a revised – and to some extent rewritten –
version of F. T. Kugler's celebrated *Handbook of Painting*. He also
hunted assiduously for fine pictures – on behalf of the National
Gallery in London, his brother-in-law Lord Wimborne at Canford
(the Guests had by now been raised to the peerage), and not least
for himself. His own remarkable collection – open on request and
mentioned in both Murray and Baedeker – hung on the *piano nobile*
of Ca' Cappello, in a special suite of rooms whose walls were
covered in red, yellow and green damask; it included works by
Giovanni and Gentile Bellini and Vittore Carpaccio, together with

★ Lina Waterfield, *Castle in Italy*, Chapter VIII.

a painting by Cima di Conigliano which Ruskin praised as 'the finest he had ever seen'. Layard loved to tell the story of how he had been approached by an old man carrying a picture wrapped in brown paper, which he was offered for the equivalent of £5. Suspecting it to be just another of the countless daubs or forgeries that he was shown every day, he refused to look at it, finally shaking the man off by taking refuge in his gondola. When he reached home, however, the picture was lying on his doorstep; and he unwrapped it to find Gentile Bellini's superb portrait of the Sultan Mehmet II. Layard kept it in a special room of its own; it can now be seen at the National Gallery in London.

His other preoccupation, at least after 1888, was the establishment of an English church in Venice. As early as 1873 the local English chaplain – obliged to hold his services wherever he could beg, borrow or steal an adequate space – had complained of overwork: in the previous year Venice had become the terminus for Indian mail steamers, and was consequently now an important staging-post on the India route. Passengers from visiting ships often swelled his congregations to 200, sometimes even more. The situation was growing steadily worse, and on 30 April 1888 a letter appeared in *The Times*, signed by the Bishop of Gibraltar, Layard and Alexander Malcolm,★ a Scottish businessman who now owned the Palazzo Benzon, where Byron had been an *habitué* seventy years before:

> The need of a suitable English church has long been felt at Venice. The palace in which, till the present year, the services were held has lately been sold, and we have been obliged to look elsewhere for accommodation. At the present moment the services are conducted in a room lent to us without charge by the Venezia-Murano Glass Company. But this is merely a temporary arrangement, as during the spring and autumn, when large numbers of English and American visitors are here, the room is too small for the wants of the congregation.

★ Malcolm's activities in Venice were by no means always beyond reproach. He was much involved in the sale of Venetian antiquities, and is known to have exported to England slabs of polychrome marble taken down from the south façade of St Mark's during its restoration.

We hope to procure an existing building, conveniently situated
on the Grand Canal, and capable of being converted into a handsome English church. We calculate that a sum of £2,500 will be
required for this purpose. As the number of English residents is
small, not exceeding 50, we are obliged to appeal to our countrymen
at home for help . . .

When, a year later, little more than a third of the money had been
raised, Layard provided premises himself – a warehouse in Campo
S. Vio that he had purchased in his wife's name from his Venezia-
Murano Company. He then appealed for another £600 to convert
and furnish the building, which – though work was not finally to
be completed for another five years – was consecrated and dedicated
to St George in 1892.

Enid, according once again to Mrs Waterfield, was 'very tall,
with a regal bearing; she had lovely blue eyes and a pleasant deep
voice. Many people found her alarming. She adored her husband
with quiet devotion.' She worked indefatigably as his editorial
assistant, indexing, proof-reading and hammering away at one of
the first typewriters ever seen in Venice, at which she was adept.
Her spare moments she spent writing letters and a copious diary,
singing and playing the guitar and – with the help of a numerous
staff – running the house smoothly and efficiently. She and her
husband entertained on a vast scale: at various times they received
Queen Margherita of Savoy, Queen Alexandra, Crown Prince and
Crown Princess Frederick of Germany (she was the eldest daughter
of Queen Victoria) and their son, the future Kaiser Wilhelm II –
to say nothing of Lord Kitchener,★ Robert Browning, John Ruskin

---

★ Helen, Lady Radnor writes in her memoirs:

During the month of November [1910] Lord Kitchener came to Venice
on his way from Egypt, and stayed for two or three days with Lady Layard.
I met him at dinner there one night . . . We talked and laughed incessantly
that evening, from the beginning to the end of dinner, which I am not
sure met with the approval of our hostess! After dinner, when I was saying
'good-night', I asked Lord Kitchener if he would like to see an old Italian

and the constant flood of visitors who were either staying in Venice or passing through on their way to Egypt, India or the Far East. There were formal receptions on Tuesday evenings and a *soirée musicale* every Friday.

When Queen Victoria celebrated her Golden Jubilee in 1887, the Layards outdid themselves. The balconies of Ca' Cappello were decorated with immense hangings of silk and velvet, embroidered by Enid with the arms of her and her husband's various families. They also organized festivities on the Grand Canal, moonlight picnics on islands in the lagoon and, on 21 June, a magnificent dinner in the palazzo for all the English residents of the city. None the less, there were complaints. There is no doubt that Enid was a martinet: she insisted on absolute punctuality and forbade smoking. Moreover the food, though served by gold-sashed gondoliers, was generally agreed to be vile. No wonder that Ca' Cappello was nicknamed 'the refrigerator'; many of the guests later commented that it seemed to lack any intimacy, and felt more like an Embassy than a private house.

Pillar though he was of the British colony in Venice, Layard was careful not to cut himself off from England. He kept up a continual correspondence with many friends, to whom he confessed that 'like the old hunter turned out to grass, he still wanted to look over the

---

'Sala', if so to come and see mine, adding that I should be at home the following afternoon. He thanked me, and said he would be delighted to come. Lady Layard overheard this, and said, 'I am afraid we cannot do that, as I have settled to go elsewhere.' Whereupon, Lord Kitchener turned to her and said civilly, but also very determinedly, 'I have just told Lady Radnor that I will go and see her tomorrow, and I should like to do so.' He came, and after he had been with me about half an hour my gondolier came and said, 'The gondola is at the door, Milord.' 'Whose gondola?' asked Lord Kitchener. 'Lady Layard's,' replied Giovanni. 'Oh very well, tell it to wait,' was his answer: and I am afraid that it did have to wait, for quite a long time.'

Lady Radnor was a regular visitor to Venice between 1900 and 1913 – when, at the age of sixty-seven, she found that she could no longer get in and out of her gondola.

fence when the hounds were in cry'. In the year of the Jubilee he was bitterly disappointed not to receive the peerage he had expected, and wrote to his friend Sir William Gregory:

> I am a Privy Councillor and G.C.B.; I have been an Ambassador and a Minister; twice Under–Secretary for Foreign Affairs and First Commissioner of Works; I obtained Cyprus for England; have made discoveries which distinguished the Victorian era, am a corresponding Member of the French Academy, an honorary D.C.L. and honorary member of I don't know how many learned societies, English and foreign. I don't think I shall be charged with vanity or presumption if I venture to doubt whether there are many persons who have more qualifications and claims . . .

The fact was that Queen Victoria had never forgiven him for writing a dispatch which she considered disrespectful of a fellow sovereign – even if that sovereign was that odious Ottoman, Sultan Abdul-Hamid. It was a sad irony for one who had spent his life defending the Turkish cause, but he managed nevertheless to look on the bright side: 'Had I been put in the House of Lords,' he told Lady Gregory, 'I should have considered it my duty to reside in England, which certainly would not have contributed to my health or happiness.' Another disappointment was being passed over as a Trustee of the British Museum; Layard was, however, immensely gratified when a group of his friends – they included the Empress Frederick, Prime Minister Lord Salisbury and, more surprisingly, Mr Gladstone – commissioned a portrait bust of him in bronze by the leading sculptor of the day, Sir Edgar Boehm, to be placed in the Museum. Boehm insisted that for the discoverer of the stones of Nineveh only marble was good enough, and the bust was duly unveiled in the boardroom on 11 June 1891.

Alas, little more than a year later, Layard's relations with the Museum were at their worst. The cause of his anger was the appointment as Acting Keeper of the Department of Egyptian and Assyrian Antiquities of a certain E. A. T. Wallis Budge. Of Budge's scholarship there could be no doubt: he could read both Egyptian hieroglyphics and Assyrian cuneiform and knew all the principal Mesopotamian excavations a good deal better than Layard himself, who had not visited them for forty years. What Layard could not forgive was Budge's treatment of his old friend and colleague Hormuzd Rassam. Rassam had become Layard's secretary and interpreter at the age of seventeen; thereafter, thanks to his quick intelligence and immense enthusiasm, he had made himself one of the leading archaeologists in his field. To Budge, however, he was simply a 'native'; and when in Baghdad Budge had uncovered a thriving market in Assyrian antiquities he had instantly accused the 'native watchmen' – who, he claimed, were not only the employees of 'the native Mr Rassam' but also his relatives. Back in London in 1892, he published a new *Guide to the Exhibition Galleries of the British Museum* and attributed the Assyrian collection to 'Layard, [Sir Henry] Rawlinson and others', ignoring Rassam altogether.

Layard sprang to the defence of his friend, 'one of the honestest and most straightforward fellows I ever knew'. In a letter to *The Times* of 27 July 1892 he protested that Rassam was the victim of a 'great injustice', and that 'a deliberate attempt was being made to deprive him of the credit which is his due'.

> During his employment with the Trustees of the British Museum, Mr Rassam discovered the remains of five Babylonian palaces and temples, and of three temples and one palace in Assyria . . . I cannot for a moment believe that so distinguished and honorable body as the Trustees have countenanced this treatment of Mr Rassam, who during very many years rendered them the most loyal, the most devoted, and the most disinterested service, and to whom they and the public owe some of the most important and precious monuments and records, illustrative of sacred and profane history, of which they are the guardians.

Shortly afterwards Rassam brought a libel action against Budge, whose subsequent apology was denounced by Layard as 'mean, shuffling and untruthful'; and the following year the case was heard in London. Layard himself gave evidence, but although technically

Rassam won his case, it proved a Pyrrhic victory: he was awarded only £50 of the £1,000 for which he had asked.

And Layard's reputation also suffered. The magazine *Nature* demanded an inquiry into how Assyrian antiquities came into private hands, such as those presented to Canford Manor by Sir Henry Layard; and one of his obituarists was to write that 'he could hardly claim to be a scholar at all, and his want of the true archaeologist's feeling was sufficiently shown by his presenting to his friends neatly cut tablets containing fragments of cuneiform inscriptions, which of course left serious lacunae in priceless historical documents'. Layard had perfectly adequate answers to both accusations. The Sultan's *firman* having been issued to him personally, all his findings were technically his property; but instead of selling them for his own profit he had presented them to the nation. Moreover, there had been a vast quantity of excavated material that the Museum had not been prepared to pay for; what would have become of it if Sir John Guest had not offered to foot the bill? As to the second charge, Layard had been obliged to reduce the weight of these vast slabs of stone in order to be able to float them on rafts to Basra, and he had taken care to cut out only pieces from the standard, endlessly repeated inscriptions, which were consequently of little or no historical value. But – at least in public – he held his peace.

On 9 March 1894 Henry and Enid Layard celebrated twenty-five years of marriage with a dinner-dance at Ca' Cappello. 'When I married,' he wrote, 'I could not have believed that I should reach my silver wedding. Well, I have been very fortunate, and I can say, what few married men can say, that my wife and I have never been separated by one single day and that we have never had a quarrel.' Less than four months later he was dead. On 3 April his doctor tentatively diagnosed a malignant tumour in the groin and advised his immediate return to England for a specialist opinion. His fears were confirmed, and it soon became clear that the patient was not going to recover. He died, in their London house at no. 1 Queen Anne Street, on 5 July and was buried four days later in the cemetery at Woking. He was seventy-seven.

★

Enid Layard, still only fifty, returned to Venice, where she spent most of her time until her death in 1912 – another eighteen years. Her life continued much as it had always been, with feverish entertaining and a formidable range of charitable activities. 'Weekly at the Seamen's Institute,' wrote Laura Ragg, wife of the English chaplain, 'she would listen patiently to innumerable ballads and join in the chorus of rather vulgar comic songs; and she valiantly put up with the odour of coarse tobacco clinging to the rooms.' Occasionally she took up her guitar and performed herself – although, one suspects, with a rather different repertoire. She also created, on the Giudecca, what was known as the Ospedale Cosmopolitano – the Cosmopolitan Hospital – in which foreign sailors could be treated by doctors and nurses speaking their own language. But by far the best vignette of her life in Venice in the first years of the twentieth century has been provided by her nephew Rowland Burden-Muller, who was born in 1891.

> In those days I saw more of Venice, where Aunt Enid lived at the Palazzo Ca' Capello mourning, in widow's weeds *à la* Maria Stuart, a husband who had died some years before, after a useful life discovering the Ruins of Nineveh and later as Ambassador to the Porte. However, her mourning did not preclude an active social life, with receptions every evening during the month of April; her own on Thursday evenings, the Brandolins on Friday, with remaining evenings taken by the Noces, della Grazias, Morosinis and others. To these, at 14, I was taken so that I should learn to conduct myself appropriately in polite society. On returning home at 1.30 a.m. I was made to stand beneath Carpaccio's *Visit of the Three Magi*, now in the National Gallery,★ and recite the names, in full with correct titles and proper precedence, of all the persons to whom I had been introduced that evening. Meanwhile Aunt Enid sipped her barley water before going to bed. The mornings started with most of us assembling in the dining room for breakfast, a meal usually interrupted for me since I had to go into the gallery and

★ Alas, it is not.

draw a faded green silk curtain over Gentile Bellini's portrait of Sultan Mohammed in order to protect it from the depredations of the parrot while taking its morning bath. I could never understand why the parrot's cage had to keep company with the Sultan.

On several mornings each week I was sent with Signor Malagola, Keeper of the Archives, 'to see the sights', occasionally accompanied by the vastly dull Princess Stephanie, widow of Crown Prince Rudolph of Austria, a lady-in-waiting and two dachshunds. My mother, fearful of my growing state, insisted on my wearing my Eton suit so as all possible use should be extracted from its cost and, being very Scotch, she insisted that I should top it with a Scotch bonnet with flowing ribbons. Thus garbed, I was taught how to row the gondola, surreptitiously, by Ricardo and Giovanni, Aunt Enid's two charming gondoliers. One might have thought that such a sight upon the Grand Canal would have attracted some attention; but the spirit of the nineteenth century still hovered over the twentieth and individuality was rampant. Also I was a Victorian child, obedient and passive and quite devoid of self-consciousness. I suppose a modern child would have rebelled or had to be sent to a psychiatrist.

In those days the campanile had just collapsed★ and there were only three motor boats in the city and no hotels on the Lido, which can hardly have changed since Byron rowed there. Aunt Enid owned a rush hut, a forerunner of today's cabanas; and sometimes we went there for a picnic. Gondolas were sent ahead with the chef and a couple of *garçons de cuisine*, and a butler and a pair of footmen who placed in position three easels for Aunt Enid, Princess Stephanie and Susie Duchess of Somerset who enjoyed painting in water-colour, thus creating a scene in the manner of Boudin. Being under 15 years of age I was permitted to bathe, and later we were served a six-course collation in the rush hut by the butler and footmen with cotton gloves, returning to Venice by sunset.

The three motor launches belonged to the Spanish Pretender, who also owned an aged white parrot reputedly over 120 years old,

★ See pp. 237–8.

to Val Prinsep, the artist son of Watts's patron from Little Holland House, and to a newly arrived American couple, not yet acknowledged by Venetian society. Often we had tea with old Mr and Mrs Eden in their garden on the Giudecca, the largest in Venice, and nearby was the small nursing home founded by Aunt Enid for British sailors. Sometimes I went out with Val Prinsep or the immensely fat and delightful Clara Montalba when they went sketching, for painting in water-colour was a fashionable vocation. The Prinsep boys were at Eton with me and occasionally I got away to see them, though Aunt Enid disapproved of the family as being 'very bohemian', and Mrs Prinsep's father, Mr Leland, had made a scandal with Mr Whistler over the decoration of his dining room.* On Sundays I sang in the choir of the English church, conducted with her fan by Helen Lady Radnor who took her pet gondolier home to Longford Castle in Wiltshire† where he rowed her on the lake as part of his duties. The organ was played by Sir Hubert Miller, and was blown by his pet gondolier who was very handsome. Then there were luncheons with Mrs Browning, Pen's wife, who, as a disciple of Dr Fletcher, chewed her food 40 times before swallowing, a method my mother made me adopt at once. Also we were taken on an inspection of the ancient island lunatic asylum,‡ where Mrs Cavendish Bentinck, arrayed in chiffon and pearls, prodded a female lunatic in the buttocks with her parasol exclaiming, 'Do tell me, what is wrong with that one?' Aunt Enid had a *penchant* for minor royalty, a social pest now fortunately extinct, and they were a cause for much entertaining. I remember a beautiful reception for mother's friend, Princess Charlotte of Saxe Meiningen, given by the Duca della Grazia at the Palazzo Vendramin – the deathplace of Wagner – where there were two footmen in eighteenth-century costume outside every door and an orchestra brought from Vienna for the occasion; but I can also remember the trouble I encountered from my mother because of the difficulty I had in saying easily

---

* His name was actually F. R. Leyland. The famous Peacock Room is now to be seen, reconstructed, in the Freer Art Gallery of Washington DC.
† Actually, to her house at Cookham.
‡ On S. Servolo.

'*grossherzogliche Hoheit*' when talking to an archduke. For a boy of 14 it was quite a mouthful. It was a period of personalities, of parties, and of palazzos still inhabited by Venetians. Receptions had replaced Ridotto but pleasure, if sedate, was in the air. Venice was gaily international, yet somewhat provincial. Of the Italians, the della Grazias, Brandolins, Noces and Countess Morosini entertained frequently, and Aunt Enid, Lady Radnor, Lady Helen Vincent and Sir Hubert Miller of the English. America was represented by the Ralph Curtises of the Palazzo Barbaro whose father was said to have had to leave Boston after losing his temper and pulling a neighbour's nose on the train. The Countess Morosini and Lady Helen Vincent were famous beauties, one dark and the other fair. The former was greatly admired by the German Emperor who sent her his portrait after visiting Venice in his yacht. Many of these figures were caricatured by 'Baron Corvo' in his book *The Pursuit of the Whole and the Past.*★ It was the period of the English occupation and before the real American invasion when Venice became a fashionable summer resort. In those days the season closed in May.

In his will, Layard − who had already in 1886 presented to the National Gallery in London three fragments of a fresco by Spinello Aretino − bequeathed to the Gallery all his pictures other than portraits, with a life interest to his wife. In 1900 she handed over − from the part of her husband's collection that had been left in their London house at 1 Queen Anne Street − another fresco, now ascribed to Montagna. After her death on 1 November 1912 most of the pictures from Queen Anne Street followed. Those from Venice were delayed by war, export difficulties and a long dispute over the precise meaning of the word 'portraits' in the will; but in 1916 they too entered the Gallery − a number of them being later transferred to the Tate. Altogether, the Layard Bequest amounted to four frescoes and seventy-eight paintings. Remembering the size, quality and quantity of the British Museum's Assyrian collec-

---

★ The writer nods here. The real title of the book is *The Desire and Pursuit of the Whole*. (See Chapter 12.)

tion, one is tempted to ask whether any one man has personally provided the museums and galleries of England with a greater volume of works of art. It seems unlikely.

11. Whistler and Sargent
(1870–1913)

For Mr Whistler's own sake, no less than for the protection of the purchaser, Sir Coutts Lindsay ought not to have admitted works into the gallery in which the ill-educated conceit of the artist so nearly approached the aspect of wilful imposture. I have seen, and heard, much of cockney impudence before now, but never expected to hear a coxcomb ask two hundred guineas for flinging a pot of paint in the public's face.

The author of this magnificent piece of abuse was John Ruskin; the recipient was James McNeill Whistler; the subject was Whistler's *Nocturne in Black and Gold: the Falling Rocket*, which was on show at the Grosvenor Gallery; and the upshot was a libel suit brought by Whistler. The legal proceedings opened on 25 November 1878 in the absence of the defendant, who was recovering from one of his increasingly severe mental breakdowns. The art critic W. M. Rossetti – brother of Dante Gabriel – and the painter Albert Moore testified on behalf of Whistler; Sir Edward Burne-Jones and William Powell Frith for Ruskin. Burne-Jones went almost as far as Ruskin himself:

For years past [Whistler] has so worked the art of brag that he has succeeded in a measure amongst the semi-artistic part of the public, but amongst artists his vanities and eccentricities have been a matter of joke of long standing.

In the end the case was won by Whistler; but the moral victory was Ruskin's. The damages sought amounted to £1,000, plus costs; the sum awarded was one farthing, with costs equally divided. Whistler's legal fees were thus considerable; his formerly lucrative portrait practice dried up; and six months later – on 9 May 1879 –

he was declared bankrupt. Worst of all, he was obliged to sell the White House, the beautiful Chelsea residence with an immense studio on which work had only recently been completed.★

When he had taken the witness stand, Whistler had testified on oath that he had been born in St Petersburg; it doubtless seemed to him a good deal more romantic than the little town of Lowell, Massachusetts, where he had in fact first seen the light of day on 11 July 1834. True, he had spent five years in Russia in his childhood while his father, a railway engineer, was building the first line between St Petersburg and Moscow; but in 1849 George Washington Whistler had died of cholera, and the family had returned, practically penniless, to America. James had then briefly attended the Military Academy at West Point – its Superintendent was a certain Colonel Robert E. Lee – but had been a hopeless failure; and after a scarcely more successful spell with the US Coastal Survey (where however he at least received a good grounding in the art of etching) he had set off to be a painter in Paris. There he had enjoyed a Trilby-like existence with a few of his English fellow students, including George du Maurier himself, Edward Poynter and Frederic Leighton;† and it was probably thanks to these friends that he had decided, around 1860, to settle in London, to begin a life of controversy, argument, litigation and endless quarrels. He was redeemed by his conversational brilliance, his eccentricity – the English dearly love eccentrics – and his caustic wit: when one of his students complained that he had trouble painting what he saw, he is said to have replied: 'Your trouble will begin when you see what you paint.' An amusing companion he may have been; but he was never an easy one. Often, as an acquaintance ruefully pointed out, it was possible to get him to do what you wanted only if you took care to treat him as a very sensitive foreign power.‡

★ Before leaving, Whistler placed an inscribed stone plaque above the front door. It read: 'Except the Lord build the house, they labour in vain that build it. E. W. Godwin F.S.A. built this one.'

† Both Poynter and Leighton were to become Presidents of the Royal Academy, with a baronetcy and a peerage respectively.

‡ W. Shaw Sparrow, *Memories of Life and Art through Sixty Years.*

Nevertheless, there was much sympathy for Whistler in the London art world after the libel action, and not a little surprise that the Grosvenor Gallery's chief rival, the Fine Art Society, should have launched an appeal to meet not his own costs but those of Ruskin, a comparatively rich man. It may therefore have been as much to defuse criticism as anything else that on 9 September the Society's manager Marcus Huish and one of the trustees, Ernest Brown, commissioned Whistler on behalf of the Society to produce twelve etchings of Venice, for which he offered a welcome advance of £150. Only ten days later, armed with a box of new copper plates, etching needles and a bottle of acid, Whistler was rowed down the Grand Canal to his lodgings near the Frari – where his mistress, Maud Franklin, was to join him in October – and embarked on one of the most brilliantly creative periods of his career. Having originally planned to stay for three months, he remained for fourteen; and during that time, quite apart from several oil paintings and about a hundred dazzling pastels, he produced some fifty etchings rather than the required twelve.

Whistler's first few months in the city were hard, largely because the winter of 1879–80 was one of the coldest in Venetian history. 'Standing in the snow with a plate in my hand and an icicle at the end of my nose' proved impossible, and he was obliged to work as best he could in a freezing studio on an upper floor of the then sadly dilapidated Ca' Rezzonico (to be restored by Pen Browning ten years later). He missed London; in a letter to his sister-in-law he wrote:

> . . . now that it has taken to snowing I begin rather to wish myself back in my own lovely London fogs! – They are lovely those fogs – and I am their painter! – Of course you know Venice is superb and if I hadn't dined horribly today – and yesterday too – and the day before for the matter of that, nothing could induce me to speak the truth and acknowledge that I am bored to death after a certain time away from Piccadilly! – I pine for Pall Mall and I long for a hansom!

But for most of the time he was far from downhearted. After all, the palace could boast two glorious ceilings by Giambattista Tiepolo and a room frescoed by Francesco Guardi.★ His social life too began to flourish. He became friends with the Curtises and – inevitably – with Katharine de Kay Bronson, of whom Ralph Curtis remembered:

> During happy years, from lunch till long past bed-time her house was the open rendezvous for the rich and poor – the famous and the famished – *les rois en exil* and the heirs-presumptive to the thrones of fame. Whistler there had his seat from the first, but to the delight of all he generally held the floor.

Above all, he was happy in his work. 'Venice,' he wrote, 'is an impossible place to sit down and sketch – there's always something far better still just around the corner'; nevertheless, he wrote to Marcus Huish that his prints would be 'superb – and you may double your bets all round'. 'I have learned,' he continued, 'to know a Venice in Venice that the others seem never to have perceived . . . The etchings themselves are far more delicate in execution, more beautiful in subject, and more important in interest than any of the old set.'

★

What was this 'Venice in Venice'? Whistler was no Canaletto: not for him the majestic sweep of the Grand Canal, the grandeur of the Salute, the sublime elegance of the Doge's Palace. He does not even seem to have been particularly interested in the architecture of the city as such, or at least in that of its principal buildings. As far as we know, he made no more than two drawings of palaces on the Grand Canal – one of which is in fact an etching – scarcely any of churches (except when seen in the far distance) and but a single

★ Not, however, the enchanting frescoes of clowns and other pictures of eighteenth-century life by Domenico Tiepolo. These were originally painted in the Tiepolo villa at Zianigo, near Mira; they were bought by the *commune* and transferred to the Rezzonico only in 1910.

interior, of a palazzo which remains unidentified. What attracted him, again and again, was what might have been called *Venezia minore*, the lesser Venice, the Venice of her own day-to-day inhabitants. This preference was not in itself particularly new; for some years already painters like Myles Birket Foster, Luke Fildes and Henry Woods had been enjoying considerable success with their *genre* pictures of the Venetian working class. But their subjects tended to be scrubbed and sanitized, and attractively posed; shades of the chocolate box, even of the jigsaw puzzle, were never far away.

For Whistler on the other hand, the people themselves were of relatively little importance. When he introduces them at all, they are usually shadowy figures, lightly sketched in with the purpose either of improving the composition or of adding a touch of human interest. Seldom do they constitute the main focus of the picture; and even when they do, they remain unrecognizable as individuals. What he looked for — first, last and always — was atmosphere. In this, he was the very reverse of Ruskin, who concentrated almost exclusively on the major buildings and then thought only of their minutiae: the foliation of a pinnacle, the significance of a sculptured detail, the curve of a cusp. Whistler cared for none of these things. To his eye, the magic of Venice lay in the little back canals, the bridges that crossed them, the hidden *calli* and dark *sottoportici* of perhaps S. Polo or S. Croce, from which any self-respecting, Baedeker-wielding tourist — in the unlikely event of his finding his way there at all — would recoil with a sniff and a shudder. So obscure, indeed, were most of the subjects — particularly where the etchings are concerned — that many have been only recently identified. One or two still keep their secrets today.

This problem is largely due to Whistler himself, who hardly ever even hints at a precise location. Edith Bronson remembered:

What would be the use, he would ask, of his ferreting out some wonderful old bridge or archway, and thinking of making it immortal, if some second-rate painter-man were to come after him and make it commonplace with his caricatures?

The Times's art critic Harry Quilter recalled an entirely characteristic scene:

> I had been drawing for about five days, in one of the back canals, a specially beautiful doorway, when one morning I heard a sort of war-whoop, and there was Whistler in a gondola, close-by, shouting . . . 'Hi, hi! what? what? Here, I say, you've got my doorway!' I replied, 'It's my doorway, I've been here for the last week.' 'I don't care a straw, I found it out first.'

Such titles as *The Doorway, The Garden, The Steps* or *The Balcony* tell us no more than we can see for ourselves. Often too – and perhaps deliberately – Whistler tends to blur what might otherwise have been an easily recognizable part of the background. And the problem of identification is made no easier by the fact that an etching, unlike a painting or a pastel, provides us with a mirror image of the subject, and he saw no reason to reverse his plates. No less an authority than Walter Sickert went so far as to suggest that the etchings might themselves be reproduced in reverse:

> Let there be a brief, careful topographical note to each, by someone who knows Venice well from San Simeone Profeta to San Pietro di Castello. Let us enjoy, *for the first time*, without having to reverse them in a looking-glass, the witty comments of the hand that flew like a swallow over the surface of the copper in lyrical appreciation of the loveliest city in the world. I do not want to think I am looking along the Riva towards the Via Garibaldi when I am really looking towards the Ducal Palace. It worries me, and spoils my pleasure to see the Salute on the Giudecca and San Giorgio on the Zattere. Whistler is great – but so is Venice.

In fact, owing to the obscurity of most of the sites, it is only in the two etchings of the Riva degli Schiavoni that the reversing process seems to make much difference.

In the summer of 1880 Whistler and Maud Franklin left their lodgings near the Frari to join a group of young American painters led by Whistler's friend Frank Duveneck, who had settled in lodgings in and around Casa Jankowitz – now the Pensione Bucintoro – at the far end of the Riva next to the church of S. Biagio. The upper, west-facing windows of their single studio room afford a magnificent view all the way down to the Doge's Palace, with the Salute in the distance and, further round to the left, the island of S. Giorgio Maggiore; and the etchings done from these windows are both little masterpieces of their kind – although here above all, as Sickert complained, the looking-glass image can be strangely troubling. Fortunately for us, Whistler also painted – though not always with his own materials. Henry Woods reported:

> He uses all the colours he can lay his hands upon; he uses a large flat brush which he calls 'Matthew', and this brush is the terror of about a dozen young Americans he is with now. Matthew takes up a whole tube of cobalt at a lick; of course the colour is someone else's property.

Of all Whistler's work in Venice it is his pastels that are the most easily approachable. His friend Otto Bacher – one of the 'Duveneck boys' who left a delightful memoir of their time together★ – remembered how, when he set off in the mornings in his gondola,

> he always carried two boxes of pastels, an older one for instant use, filled with little bits of strange, broken colours of which he was very fond, and a newer box with which he did his principal work. He had quantities of vari-coloured papers, browns, reds, greys, uniform in size.
>
> In beginning a pastel he drew his subject crisply and carefully in outline with black crayon upon one of those sheets of tinted paper which fitted the general colour of the motive. A few touches with sky-tinted pastels, corresponding to nature, produced a remarkable effect, with touches of reds, greys and yellows for the buildings here

★ *With Whistler in Venice.*

and there. The reflections of the sky and houses upon the water finished the work. At all times he placed the pastels between leaves of silver-coated paper ... Taken as a whole, the pastels are as complete a collection of pictures of Venice and its life as can be found.

To what extent, both in his choice of subjects and in his treatment of them, was Whistler influenced by Ruskin? When he arrived in Venice in September 1879, his disastrous litigation was less than a year in the past, his bankruptcy only four months; it is inconceivable with a character such as his, that he should not still have been haunted by the ghost of his arch-enemy. He must have had at least a cursory acquaintance with *The Stones of Venice* – few people, then as now, managed to get all the way through those three brilliant but impossible volumes – and he would certainly have known of Ruskin's passion for Venetian Gothic and his detestation of the Renaissance.★ Is it purely coincidental that he seems almost wilfully to ignore the former, even going so far as to omit any suggestion of the Doge's Palace – described by Ruskin as 'the central building of the world' – from his exquisite etching of the Piazzetta? Or that the only work which betrays any real interest in architectural detail is his depiction (in *The Doorway*) of the early Renaissance Palazzo Gussoni?

The Duveneck boys transformed Whistler's time in Venice – and probably Maud's as well. With no work to occupy her she must have spent those first months bored out of her mind – particularly since there would have been no question of her being received by the Curtises or the Bronsons, let alone in any Venetian household. This gang of young artists, however, who idolized Whistler – when he was not using their painting materials – cared not a fig about irregular relationships; and Maud, who was in all probability the only woman in the group, must at last have begun to enjoy herself. (Curiously enough, Bacher does not mention her.) As for her lover, who needed a constant audience to admire him,

★ See Chapter 5, pp. 89–90.

flatter him and laugh at his wit, he was in his element. Night after night he could be seen sitting at Florian's, wearing his invariable white duck trousers, dark jacket and broad-brimmed brown hat, tilted far back on his head to show off his thick, curly hair with its famous snow-white streak. True, he was working as hard as he had ever worked in his life; but he had promised his strictly Sabbatarian mother – she was a McNeill, originally from the island of Skye, a member of one of the many families that had emigrated en masse to America after the defeat of Bonnie Prince Charlie at Culloden* – that he would never paint on Sundays, and these he devoted exclusively to the entertainment and amusement of his friends.

In the early autumn of 1880, Marcus Huish summoned Whistler back to London: he needed the etchings, he explained, for an exhibition – 'Twelve Great Etchers' – that he was planning to open in a few weeks' time. Whistler, for his part, was willing to go. He felt that he had exhausted the possibilities of Venice; he was unwilling to face another Venetian winter; and he too was anxious to print his etchings. There was only one problem. As usual, he was penniless; indeed, he was in debt. He therefore wrote to Huish asking for £100. Huish, who was probably by now bitterly regretting ever having sent Whistler to Venice at all, dispatched a cheque for £50. It might well have been enough, but Whistler was adamant: he needed a hundred, he had asked for a hundred, and a hundred was what he proposed to get. Finally Huish caved in, but not until it was too late for the etchings to be included in the exhibition.†

It was the beginning of November by the time Whistler and Maud were finally ready, and their friends were determined to see them off in style. They chartered a vast barge, which they decorated with flowers, fruit and sheaves of wheat, and hung with Japanese lanterns. Oarsmen were stationed fore and aft; in the centre was a dining-table, at the head of which stood a splendid throne for the guest of honour, topped with the American flag. Starting in the

---

* She must also be – with the sole exception of the Virgin Mary – the most celebrated mother in the history of painting.

† Was this, one wonders, Whistler's secret objective, so that he could have a show of his own?

evening from the Riva, the boat sailed out into the lagoon and onward up the Grand Canal. A sudden rainstorm obliged it to shelter for some time under the Rialto Bridge, but there was no dampening of the spirits; the party continued till morning, when a somewhat shaky couple boarded their train. It was a fine send-off, but it was no finer than Whistler had deserved; for the body of work with which he returned to England was richer and more varied than that of any other visitor to Venice during the nineteenth century, while his influence was to remain supreme until well into the twentieth.

Back in London, he drove at the earliest possible moment to the Fine Art Society to see its exhibition.

> Nobody expected me. In one hand, I held my long cane; with the other, I led by a ribbon a beautiful little white pomeranian dog – it, too, had turned up suddenly. As I walked in I spoke to no one, but putting up my glass, I looked at the prints on the wall. 'Dear me! dear me!' I said, 'still the same old sad work! Dear me!'

Then he settled down to the business of printing. Most etchers tended to leave this work to professionals, but Whistler always insisted on doing it himself. There was, he maintained, as much skill involved with the printing press as with the engraver's needle, and he could trust no one else. That way, too, he was able to ensure that every proof was unique. By the end of November the job was done, and the twelve best Venetian etchings were hung in a small room at the Fine Art Society. The last word may perhaps be given to Whistler's old enemy Harry Quilter, who – despite the way Whistler had treated him in Venice – was able to write in the *Spectator*:

> What has been done, and done with a cleverness so great as to be almost genius, is to sketch the passing, everyday aspect of canal, lagoon and quay; to give, in fact, to those who have not seen the city some notion of that outside aspect, in which wealth and poverty, grandeur and squalor, life and death, are so strangely mingled.

Did James NcNeill Whistler, during his stay in Venice, run into his young compatriot and fellow painter John Singer Sargent? There is no record, oddly enough, of the two having met while they were there; on the other hand we know that Sargent arrived with his parents at the Hotel d'Italie on Campo S. Moisè – now the Bauer-Grünwald – in the late summer of 1880. He almost immediately found a studio, just as Whistler had, in the Palazzo Rezzonico; and since Venice is a small city and Whistler was to remain there until mid-November, it seems almost incredible that the paths of the two men did not cross. There is even a picture by Sargent – to which he gave the title *Venise par temps gris* – painted from exactly the same viewpoint as one of Whistler's etchings, the window of the Casa Jankowitz, in which he and Maud Franklin lived with the Duveneck boys. Is it too fanciful to suggest that Whistler invited him up to show him the magnificent view down the Riva, and that Sargent subsequently decided to paint it for himself?★

For Whistler, this was his first and last visit to Venice; for Sargent, twenty-two years younger, it was already his fifth. Now twenty-four, he too was an American expatriate; but whereas Whistler had spent most of his youth in the United States, Sargent had never yet set foot there. His parents, a moderately well-to-do Philadelphia doctor named – rather surprisingly – FitzWilliam Sargent and his wife Mary had crossed the Atlantic in 1854 to recover from the death of a two-year-old daughter; they were to remain in Europe, constantly on the move and living in hotels or rented apartments, for the next half-century. Soon after their arrival they settled temporarily in Florence, where their son John was born on 12 January 1856.†

The family had first come to Venice when he was only a few months old; then in May 1870, when he was fourteen, they had stayed a fortnight, being eventually driven out by a premature heat

★ Sargent's picture is in fact dated 'c.1882', but could easily be two years earlier. And even if the date is correct the suggestion is not invalidated.

† This, at least, was the day on which he celebrated his birthday; but no birth certificate has ever been found, and Sargent's father was always uncertain of the precise date.

wave; three years later in the summer of 1873 they were there again, on what was to be, for the brilliantly precocious young painter, his first formative visit. In March 1874 he wrote to his cousin Mary Austin:

> I have learned in Venice to admire Tintoretto immensely and to consider him perhaps second only to Michael Angelo and Titian, whose beauties it was his aim to unite.

He went on to recommend a book

> to my artistic cousin Mary, [if she] would like to read about Tintoretto, and know the opinion his contemporaries had of him, before his pictures had blackened and faded, and before the great pictures on the ceiling of San Rocco in Venice were used as sieves for rain water which was collected in buckets on the floor.

The Sargents had intended to go back to Venice the following summer, but reports of a growing cholera epidemic led them to change their minds. They went instead to Paris, where John could attend what was perhaps the best art school in Europe – in the studio of Charles-Emile-Auguste Durand, known professionally – if somewhat preciously – as Carolus-Duran. 'I am sorry to leave Italy – that is to say, Venice,' he wrote that autumn, 'but on the other hand I am persuaded that Paris is the place to learn painting in. When I can paint, *then* away for Venice!'

It was at about this time that a 22-year-old American art student named Julian Alden Weir wrote to his mother:

> I met this last week a young Mr Sargent, about eighteen years old and one of the most talented fellows I have ever come across; his drawings are like the Old Masters, and his color is equally fine. He was born abroad and has not yet seen his country. He speaks as well in French, German [and] Italian as he does English, [and] has a fine ear for music . . . Such men take one up, and as his principles are equal to his talents, I hope to have his friendship.

Sargent remained technically a pupil of Carolus-Duran for the next five years; but already in the spring of 1878 he was back in the city he loved – or so at least we are informed by the painter Mary Cassatt, who refers to a 'Mr Sargent' in connection with a newly founded Society of American Artists. This, however, is the only evidence. We know nothing of where he lived or how long he was in Venice. But by this time, at any rate, there was no doubt that he had realized his ambition. At the age of twenty-two he could paint with greater skill and assurance than most painters ever achieve. To no less an authority than the sculptor Auguste Rodin, he was 'le Van Dyck de nos jours'; to his friend Henry James, his work offered

> the slightly 'uncanny' spectacle of a talent which on the very threshold of its career has nothing more to learn . . . Perception with him is already by itself a form of execution . . . It is as if painting were pure tact of vision, a simple manner of feeling.

James went on to refer to 'his knock-down insolence of talent'.

> It is the old story; he expresses himself as no one else scarce begins to do in the language of the art he practises . . . Beside him his competitors appear to stammer.

The 1880 visit – Whistler or no Whistler – was the one during which we see Sargent putting down his roots in Venice. Though he never possessed a house or apartment there he now became essentially a Venetian, dividing his time between his studio in the Ca' Rezzonico – where he became a close friend of his older colleague Giovanni Boldini – and his gondola, from which he endlessly sketched in company with his sister Emily. He loved gondolas, not only for their intrinsic beauty but also for the low viewpoint that they afforded; time and again we see the *ferro* – that characteristic prow – in the foreground of a watercolour. With the coming of autumn his family departed, but John could not drag himself away. He moved to the Hotel all'Orologio, at no. 290

Piazza S. Marco, next to the Clock Tower, from which, in late October, he wrote to his friend Vernon Lee: 'There is plenty of work to be done here, and the only thing I fear is the *ennui* of living almost alone in a wet and changed Venice.' This, none the less, is what he seems to have done; it was February 1881 – perhaps even March – before he left.

But if Sargent was indeed lonely in Venice that winter, it was for the last time. He probably already knew the Bronsons at Ca' Alvisi; Mrs Bronson, as we are well aware, made it her business to take up any of her compatriots who might find themselves in the city – but in 1881 Daniel and Ariana Curtis moved into Palazzo Barbaro. Daniel Sargent Curtis was FitzWilliam Sargent's first cousin; Ariana was English-born, the 'brutally intelligent'★ daughter of Admiral Ralph Randolph Wormeley RN, who was in turn a great-nephew of George Washington's attorney-general. Sargent was one of their earliest guests, and in later years one of the most regular; on his very first visit in 1882 he settled down to a portrait of 'the dogaressa', as he called her. Their son Ralph was also a painter, who had studied at the same time as Sargent in the studio of Carolus-Duran. He was talented but spoilt: the unashamed luxury of the Barbaro, with its superb furniture and its pictures, its spacious garden – a rarity in Venice – its huge and highly trained staff and its fleet of gondolas, encouraged his playboy nature and disinclined him to work harder than was absolutely necessary.

Sargent, by contrast, worked very hard indeed. Despite his huge frame – which, as a friend marvelled, 'would have done credit to a Japanese wrestler' – there was a wonderful gentleness about him – reminiscent, as *The Times* was later to put it, 'of a good giant in a fairy story'. His appetite was prodigious: a fellow guest reported admiringly, 'he can put away more food at a sitting than any man in London . . . He ate during the best part of two hours with a steadfastness and concentration such as I have never before or since seen equalled at a meal.' At the same time he was strangely shy; and yet again, paradoxically, he loved social life. For the rest, his sense

★ Stanley Olson, *John Singer Sargent: His Portrait.*

of humour, his musicianship – he was a brilliant pianist who could read anything at sight – and his fascination for the ridiculous or the bizarre made him endlessly entertaining company.

Sargent's work in Venice was strongly influenced by that of Whistler: more so, perhaps, than he would have liked to admit. Like his compatriot, and unlike the hordes of foreign artists who descended on the city every spring, he remained unseduced by the things that most people came to see. Of the churches or the palazzi we are allowed only an occasional glimpse, and then only in part, as a backdrop to the main scene; never do they figure as subjects in themselves. Like Whistler too, Sargent prefers to show us every-day life in Venice, and in particular that of Venetian working-class women going about their daily business. Of these, *The Studio* wrote:

> Mr Sargent, tiring of over-dressed beauties for the nonce, has picked up a few of the slouchiest specimens of woman-kind that Venice produces, but serves them up with such a skilful turn of the wrist, and such a dexterous toss of the pan, that with our eyes shut we should almost take them for duchesses.

He usually depicts these women either in small *campi* and *calli* with occasional groups of rather sinister men, or in almost bare interiors of large and apparently deserted palazzi. Here is Henry James again:

> There stands out in particular, as a pure gem, a small picture exhibited at the Grosvenor, representing a small group of Venetian girls of the lower class, sitting in gossip together one summer's day in the big, dim hall of a shabby old palazzo. The shutters let in a chink of light; the scagliola pavement gleams faintly in it; the whole place is bathed in a kind of transparent shade; the tone of the picture is dark and cool. The girls are vaguely engaged in some very humble household work; they are counting turnips or stringing onions, and these small vegetables, enchantingly painted, look as valuable as magnified pearls. The figures are extraordinarily natural and vivid;

wonderfully light and fine is the touch by which the painter evokes
the small Venetian realities . . . and keeps the whole thing free from
the element of humbug which has ever attended most attempts to
reproduce the idiosyncrasies of Italy.*

For the rest, Sargent is endlessly fascinated by the visual joys of
Venice: the ever-changing light, the reflections of buildings in the
water, the unknown corners, the anonymous doorways, the sense
of the all-embracing sea. This above all he never allows us to forget;
far more than Whistler's, his Venetian pictures are full of boats,
masts and spars.

He often spoke of his intention of painting a really important
canvas of Venice for the Paris Salon, the exhibition of work by
living artists which was held annually in May at the Palais des
Champs-Elysées; oddly enough, he never did so. The nearest he
came to it was to show two watercolours, both called *Vue de Venise*,
in the Salon of 1881. Of these one critic wrote: 'Only impressionist
sketches, but what light! What sparkle!' The larger, often gloomier
oil paintings, though shown at many other exhibitions in Europe
and America, were never really popular; they were too much
at variance with the way most people thought about Venice.
Sargent was to include at least three in his first one-man exhibition,
held at Boston in 1888; but eventually, unable to find buyers, he
gave most of them to his friends in the art world. (Two went to
Mr F. W. C. Bechstein, in return for one of his company's upright
pianos.)

The American connoisseur and collector Martin Brimmer wrote
to a friend at about this time:

Young Sargent has been staying with [the Curtises] & is an attractive
man . . . He had some half-finished pictures of Venice. They are
very clever, but a good deal inspired by the desire of finding what

---

*James's memory is playing him tricks. None of Sargent's surviving paintings
fits this description entirely; the nearest is the one which he called *Venetian
Women in the Palazzo Rezzonico*, probably dating from 1880.

no one else has sought here – unpicturesque subjects, absence of color, absence of sunlight. It seems hardly worthwhile to travel so far for these. But he has some qualities to an unusual degree – a sense of values & faculty for making his personages move.

Sargent may have been disappointed by the lukewarm reactions of the critics, but he was unrepentant. That winter he wrote to Mrs Curtis:

> You will perhaps see how curious Venice looks with snow clinging to the roofs and balconies, with a dull sky, and the canals of a dull opaque green, not unlike pea soup, *con rispetto*, and very different from the *julienne* of the Grand Canal in summer.

That was in 1898; over the next fifteen years he was to pay nine more visits to Venice, staying almost invariably with the Curtises at the Barbaro. By then he was growing tired of portraits, and in Venice he painted scarcely any. There was that of Ariana Curtis; there could have been one of Robert Browning, if the poet had only taken any of the hints that the painter dropped. The famous portrait of Isabella Stewart Gardner – who was to accumulate over fifty of his works – was painted in Boston; and we are left only with *An Interior in Venice*, the enchanting group portrait of the Curtises in their drawing room, painted in 1899 and now hanging in the Royal Academy at Burlington House. Mrs Curtis apparently disliked it for making her look so old, and making her son Ralph so 'slouchy'; and an even more curious comment was made by the critic Roger Fry:

> Sargent is too fond of the sparkle and glitter of life to give us any sense of the dreamy gloom of a seventeenth-century palace. He appears to harbour no imaginations that he could not easily avow at the afternoon tea he so brilliantly depicts.

After 1913 there were no more visits to Venice. By then, Sargent confessed, he had become a little disillusioned with the city, now marred by 'the swarms of larky smart Londoners whose goings-on fill the Gazette'. He preferred London, where he settled in Whistler's former studio at 31 Tite Street, Chelsea which – despite the fact that his predecessor had painted it a shade of yellow so savage that it gave visitors the sensation of standing inside an egg – he had happily acquired in 1886 when Whistler had moved to 454 Fulham Road.

How did the two men really get on? Fundamentally, relations between them seem to have been cordial enough. They shared a genuine love of the byways and back canals of Venice; and there can be no doubt that they admired each other's work. When Sargent was still little known in England, Whistler was one of the first to bring him to public notice; Sargent for his part used to say that Whistler's handling of paint was 'so exquisite that if a piece of canvas were cut out of one of his pictures one would find that it was in itself a thing of beauty by the very texture and substance into which it had been transformed by his brush'. Temperamentally, however, they differed profoundly: Whistler, acutely conscious of his own genius and fiercely intolerant of any ideas or opinions other than his own, was perhaps more than a little jealous of Sargent's popularity and sophistication; 'Not that he isn't charming and all that,' he wrote to a friend on 16 July 1899, 'only a sepulchre of dullness and propriety.' The remark was as inaccurate as it was unkind. Sargent was anything but dull; nor was he one jot less dedicated a painter. But he was gentle and easygoing, as happy to converse in any one of three or four languages – or, better still, to play the piano – as to sit at his easel. Explosive characters like Whistler's were not for him.

One suspects that somehow, even in the artistic life of turn-of-the-century London, they saw comparatively little of each other. In any case, Sargent was to outlive Whistler – who died in 1903 – by twenty-two years. On the evening of 14 April 1925 he attended a dinner given by his sister Emily at 10 Carlyle Mansions; it was a farewell party, since he was due to leave for America the following day. At ten thirty the guests left, and he returned to Tite Street. When the maid knocked at his door the next morning she found him dead. He was sixty-nine years old. Beside him lay an open book, which Whistler, we may be quite sure, would never have read: it was the *Dictionnaire philosophique* of Voltaire.

12. Corvo
(1908–13)

I came to Venice in August for a six-weeks' holiday; and lived
and worked and slept in my *barcheta* almost always . . . I went
swimming half a dozen times a day, beginning at white dawn,
and ending after sunsets which set the whole lagoon ablaze
with amethyst and topaz . . . One day, I replenished my stock
of provisions at Burano; and at sunset we rowed away to find
a station for the night. Imagine a twilight world of cloudless
sky and smoothest sea, all made of warm, liquid, limpid helio-
trope and violet and lavender, with bands of burnished
copper set with emeralds, melting, on the other hand, into
the fathomless blue of the eyes of the prides of peacocks,
where the moon rose, rosy as mother-of-pearl. Into such glory
we three advanced the black *barcheta*, solemnly, silently, when
the last echo of *Ave Maria* died.

Frederick Rolfe

In the London *Star*, on 29 October 1913, there appeared the
following announcement:

A curiously interesting and almost mysterious character has passed
away in the person of Mr Frederick Rolfe, who was found dead in
his bed at Venice a few mornings since. Mr Rolfe was the author,
under his own name, of various novels in which an extraordinary
amount of very ill-assimilated learning was displayed, and the life
of the Italian priesthood, rural as well as at the Curia, was portrayed
with an insight and an appearance of exact knowledge which
impressed the critics.

Under the name of Baron Corvo, an Italian title which he
claimed to have acquired through the gift of some estates by a

former Duchess of Cesarini-Sforza, he wrote verses and controversial articles on Catholic ritual and Italian politics. He used to
state that he had been at one time in priest's orders, but this, we
believe, was denied by the authorities of his Church.

A devout Catholic in doctrine, he was at issue with the hierarchy
over Italian matters, being a strong opponent of the temporal power.
He compiled an elaborate genealogical table to show that the King
of Italy was the legitimate King of England, and fantastic as the idea
may appear, the scholarship and research involved were frankly
acknowledged by antiquarian and heraldic criticism.

All this was true as far as it went, but it went nowhere near far
enough. Frederick William Serafino Austin Lewis Mary Rolfe may
have possessed more than a touch of genius; unfortunately he was
himself possessed by a devil which allowed him no rest, which
made friendship impossible and his ultimate destitution inevitable.
All his life, in his efforts to alleviate a poverty which sometimes
involved a whole week without food, he would write, in his
strangely medieval hand, long letters detailing his misfortunes –
always the fault of others – and begging for assistance; but almost
invariably, if that assistance was offered, he would fling it back,
showering the unfortunate donor with pages of invective and abuse.
For the last five years of his life, during which he never left Venice,
his devil brought him – according at least to his own account – to
depths of privation and despair that few if any visitors to the city
have ever known. To his compatriots in the resident English colony
he was a continual thorn in the flesh: at once an embarrassment, a
perennial problem and a source of vague guilt. He was not so much
an irritant: he was a pain.

A Londoner, born on 22 July 1860 at 61 Cheapside to a family
of piano manufacturers, he was already forty-eight when he arrived
for the first time in Venice, carrying his few belongings in a
wicker laundry-basket. By then he had written three major books,
including his best-known work, *Hadrian the Seventh* – which, more
than any other, provides the key to his extraordinary personality.
It is the story of George Arthur Rose, a fervent Roman Catholic

who has nevertheless been rejected for the priesthood, and whose rejection has made him lonely, deeply embittered, and – as he himself puts it – 'as touchy as a hornet with a brand-new sting'. One day he receives a surprise visit from a cardinal and a bishop, who tell him that the Church wishes to make restitution for his sufferings by granting him his long-sought ordination. With characteristic gracelessness, he agrees; and soon afterwards he finds himself in Rome, attending the bishop at a papal conclave. For a long time the assembled cardinals have been in deadlock; suddenly, to his astonishment, he finds that he has been elected Pope. He instantly sets about a radical reform of the Papacy, renouncing its claim to temporal sovereignty and selling the Vatican treasures for an immense sum, which he distributes among the poor. Finally, one day when returning from the Quirinal, he is assassinated.

> How bright the sunlight was, on the warm grey stones, on the ripe Roman skins, on vermilion and lavender and blue and ermine and green and gold, on the indecent grotesque blackness of two blotches, on apostolic whiteness and the rose of blood.

Since Frederick Rolfe was one of the most completely self-centred men who ever lived, all his work is to a greater or lesser degree autobiographical. He is George Arthur Rose, just as in his later work he figures as Nicholas Crabbe. The second half of *Hadrian the Seventh* is clearly wishful thinking; the first provides us with an all-too-accurate self-portrait. Rolfe too – a devout Catholic convert – had been rejected by the Church. Indeed, it had forcibly expelled him from the Scots College in Rome on the grounds that he had no divine vocation;★ and that humiliation, together with what he considered the obvious injustice he had suffered, had blighted his life. The only good – if good it was – to come out of his stay in Rome was the friendship of the elderly Duchess Sforza-Cesarini. She was English by birth – her first cousin once

★ One of his habits to which the College objected was that of saying his office in the bath.

removed, Lord Curzon of Kedleston, was shortly to be appointed
Viceroy of India – a devout Catholic and a socialist; and she took
the disappointed young seminarian under her wing. Whether or
not she really endowed him with a title is less certain; he himself
gave at least three different explanations for it at various times.
Romantic and somehow a little sinister, it suited him well; but he
soon tired of it, preferring to sign himself 'Fr. Rolfe', with its faintly
ecclesiastical overtones.

Returning to his homeland, he spent a year or two in Aberdeen,
eking out a precarious living as tutor, painter and photographer; in
this last occupation he claimed to have made significant contributions to the new science of submarine photography and also to
have invented an early form of colour printing. He also began
seriously to write, though authorship at this time proved no more
successful than any of his other activities.* Once again forcibly
evicted from his lodgings, he moved to the shrine of Holywell in
Wales, painting religious banners for use in the regular parades
in honour of St Frideswide. Everywhere he made enemies; he
was none the less astonished when, on 8 November 1898, there
appeared in the *Aberdeen Free Press* the first of three anonymous
but impressively well researched articles which tore his reputation,
such as it was, to shreds. It accused him, *inter alia*, of having been
discharged from virtually every post he had ever held; of being a
confidence trickster who had contracted enormous debts under
false pretences; of assuming a title of nobility to which he had no
conceivable right; and of passing bad cheques. Gleefully, it described
his eviction from his Aberdeen lodgings:

> One evening about 6 o'clock the landlord besought the aid of a
> fellow-workman. They entered the Baron's bedroom, and the
> Baron was given ten minutes to dress and clear out. He refused to

* He later told his friend Sir Harry Luke that during 'one of his periods of
homeless destitution' he wrote the first set of the *Tales That Toto Told Me* in one
of London's public lavatories, on the paper supplied by the establishment. He
maintained that it was only by means of its unusual format and appearance that
his manuscript at last caught the editor's eye (D. Weeks, *Corvo*, p. 117).

move, and when the ten minutes was up he seized hold of the iron bedstead and clung for dear life. He was dragged forth, wearing only his pyjamas, out to the staircase, where he caught hold of the banisters, and another struggle ensued. Thence he was carried down the long staircase and was shot on to the pavement, as he stood, to the wonderment of passers-by. His clothing was thrown after him, which he ultimately donned – and that was the last of Baron Corvo in that particular locality.

The effect of these articles on Rolfe was second only to that of his failure to become a priest. In January 1899, without a penny in the world and on the verge of a nervous breakdown, he entered the Holywell workhouse; then, a month later, he discharged himself and walked the 140 miles to London.

★

The events of the next eight years of his life followed much the same depressing pattern, and need not concern us here. We may therefore pass on to November 1907, when Rolfe wrote a begging letter to Richard MacGillivray Dawkins, later to hold the chair of Byzantine and Modern Greek at Oxford.★ The correspondence unexpectedly flourished, to the point where Dawkins suggested that the two might travel together to Venice the following summer. Knowing the state of his friend's finances, he offered to advance the necessary money, to be repaid – theoretically at least – from Rolfe's future writing and photography.

They arrived in the heat of a Venetian August and took rooms for six weeks in the Hotel Belle Vue et de Russie next to the Clock Tower, with a splendid view of the Piazza – a Piazza that would

★ 'Of [Dawkins's] powers as a lecturer it was difficult to judge as he had managed over the years successfully to discourage anyone from reading modern Greek. When, very occasionally, some misguided female student, despite every obstacle he could devise, inscribed herself for the course, his first, and last, lecture of the academic year was always of such shattering indecency that the unfortunate young woman immediately decided to take up Icelandic' (Osbert Lancaster, *With an Eye to the Future*, London, 1967).

look strange to us today since there was no campanile. The former one had collapsed six years before, on 14 July 1902 at eight minutes past ten in the morning, and had not yet been replaced.★ Almost immediately, however, they began to quarrel – no one could ever live amicably with Rolfe for more than a few days – and well before the six weeks were up Dawkins returned to England. He later explained:

> I had a lot of other things to do; Rolfe had literally not another thing in the world to do but impress his so carefully cultivated personality on people and bully them into supporting him; his work was done only for the sake of his own self; the desire to make a figure in the world was always with him. I doubt whether he had any remotely disinterested feeling for anyone else . . .
>
> It did not take me long to discover that Rolfe's idea of being helped along was to be allowed to spend as much as he pleased . . . He became extremely tiresome; tried a sort of worrying bullying, and in short I did not stay long in Venice but left him with enough money to get home . . . but this he would not do. On various pretexts he stayed on in Venice, naturally running up bills. These I never paid but sent him some few pounds to clear himself; what I reckoned would be enough. By this time I was thoroughly sick of this sort of shiftiness and determined that he should no longer take advantage of me. So I entirely shut off supplies. He then started a series of letters describing his troubles, starvation and so on. But he had succeeded in making me thoroughly angry; he had fooled me by making excuses not to leave Venice and so get more money from me; I was determined to put a stop to it all and let him go on writing. I think I never left a letter unanswered, but my answers were brief.

In his description of Dawkins, Rolfe was even less charitable:

★ The new campanile, an identical replica of its predecessor, was to be inaugurated on St Mark's Day, 25 April 1912. (My mother, who had first seen the Piazza in the same year as Corvo, always maintained that it looked much better without.)

He belonged to that class of men which I (following Aristotle) call the Fusidowls, the Born Slaves, creatures absolutely incapable of performing a noble (*i.e.* a free) act themselves or conniving at such performance on the part of others. He was of the revolting flabby carroty freckled mug-nosed bristly blubber-mouthed species, toothed of Senigaglia cheese-colour ... His conversation was a hectic gabble, produced in the voice of a strangulated Punch, punctuated with screams & stamps of rage in public piazzas ...

After Dawkins's departure Rolfe stayed on at the Belle Vue. He was quite unable to pay his bills; but the proprietor, Signor Barbieri, allowed him to run up a considerable debt, impressed both by his lordly demeanour and by the number of the letters he received, many of them in envelopes of obviously high quality. (The fact that the majority were negative replies to begging letters presumably did not occur to him.) By this time, too, Rolfe had developed a passion for the lagoon, and throughout the autumn spent hours a day on the water, either with the two young gondoliers whom Dawkins had hired and he had befriended or – more often – rowing himself, Venetian style (standing up and facing forward), in a borrowed *barcheta*. One day, in a burst of unexpected generosity, he approached Lady Layard's hospital on the Giudecca with an offer to take convalescent patients in the afternoons for a row in the sunshine. He wrote:

They think no end of me. So does the matron, Miss Chaffey. Now Lady Layard (Queen of England in Venice), who adores the hospital, does so too. I choke 'em all off. What's the good of making new friends when you may be denounced at the *questura* for debt any day?

With the approach of winter, these activities ceased; but then, at 5.20 a.m. on Monday 28 December 1908, south Italy and Sicily were struck by the most catastrophic earthquake Europe had ever known, measuring no less than 7.5 on the Richter scale. Its epicentre was in the Straits of Messina, which city was almost completely demolished: in the space of a few minutes its population of 150,000 was reduced to a few hundred, while the total number of casualties throughout Italy was estimated at nearly a quarter of a million. Faced with many thousands of survivors without homes, food or clothes – since most of them had been in bed when the disaster occurred – the Italian government launched an urgent appeal throughout the north. The response was immediate, and for several weeks Rolfe – genuinely motivated by charity for perhaps the first time in his life – was occupied during every waking hour, rowing from house to house to collect all the supplies that could be found for urgent dispatch to the devastated areas.

A few weeks previously, Canon Lonsdale Ragg, his wife Laura and their small daughter had also settled into the Belle Vue. For the past three years Canon Ragg had been the Anglican chaplain in Venice; he and his family had a flat of their own in the city, but it was unheated and for some three months in the winter they sought the comfort of the hotel. There they befriended Rolfe, as far as he allowed them to do so, and in due course took him to one of Horatio Brown's Monday evening parties. It was not a success. Faced with a roomful of strangers, he froze: all his old prickliness came to the surface, and he rejected every attempt to draw him into conversation. He was to return to the Ca' Torresella on only two occasions, driven by hunger and 'in the frantic hope of finding a biscuit or a sandwich'. Ragg did not give up. Again and again he tried to help, and did his utmost to persuade Barbieri to keep Rolfe on at the Belle Vue, genuinely believing that the author of *Hadrian the Seventh* would sooner or later produce another masterpiece and put an end to his financial problems once and for all; but every attempt at assistance was met with the usual torrent of invective.

By the coming of spring the proprietor's patience was exhausted; and on 14 April 1909 Rolfe found himself cast out on to the street. It was an experience to which he was by now well accustomed. On past occasions, however, he had usually had somewhere else to go; this time he was left, literally, without a roof over his head. All he had was the open *barcheta*, and for the next fortnight this was his only home. Then, fortunately, he once again ran into Canon Ragg, who somehow prevailed on him to accept an invitation to dine as his guest in a restaurant and who informed him during dinner that he would shortly be leaving Venice with his family, having accepted the living of Tickencote in Rutland. Their belongings were already packed and would be shipped in a few days; meanwhile they were staying with the Curtises at Palazzo Barbaro. They had left their flat, which might no longer be furnished but was at least empty; and Ragg persuaded Rolfe that he would be doing them a favour if he occupied it. This Rolfe did until 7 May; but then, wrote Ragg,

he became familiar with our future address . . . & when I arrived on the scene I found insulting *postcards* awaiting me! So far as I know they failed in their object: & in any case I felt no real resentment. But it was distinctly embarrassing. I fancy my crowning offence was introducing him to a representative of Rothschild's in Paris, a man whom all my friends admired, & who, it was thought, could unravel his financial problems if they could be unravelled at all. They met & had their talk: & for some reason Rolfe's bitterness seemed to increase from that moment.

The reason was not far to seek. With his usual reluctance, Rolfe had agreed to consult the banker – an elderly man named Hardcastle – who, having listened to his problems, had declared that all he needed was a 'financial partner'. There and then he wrote a note to a contact in England, introducing Rolfe and outlining the arrangements necessary. Below his signature he scribbled the words 'late of Rothschild's'. Rolfe was impressed, encouraged and – for once in his life – genuinely grateful. He went straight to the Belle Vue and told the proprietor the news. Barbieri expressed his delight and pointed out that in such circumstances there was no longer any reason why the outstanding account – which now amounted to some 2,000 lire – should not be settled. All that Rolfe needed to do was to sign a bill for 3,500 lire; he could then return to the hotel with the certainty of remaining for another six months. Weak with relief, Rolfe signed.

A few nights later he was awakened with the news that the *signor inglese* was downstairs. There indeed was Hardcastle, obviously extremely drunk, who had arrived shortly before midnight to discuss his new friend's problems with the landlord. Barbieri had reassured him that all was now well, and had showed him the signed bill; Hardcastle had taken one look and torn it to pieces. Such a document, he shouted, should never even have been requested, let alone signed. When Barbieri finally managed to get rid of him – it was by this time around 2.30 a.m. – he had succeeded only in completely destroying Rolfe's credit. The next morning after breakfast Rolfe was once again asked to leave. Naturally, perhaps, he blamed poor Ragg – particularly when, after making inquiries, he discovered that Hardcastle too was something of an impostor, having worked for Rothschild's only briefly, in a very humble capacity, some forty years before.

★

The Raggs however, had been able to do Rolfe one real favour before they left Venice; and it was a favour greater than they knew. Shortly before their departure they had persuaded him to accompany them to an opera at the Fenice, where they had met a certain Dr Ernest van Someren and his heavily pregnant young American wife Ivy. Rolfe did not immediately follow up this first meeting, but some weeks later he called on the van Somerens in the Palazzo Corner-Mocenigo★ and told them that he was homeless and starving. They immediately invited him to live with them, and on 26 June he moved in. He was to remain there for the next nine months. His room was small, little more than a partitioned space on the first-floor landing; but it had a large window and was a considerable improvement on an open boat. In return for a few domestic chores he was given a small allowance – enough for tobacco, for paper, for stamps to fund the long and furious letters which he sent off to the world at large (and the unfortunate Raggs

---

★ This mid sixteenth-century palace, the work of the architect Michele San-micheli, stands on the Campo S. Polo, no. 2128a. Its main front, however, faces the Rio S. Polo, and can best be seen from the nearby bridge.

in particular), and for the vast quantities of vermilion ink that were necessary to fill his perfectly enormous fountain pen. On many an evening, Ivy van Someren recalled, when the doctor was out making his calls, she and Rolfe

would linger over our coffee talking about life and books . . . He was replete with recondite information and delighted to have an attentive listener. Perhaps his chief subject was Roman Catholic ritual and I was interested to learn the origin and meaning of certain ornaments, insignia, robes, utensils, and so forth. He would explain at length the significance of a button on a priest's cassock, the shape of the traditional mitre, the use of a certain dye for the cardinal's red robe and other details of which even most Catholics are ignorant . . .

Once I asked him plaintively: 'Isn't there anybody in the world you really like?' He stared at me as if trying to think of someone. At that time I believe he did like and admire my husband, but he was too cantankerous to admit anything of the kind.

Rolfe looked the scholar he was. His pointed nose, thin lips and pale skin suggested the learned ecclesiastic even in his usual dress – a white turtle-necked sweater (he had two of these which my housemaid washed regularly) and a well cut tweed coat and trousers. He was neat and complacent about his appearance and kept his granite-grey hair cut short, paying the barber from the ten lire a week my husband sent to his room in an envelope. He never acknowledged its receipt . . .

Gratitude certainly was not one of his strong points: he preferred to complain. There was a good deal of unnecessary troublemaking too, and endless self-pity:

. . . I have had no change of clothes since August 1908. I live and sleep in the open landing of a stair in this barrack of a palace. I have walked the city many nights, wet and fine, before I found this refuge – have been six consecutive days without food, half-starved for weeks together on two rolls (at three *centesimi* each) a day, and endured all the extremes of penury short of prison and the *Asili dei*

Senza Tetto.★ All my pawn-tickets of the *Monte di Pietà* have expired, save one. Now and then I contrive to get a job as a private gondogliere [*sic*]: at present I chop and saw and carry logs, work a cream-separator, light fires, and fill boilers. My mother in England works for a living at 75; my sister has become blind; and we have not met for three years.

One would hardly guess from the above that he was by now dining with the van Somerens almost every evening, except when they had guests whom he did not know; at such times he preferred to take a tray to his room. In the heat of the summer his hosts left for the mountains, leaving him with their servants. When they returned he protested volubly about the food they had provided – Dr van Someren was a nutritionist and had strong views on diet – and accused the cook of having given him 'short commons'. ('Incidentally,' wrote Ivy later, 'I may state that he ate through my winter's supply of marmalade!') Apart from that he gave no trouble, spending most of the day writing.

The book which was now rapidly taking shape was to be, after *Hadrian the Seventh*, his best-known work. *The Desire and Pursuit of the Whole* is even more autobiographical than *Hadrian*, since most of it consists of an only very lightly disguised account of Rolfe's life in Venice. It is consequently a *roman à clef*: even when he changes the names of his characters he is careful to leave fairly obvious clues as to their identity – thus Dawkins becomes Macpawkins, Barbieri (barber) becomes Parrucchiero (wig-maker), Hardcastle becomes Sappytower, the Scotsman Horatio Brown becomes 'merry magenta Mactavish' of the 'Palazzo degli Incurabili'. It is less clear why the Raggs should be renamed the Wardens, or Lady Layard Lady Pash; but every Englishman living in Venice at the time would have recognized them instantly. To say that the portraits of these – and several others – were unflattering would be an understatement; in almost every case Rolfe's pen had been dipped in unadulterated vitriol. Naturally he spoke of his work from time to time to Mrs

★ Asylums for the Homeless.

van Someren, to whom – most improbably – he had taken a liking; equally naturally she expressed the hope that she might be allowed to read the unfinished manuscript; and at last he agreed, provided only that she promised not to show it to her husband.

The decision proved his undoing. Mrs van Someren was appalled to see all her friends – and by extension herself – mercilessly and undeservedly torn to pieces, and felt that in the circumstances she was justified in breaking her promise. She showed the manuscript to the doctor, whose reaction was predictably the same as hers had been, and together they confronted Rolfe with an ultimatum: either he abandoned the novel or he left their house. The following morning – it was Saturday 5 March 1910 – he packed his few belongings and took them, together with his precious manuscript, to the Bucintoro rowing club. He wrote to a friend:

> Row with pious doctor, and left house on Saturday. Ate last on Friday evening. Walking all night on Lido beach beyond Excelsior. Often questioned by Police who are on watch to see that no one evaporates salt from the sea. Say that one is writer studying the dawns. So far satisfactory. But the cold is piercing and two nights have made me stiff as a post . . . Something must be done. But spirits and determination undimmed.

Meanwhile, he made no secret of what he thought of the van Somerens. 'Within a few hours of his departure,' wrote Ivy,

> he began the long bombardment by post of my husband, sometimes in Italian on postcards, sometimes in English; abuse, but not vulgar abuse, no, learned sermons on the hypocrisy of professed Christians, on the venom of human snakes, the imitators of ancient criminals – all oblique references to the Doctor's or our friends' deeds. All these communications were written with scarlet ink in his beautiful handwriting, copied, he told me, from the poet Petrarch's script.

How he succeeded in persuading the long-suffering Barbieri to receive him back in the Belle Vue we shall never know. It may be that members of the British colony – still unaware of his treatment of them in his novel – organized a subscription on his behalf; though even in such an event it would have been a hard task to persuade him to accept it. More probably the poor publican, seeing the lamentable condition of his former client, simply felt that he had little choice. By this time he had acquired a few additional rooms adjoining the neighbouring Clock Tower, and in one of them, 'an empty attic', he allowed Rolfe to sleep.

It was very nearly too late. Those bitter, starving nights on the Lido had seriously affected his health. Pneumonia set in, and on 21 April the British Consul in Venice telegraphed the Foreign Office: *Fr Rolfe dangerously ill penniless Hotel Belle Vue here.* A few days later he was rushed to Lady Layard's hospital, where he received the last rites of the Church. Somehow – thanks as much, probably, to his own grim determination as to anything else – he survived to receive a visit from Queen Alexandra, who was staying with the Layards and chanced to be touring the hospital; and on 11 May he was back by the Clock Tower. 'I'm just pinned down to my room,' he wrote on 11 July 1910,

> a back room on the first floor of that narrow alley which leads from Piazza to Calle Larga [di S. Marco], so close to the ground that I can touch the hats of the whores and drunks who roar there all night long, where never a ray of the sun has ever come, so dark that I can't see to write there on these brilliant days without the light on, and a playground of *rats*, of which I have just trapped and drowned in the slop-pail the *thirty-sixth since July 1st!!!*

Fortunately perhaps for the British colony, *The Desire and Pursuit of the Whole* was not published until 1934, by which time most of those whom it crucified were safely in their graves. But the novel, despite the hatred and bitterness that inform almost every page, does not bear its title and subtitle for nothing. The title is a reference to a sentence in the *Symposium* of Plato: 'The desire and pursuit of the whole is called love'; the subtitle is, quite simply, *A Romance of Modern Venice*. In other words, this is primarily a love story: the love of the hero, Nicholas Crabbe, for Zilda, the seventeen-year-old orphan girl whom he has rescued from the Messina earthquake, who determinedly attaches herself to him, and who on their return to Venice becomes his dedicated servant and gondolier. But the story is not quite as simple as that; because except at the beginning of the book and in the last few pages, Zilda is effectively Zildo, a boy.

> In describing the weird gymnastics in which his mind engaged during these wave-running fateful hours of darkness, he always laid singular and particular stress upon the influence of her phenomenally perfect boyishness . . . She looked like a boy; she could do, and did do, boy's work, and did it well; she had been used to pass as a boy, and to act as a boy; and she preferred it: that way lay her taste and inclination: she was competent in that capacity. There was nothing in her to inspire passion, sexual or otherwise; no one could help noticing and admiring her qualities of springlikeness, of frankness, of symmetry, of cogency: but, in other respects, she was negligible as a boy. A youth knows and asserts his uneasy virility; a girl assiduously insinuates her feminility [*sic*]. Ermenegilda Falier★ came into neither category. She was simply a splendid, strapping boy – excepting for the single fact that she was not a boy, but a girl.

Why, then, is she defeminized? Surely because Rolfe, an active homosexual, would have found a heterosexual love story impossible

★ It says much for the author's snobbery that he should make his heroine – born of humble parents in Venice but brought up by relations in Calabria – a member of the family of Falier, which in its early history provided the Most Serene Republic with no fewer than three Doges. The first, Vitale (1084–96), presided in 1094 over the consecration of St Mark's, where his tomb may still be seen in the narthex; and the second, Ordelafo, remodelled and enriched the great golden altar-screen known as the *Pala d'Oro*, on which he is clearly depicted. The reign of the third, Marin, though the most celebrated, was also the least distinguished. He was beheaded on a charge of treason on 18 April 1355, aged seventy-six – the only Doge in Venetian history to have met such a fate. Byron was to make him the subject of a play, and the Wallace Collection possesses a splendid portrayal, by Delacroix, of the execution.

to sustain. His own passion, as we shall shortly see, was for strapping young gondoliers; and the love for young Zildo – who is just such a one – that slowly develops in the reluctant heart of Nicholas Crabbe is, like everything else in the book, taken from life. This makes it all the more surprising that their love remains unspoken and chaste – until the very last page. Then, when Zildo has saved his master's life, 'he' becomes 'she' and the two fall into each other's arms. In the stress of the moment, the author's normally brilliant style deteriorates badly:

> Lips clung to lips, and eyes looked to eyes, long. Breast pressed breast★ and heart beat unto heart. Halves, which had found each other, were joined and dissolved in each other as one.

In that last sentence the title of the novel is explained. Perhaps, too, the answer is given to the other question still remaining: why, if Zildo has to be a boy, does the author not make him a real boy in the first place? Simply because Plato's conception of the two halves clearly requires them to be male and female, in order to achieve complete sexual union; it follows that the boy must, anatomically, be a girl.

There is little doubt, however, that the author would have preferred otherwise. Venice is a small city, in which rumours spread fast; and by the time he was taken in by the van Somerens his weakness for young gondoliers was an open secret. It is confirmed by a series of eighteen letters, five postcards and a telegram which he wrote between October 1909 and August 1910 to an elderly bachelor in Falmouth named Charles Masson Fox. The two must have met in Venice just before the correspondence began, and quickly discovered their shared interest. As always with Rolfe, they are nearly all begging letters; but they are also essentially those from one homosexual to another, concerned with the behaviour of a small group of adolescent Venetian boys who had probably lost their innocence long before Rolfe and Fox entered their lives. In

---

★ It is not recommended to attempt reading these last three words aloud.

the earlier letters, written from the van Somerens', the author describes his own almost unbearable frustration. In 1890 he had vowed himself to twenty years of chastity:

> I'm sure you can imagine far better than I can tell you the most tantalizing tortures which I suffer . . . To have been offered the very thing that I have been yearning and still burn for, offered unreservedly, and not to be able even to touch it . . .

The vow theoretically came to an end in January 1910, but on 28 November 1909 he seems to have jumped the gun. Now for the first time he describes – and in remorseless detail – his own performances, on one occasion 'thrusting 242 times fiercely and more fiercely'. (Which of the participants, one wonders, was counting?) His letter concludes:

> He says that Peter and Zildo [note the name] love each other and do everything to each other but to no one else, though he and Peter once had a whole summer night together on the lagoon in P's father's gondola. P. also is in much request among women but cannot spit more than twice a night. Whereas Amadeo has done it 8 times and vows that he could do 12 with a hot patron! Comments please.

Alas, Fox's comments will never be known, Rolfe having destroyed all his replies – as, incidentally, he had instructed Fox to do to his own letters. We can only be grateful that these instructions were disobeyed: in doing so Fox enabled a spotlight to be turned on to yet another facet of the strange, tormented soul of Frederick Rolfe.

The Venice Letters, as they are called, were published for the first time as recently as 1987. Before then they had been known only to a very few, often in corrupt versions, and in the years immediately following their first appearance they were spoken of in hushed tones of horror and disgust. A. E. Housman – whose own tastes were well enough known – reported to his publisher that he had been 'more amused with things written in urinals', while Rolfe's first biographer, A. J. A. Symons, went further still:

As I read my hair began to rise . . . [These pages] gave an account, in language that omitted nothing, of the criminal delights that waited for the ignoble sensualist to whom they were addressed . . . What shocked me about these letters was not the confession they made of perverse sexual indulgence . . . but that a man of education, ideas, something near genius, should have enjoyed without remorse the destruction of the innocence of youth; that he should have been willing for a price to traffic in his knowledge of the dark byways of that Italian city; that he could have pursued the paths of lust with such frenzied tenacity: these things shocked me into anger and pity.

But many of us would probably feel more sympathetic to the views of Pamela Hansford Johnson* when she wrote:

I do not think *The Venice Letters* can be written off as easily as some would like – neither for good nor for ill. For there really is something splendid, almost mythological, about their ramping sexuality; it was so extremely wholehearted, as everything about him was. If one must read this kind of thing, Rolfe is incomparably better at it than Henry Miller. And there are a few passages of descriptive splendour as fine as anything in *The Desire and Pursuit of the Whole*, where the physical beauty of Venice is expressed as no one else ever did it, before Rolfe or after him.

It is only fair to add that doubt has been cast on the veracity of these letters. One of Rolfe's two most recent biographers† has argued at some length that the writer was merely dressing up his incessant demands in such a way as to amuse and excite their recipient, and in the hopes that they might stimulate (*inter alia*) his generosity. If so – and the idea anyway seems highly unlikely – they failed. The very last letter – or at least, the last to have survived, written on 21 August 1910 – asks for £5, but there is no evidence that this money was ever sent. Everyone from whom Rolfe tried to extract

* Author of *The Unspeakable Skipton*, a brilliant fictionalized portrait of Rolfe.
† Donald Weeks, *Corvo*.

money, even those who were generous at the start, saw through him sooner or later; and Charles Masson Fox was no exception.

★

But just at the moment that Fox was fading out of the picture, a new victim presented himself. This was the Reverend Justus Stephen Serjeant, formerly of Christ's College, Cambridge, and now Rector of Warboys in Huntingdonshire.★ He arrived in Venice towards the end of August 1910 and as an enthusiastic admirer of *Hadrian the Seventh* immediately sought out Rolfe, who told him the story of his life. Serjeant seems to have been genuinely moved, and tentatively suggested that they might enter a form of partnership. A considerable inheritance was, he believed, on its way to him; with this he proposed to pay Rolfe a regular salary while he worked on the various books he was contemplating, in return for a share of the profits. Rolfe accepted with alacrity; unfortunately the money did not come as quickly as he had hoped, and two more cruel winters were to be endured before the first cheque arrived.

In January 1911, with Venice in the grip of the first of these winters, he once again fell seriously ill; and Barbieri's secretary, knowing of Queen Alexandra's visit to Lady Layard's hospital while he was a patient, took it upon herself to write to Buckingham Palace requesting help for

> Mr Fred. W. Rolfe, who after being unable to satisfy his living expenses since last spring is now wandering homeless on the Lido island in this piercing cold . . . He will not ask anyone for help and my position of hotel secretary does not allow me to give him any assistance, especially because I am employed by his creditor.

★ It is not entirely clear why A. J. A. Symons in *The Quest for Corvo* refers to him as 'The Rev. Stephen Justin'. He called on him at his home and persuaded him to give him free run of his correspondence with Rolfe, so he can hardly have been completely mistaken. But Rolfe himself gives his name as Serjeant in a letter written in August 1913, and it is as Serjeant that he is listed in *Crockford's Clerical Directory* of 1911 – where, incidentally, there is no reference to a Justin. He presumably asked Symons to disguise his name, fearing unpleasant publicity.

The Queen immediately responded with £10, which she sent to the Consul with the request that it 'be laid out for Mr Rolfe's benefit'. Enclosing Rolfe's receipt on 11 February, the Consul explained – somewhat presumptuously, it may be thought – that he had decided not to mention the source of the gift since, as he put it, 'the case is a most difficult and delicate one'.

Whether Rolfe had by this time left his room by the Clock Tower is, despite the secretary's letter, open to doubt. Had he done so, and had he really been 'wandering homeless' on the Lido since the beginning of the year, there is no way in which he could have survived; and Barbieri, although he would certainly not have believed Rolfe's assurances of a coming upturn in his fortunes and must long have accepted the fact that his bill would never be settled, is unlikely to have thrown him out of a room that he had given him in the first place only out of charity. Be that as it may, by the early spring Rolfe had abandoned it and taken once again to his open boat, where he could at least – when the weather permitted – enjoy the sunshine and the lagoon he loved. But his life continued hard. It was almost certainly in October 1911* that he wrote to Serjeant:

> I've been literally fighting for life through a series of storms. Do you realize what that means in a little boat, leaky and so coated with weed and barnacles by a summer's use, that it is almost too heavy to move with the oar, and behaves like an inebriate in winds or weather? . . . And storms get up on this lagoon in ten minutes, leaving no time to make a port. I'm frequently struggling for 50–60 hours on end. Results: I've lost about 300 pages of my new MS. of *Hubert's Arthur*.† Parts were oiled by a lamp blown over them:

---

* The letter bears no precise date, but all the evidence points to this time. Symons suggests that it was written early in September 1913; but by then, as we shall soon see, Rolfe was comparatively affluent.

† A historical romance, in its first version the joint work of Rolfe and his friend Harry Pirie-Gordon – the 'Prospero & Caliban' of the title page – which was completely rewritten by Rolfe, with many changes and a new ending, after the two quarrelled. It tells of how Arthur, Duke of Brittany, instead of being

winds and waves carried away the rest. At every possible minute I am rewriting them: but, horrible to say, grey mists float about my eye-corners just through sheer exhaustion. The last few days I have been anchored near an empty island, Sacca Fisola, not too far away from civilization to be out of reach of fresh water, but lonely enough for dying alone in the boat if need be. Well, to shew you how worn out I am, I frankly say that I have funked it . . . If I stay out on the lagoon, the boat will sink, I shall swim perhaps for a few hours, and then I shall be eaten alive by crabs. At low water every mudbank swarms with them. If I stay anchored near an island, I must keep continually awake: for, the moment I cease moving, I am invaded by swarms of swimming rats, who in the winter are so voracious that they attack even a man who is motionless. I have tried it. And been bitten. Oh my dear man you can't think how artful fearless ferocious they are. I rigged up two bits of chain, lying loose on my prow and poop with a string by which I could shake them when attacked. For two nights the dodge acted. The swarms came up (up the anchor rope) and nuzzled me: I shook the chains: the beasts plopped overboard. Then they got used to the noise and sneered. Then they bit the strings. Then they bit my toes and woke me shrieking and shaking with fear.

Now this is what I have done. I am perfectly prepared to persevere to the end. So I have taken the boat to a 'squero' to be repaired. This will take a fortnight. When she is seaworthy again I'll go out and face my fate in her. Meanwhile I'm running a tick at the Cavaletto, simply that I may eat and sleep to write hard at restoring the 300 odd pages of *Hubert's Arthur*. When that is done, the boat will be ready. I will assign that MS. to you and send it.

My dear man, I am so awfully lonely. And tired. Is there no chance of setting me right?

---

murdered by King John, escapes to Jerusalem, which he recovers from the Saracens. Finally he is acclaimed King of England, but is killed while expelling the French claimant from the country. Dedicated, jointly and rather surprisingly, to Rudyard Kipling and Gabriele d'Annunzio, this virtually unreadable work was published only in 1935.

How true is all this? Was he (as has been suggested) deliberately subjecting himself to an endurance test? And even if he were, could all these tribulations have been really as appalling as he makes out? It must never be forgotten that he was a novelist, with a novelist's imagination. He was also – not to put too fine a point on it – a confidence trickster of long experience. Certainly he knew the meaning of poverty – dire poverty; but we may be sure that the stories of his sufferings lost nothing in the telling.

It was another five months before he was to receive his first cheque from Serjeant; but when this finally arrived at the beginning of March 1912 – to be followed by others, rising by the end of the year to a total of £1,000 – his whole life changed. He settled his debts; he got himself a decent room in the Hotel Cavaletto;* he dyed what remained of his hair ginger; he even managed to buy himself a boat, whose sails he painted himself with a naked boy, bearing a shield emblazoned with the cross of St George, and his motto – 'Stand not in my Way, nor Follow me too Far' in both Latin and Greek; and he travelled to Florence for six weeks to gather material for a projected book about Botticelli. He even had his portrait painted by Gaele Covelli, a painter who – although his name is now largely forgotten outside Italy – in his day enjoyed considerable success.

But there was no creative writing. A few false starts perhaps – *The Desire and Pursuit of the Whole* was copied out yet again in his ever more affected calligraphy – but of the new books that he had promised Serjeant he gave no sign. Meanwhile the begging letters began again: back at Warboys, the poor rector was inundated with ever more urgent requests – some of them read more like demands – for £50 here, £50 there, until at the end of 1912 his patience was exhausted and he finally wrote to say that he would send no more. This time, however, Rolfe could afford to accept the refusal philosophically. His credit in Venice was good at last; and he had recently persuaded an English publisher, Rider & Son, to accept a

---

* This fourteenth-century building still stands on the Bacino Orseolo, immediately behind the north-west corner of the Piazza.

novel, *The Weird of the Wanderer*, on which – since it had been written two years before he came to Venice – Serjeant had no claim. Early in 1913 he left the Cavaletto, whose proprietor had found him a small apartment in Palazzo Marcello on the Grand Canal – it stands next to Wagner's Vendramin-Calergi – in which he was to live for the remaining months of his life, in a room dramatically hung with copious lengths of scarlet cloth from Rome.★

Every evening he would return to the Cavaletto for dinner; and it was there that he met a fellow Englishman who confessed to him that he was almost destitute. Rolfe immediately invited him to Palazzo Marcello, and settled him into the room adjoining his own. He and his guest – whose name was Thomas Pennefather Wade-Browne – soon became inseparable. Inevitably their relationship was the subject of much whispered speculation among the British colony – though Wade-Browne, at forty-three, was not likely to have had much appeal for his new friend. They spent many hours of each day cruising in the lagoon, and with the coming of summer they were venturing far out into the Adriatic for weeks at a time, returning only for a day or two every month to take on fresh provisions.

Rolfe's last summer was probably the happiest of his life; but it could not last for ever. At the end of September, with the weather growing colder and the winter storms beginning to threaten, the two settled back in Palazzo Marcello. On the evening of Saturday 25 October they dined together as usual at the Cavaletto, returning on foot soon after nine o'clock and bidding each other goodnight as usual. The following morning Wade-Browne knocked at his friend's door, but there was no reply. An hour or two later he knocked again; still there was silence. Finally, at around three o'clock in the afternoon, he went into the room. Rolfe, still fully dressed, was lying dead upon his bed. 'It would seem,' the British Consul subsequently wrote to Herbert Rolfe, his brother,

★ In this palace – it is at S. Marcuola, Cannaregio no. 2137 – the most aristocratic of Venice's composers, Benedetto Marcello, had been born on 24 July 1686. Rolfe liked to claim that it was also the place of his death, but in fact Marcello died in Brescia in 1739, on his fifty-third birthday.

that he had died in the act of undoing his boots and fallen on the bed, knocking down the candle which, fortunately, went out. The English doctor was called in [Dr van Someren, presumably] but could do nothing beyond helping Mr Wade-Browne to notify the authorities and summon your brother's usual medical attendant . . . The following morning the hospital doctor certified that the cause of death was in all probability heart failure. This diagnosis was subsequently confirmed.

That same Consul, Mr Campbell – later Sir Gerald Campbell, GCMG – had himself been in Venice only a few months. He writes in his memoirs:

Soon after I had installed myself in a temporary office overlooking the Piazza San Marco I was visited by an interesting, but not especially polite, Englishman called Rolfe, who did not disguise the fact that he had not liked my predecessor, but was inclined to think better of me and would call to see me again if I measured up to his first impression. I naturally made enquiries about him and discovered that he was an eccentric author also known as Baron Corvo. His latest escapade had been to dress up as a Cardinal and, in this rig and a gondola, to have waited outside the English Church where the funeral service for the highly respected Lady Layard was being held. When her coffin was brought out and placed on a funeral gondola, he followed it up the Grand Canal, hurling insulting epithets to the disgust of the mourners.

He little knew, perhaps he did not care, that the next time I should see him, after his one and only visit to me, would be in the morgue . . .

This story, reported by the Consul only at second hand, is almost certainly unfounded. There is no mention of it in the Venetian newspapers of the time, nor any by Mrs van Someren or Mrs Ragg, who was back in Venice some three months later, at the beginning of 1913. Such behaviour would have been the act of a madman, and Rolfe was by no means mad; moreover it would have been most uncharacteristic of a man who was always acutely conscious of his dignity. Finally, although he pilloried 'Lady Pash' in his novel – as he did almost everyone else – he bore her, so far as we know, no particular grudge.

True or not, the fact that the story was circulated at all, that it was told to the British Consul in good faith and that he should have believed it tells us all we need to know about the reputation that Frederick Rolfe left behind him. Campbell's other testimony, coming to us as it does at first hand, is a good deal harder to discredit:

> Then followed a search in his room for a will or the address of some relative, and I have been described in a book written around his life and works★ as a shocked Vice-Consul, when I discovered, as I did, not his will but a large collection of incriminating letters and photographs which more than confirmed the suspicions of scandal-mongers as to his unnatural proclivities, I tried to push some of these and other *objets d'art* out of the window into the Grand Canal, but I was being closely watched by two police officers. In the end I got safely rid of most of it, but what a haul it would have been for a blackmailer!

It wouldn't, of course: the victim would have been quite unable to satisfy his demands, and it is open to doubt whether he would anyway have minded all that much. But the question is academic. Frederick William Rolfe was dead at last; and the British colony in Venice breathed again.

★ A. J. A. Symons, *The Quest for Corvo*. He actually refers to Campbell as 'a horrified Consul'.

Epilogue

With Frederick Rolfe, Baron Corvo, our story comes to an end. It might have continued for another hundred years – with Diaghilev and Stravinsky for a start, and then with the Cole Porters, with Peggy Guggenheim and Ezra Pound, with Ernest Hemingway and Carlos de Beistegui and (God help us) Elsa Maxwell – but Venice in the twentieth century was very different from Venice in the nineteenth. After the First World War it became an international playground for the rich; and after the Second, with the growth of civil aviation and the coming of mass tourism, for just about everyone else as well. As I said in the Introduction, by including the early twentieth-century Baron Corvo I have already pushed my luck; and I have no intention of pushing it any further. This book is quite long enough as it is.

And yet, as I lay down my pen after what will almost certainly be my last Venetian volume, one small doubt still lingers in my mind: have I done the place justice? In trying as I have to see Venice through foreign eyes, have I not concentrated too much on those eyes themselves, rather than on the object of their scrutiny? At one moment I even considered adding a chapter about the physical changes – some of them distinct improvements, others disastrous – that took place under Austrian rule and after the Risorgimento: among them the merciless blasting of a brand-new thoroughfare from Campo dei SS. Apostoli and Campo S. Fosca to produce the Strada Nova – a piece of vandalism of which Baron Haussmann himself would have been proud; the creation of the curiously charmless Calle Larga XXII Marzo, from the Piazza half-way to Campo S. Maria del Giglio; the filling-in of ten canals, thus transforming them into streets; the paving of forty-nine *calli*; the building of no fewer than fifty-five bridges, thirty-three of stone and twenty-two of wood; the two iron bridges over the Grand Canal, one at the Accademia and the other at the Scalzi (both replaced in my lifetime); and most remarkable of all, perhaps, the construction of a vast and astonishing bathing establishment – the *Bagni Galleggianti* of Dr Rima – which was anchored every year from May to September just off the Dogana.

But such a chapter would not have been in tune with the rest of the book; nor, strictly speaking, would it have been necessary. No city in the world has changed less over the past 200 years; and although we may deplore the disappearance of all those lovely sailing ships and barges, so beloved of John Singer Sargent and Henry James – or even, with Ruskin, the causeway that connects it to *terra firma* – the Venice of 150 years ago was already, in essence, the Venice of our own time. The old photographs say it all. I have included as many of these as possible, for no city was more beautifully and sensitively recorded in the early days of photography. They tell us much – and, incidentally, they also indicate one of the major differences between the Venice of today and that of yesterday: the astonishing stillness of the Grand Canal. Nowadays, with the *vaporetti*, the *motoscafi* and the heavy barges, the water is never at rest. Even if allowance is made for the longer time exposures which may have ironed out the minor ripples, that former glassy smoothness of the Canal leads us to an inescapable conclusion: Venice's major thoroughfare has lost its former peace – a peace, alas, which it will never regain.

For the fact must be faced: the motorboats, together with all the other innovations of the last two centuries, are here to stay. Venice in the twenty-first century cannot put its trust in oars alone – as anyone who has ever tried to deliver a television set or a deep freeze by gondola will be all too well aware. The city is after all a good deal more comfortable, both to its inhabitants and to its visitors alike, than it was in the days of Ruskin and Rawdon Brown; and progress is a tide with which we have no course but to swim. Modern times may have brought a degree of pollution unknown in the days when my father – for reasons that doubtless seemed good at the time – dived into the Grand Canal in full evening dress (white tie), struck out for the opposite shore and lived to tell the tale; and the almost constant flooding – by tourists as well as tides – is an increasing nightmare, as is the steady dwindling of the local population. These problems are hideous indeed; we can at least take comfort, however, in the thought that Venice is an incomparably happier city today than she was 150 years ago; that if she is to remain as a living, breathing, viable community rather than as a waterlogged museum she must be allowed to grow organically like her fellows; and that her future – uncertain as it still may be – is, for the most part, in safe and caring hands.

Appendix
'A Toccata of Galuppi's'

O Galuppi, Baldassaro, this is very sad to find!
I can hardly misconceive you, it would prove me deaf and blind;
But although I take your meaning, 'tis with such a heavy mind!

Here you come with your old music, and here's all the good it brings.
What, they lived once thus at Venice, where the merchants were the kings,
Where St Mark's is, where the Doges used to wed the sea with rings?

Ay, because the sea's a street there, and it's bridged by what you call
Shylock's bridge, with houses on it, where they kept the carnival:
I was never out of England – it's as if I saw it all.

Did young people take their pleasure, when the sea was warm in May?
Balls and masks begun at midnight, burning ever till midday,
When they made up fresh adventures for the morrow, did you say?

Was a lady such a lady, cheeks so round and lips so red –
On her neck the small face buoyant, like a bell-flower on its bed,
O'er the breast's superb abundance, where a man might base his head?

Well, and it was graceful of them, they'd break talk off, and afford –
She, to bite her mask's black velvet – he, to finger on his sword,
While you sat and played toccatas, stately at the clavichord.

What? Those lesser thirds so plaintive, sixths diminished, sigh on sigh,
Told them something? Those suspensions, those solutions, must we die?
Those commiserating sevenths – 'Life might last, we can but try!'

'Were you happy?' – 'Yes.' – 'And are you still as happy?' 'Yes. And you?'
Then, more kisses! – Did I stop them, when a million seemed so few?
Hark, the dominant's persistence, till it must be answered to!

So, an octave struck the answer. Oh, they praised you, I dare say!
'Brave Galuppi! That was music! Good alike at grave and gay!
I can always leave off talking when I hear a master play!'

Then they left you for their pleasure: till in due time, one by one,
Some with lives that came to nothing, some with deeds as well undone,
Death stepped tacitly and took them, where they never see the sun.

But when I sit down to reason, think to take my stand nor swerve,
While I triumph o'er a secret wrung from Nature's close reserve,
In you come with your cold music, till I creep through every nerve.

Yes, you, like a ghostly cricket, creaking where a house was burned:
'Dust and ashes, dead and done with, Venice spent what Venice earned.
The soul, doubtless, is immortal – where a soul can be discerned.

'Yours for instance: you know physics, something of geology,
Mathematics are your pastime, souls shall rise in their degree;
Butterflies may dread extinction, – you'll not die, it cannot be!

'As for Venice and her people, merely born to bloom and drop,
Here on earth they bore their fruitage, mirth and folly were the crop:
What of soul was left, I wonder, when the kissing had to stop?

'Dust and ashes!' So you creak it, and I want the heart to scold.
Dear dead women, with such hair too, what's become of all the gold
Used to hang and brush their bosoms? I feel chilly and grown old.

                                        Robert Browning

Bibliography

Bacher, Otto H. *With Whistler in Venice*. New York, 1908.

Benkovitz, Miriam J. *Frederick Rolfe: Baron Corvo. A Biography*. London, 1977.

Berenson, B., and Gardner, Mrs I. S. *The Letters of Bernard Berenson and Isabella Stewart Gardner, 1887–1924*, ed. R. Hadley. Boston, 1987.

Brackman, A. C. *The Luck of Nineveh*. London, 1980.

Bradley, J., and Ousby, I. (eds.). *The Correspondence of John Ruskin and Charles Eliot Norton*. Cambridge, 1987.

Bronson, Katharine de Kay. 'Browning in Asolo', *Century Magazine*, Vol. LIX, April 1900.

—'Browning in Venice', *Cornhill Magazine*, Vol. XII (N.S. LXVIII), February 1902 (with preparatory note by Henry James).

Brown, Horatio. *Life on the Lagoons*. London, 1884.

—*Venetian Studies*. London, 1887.

—*Venice: an Historical Sketch*. London, 1893 (later abridged as *The Venetian Republic*, London 1902).

—*John Addington Symonds: a Biography*. 2 vols. London, 1895.

Browning, Robert. *More than Friends*, letters from Robert Browning to Katharine de Kay Bronson, ed. M. Meredith. Waco, Texas, 1985.

Byron, Lord. *Letters and Journals*, ed. Leslie A. Marchand. London, 1973–82 (especially vols. 5–7).

—*The Complete Miscellaneous Prose*, ed. A. Nicholson. Oxford, 1991.

Calendar of State Papers and Manuscripts Relating to English Affairs Existing in the Archives and Collections of Venice and Other Libraries of North Italy. Vols. 1–6 ed. Rawdon Brown; vol. 7 ed. Rawdon Brown and the Rt. Hon. G. Cavendish-Bentinck; vols. 8–12 ed. H. F. Brown; vols. 13–18 ed. A. B. Hinds. London, 1864–1912.

Campbell, Sir Gerald. *Of True Experience*. London, 1949.

Charteris, Evan. *John Sargent*. London, 1927.

Clegg, Jean. *Ruskin and Venice*. London, 1981.

Corvo, Baron. *See* Rolfe, F. W.

Cosgrove, Denis. *The Iconography of Landscape: Essays on the Symbolic Representation, Design and Use of Past Environments*. Cambridge, 1988.

Daru, P. *Histoire de la République de Venise*. 9 vols. Paris, 1821.

Dictionary of National Biography.

Edel, Leon. *The Life of Henry James*. 3 vols. London, 1953–63.

Eisner, Benita. *Byron: Child of Passion, Fool of Fame*. London, 1999.

Enciclopaedia Italiana

Errera, A., and Finzi, C. *La Vita e tempi di Daniele Manin*. Venice, 1872.

Fairbrother, Trevor. *John Singer Sargent*. New York and Washington, 1994.

—*John Singer Sargent: the Sensualist*. New Haven and London, 2000.

Flagg, Edmund. *Venice, City of the Sea*. 2 vols. London, 1853.

Fugagnollo, Ugo. *I dieci giorni di Napoleone I a Venezia*. Venice, 1982.

Garrett, Martin. *A Browning Chronology*. London, 2000.

Ginsborg, Paul. *Daniele Manin and the Venetian Revolution of 1848–49*. Cambridge, 1979.

Giustinian, Sebastiano. *Four Years at the Court of Henry VIII: a Selection of Dispatches Written by the Venetian Ambassador, S.G., and Addressed to the Signory of Venice, January 12th 1515 to July 26th 1519*, tr. Rawdon Brown. 2 vols. London, 1854.

Gordon, Lyndall. *A Private Life of Henry James: Two Women and His Art*. London, 1998.

Gregory, Augusta, Lady. *Lady Gregory, Fifty Years After*, ed. Ann Saddlemyer and Colin Smythe. Gerrards Cross, 1987.

Grosskurth, Phyllis. *John Addington Symonds: a Biography*. London, 1964.

Halliday, F. E. *Robert Browning: His Life and Work*. London, 1975.

Hewison, Robert. *Ruskin's Venice*. London, 2000.

Hyde, Catherine, Marchesa di Broglio Solari. *Venice under the Yoke of France and of Austria, by a Lady of Rank*. London, 1824.

James, Henry. *Italian Hours*. London, 1909.

—*Letters*, ed. Leon Edel. 4 vols. London, 1974–84.

—*Complete Notebooks*, ed. Leon Edel and Lyall H. Powers. Oxford, 1987.

—(and others) *Letters from Palazzo Barbaro*, ed. Rosella Mamoli Zorzi. London, 1998.

Kaplan, F. (ed.). *Travelling in Italy with Henry James*. London, 1994.

Kelly, P. and Hudson, R. (eds.). *The Brownings' Correspondence*. Winfield, Kansas (in course of publication).

Kubie, Nora. *Road to Nineveh: the Adventures and Excavations of Sir Austen Henry Layard*. London, 1965.

La Forge, A. *Histoire de la République de Venise sous Manin*. Brussels, 1849.

Laver, James. *Whistler*. London, 1930.

Layard, Sir Henry. *Autobiography and Letters from His Childhood until His Appointment as H.M. Ambassador at Madrid*, ed. The Hon. W. N. Bruce. 2 vols. London, 1903.

Lorenzetti, G. *Venice and Its Lagoon*, tr. John Guthrie. Trieste, 1994.

Lutyens, Mary (ed.). *Effie in Venice: Unpublished Letters of Mrs John Ruskin Written from Venice between 1849 and 1852*. London, 1965.

McClellan, George. *Venice and Bonaparte*. Princeton, New Jersey, 1931.

Marchand, Leslie A. *Byron: a Portrait*. London, 1971.

Massie, Allan. *Byron's Travels*. London, 1988.

Miller, Betty. *Robert Browning: a Portrait*. London, 1952.

Moore, Thomas. *The Journal of Thomas Moore*. Vol. I ed. W. S. Dowden, Newark, Delaware, 1983.

Morand, Paul. *Venices*, tr. Euan Cameron. London, 2002. Translation of *Venises* (Paris, 1971).

Mount, Charles Merrill. *John Singer Sargent*. London, 1957.

Neumann, Angelo. *Personal Recollections of Wagner*, tr. Edith Livermore. London, 1909.

The New Cambridge Modern History, Vol. IX. Cambridge, 1965.

The New Grove Dictionary of Music and Musicians. 2nd edn. London, 2001.

Newman, Ernest. *The Life of Richard Wagner*. 4 vols. London, 1933–47.

Nievo, Ippolito. *Confessioni di un italiano*. New and rev. edn. Milan, 1931.

Norwich, John Julius. *Venice: the Greatness and the Fall*. (Vol. II of *A History of Venice*.) London, 1981.

Olson, Stanley. *John Singer Sargent: His Portrait*. London, 1986.

Origo, Iris. *The Last Attachment*. London, 1949.

Ormond, Richard. *John Singer Sargent: Paintings, Drawings, Watercolours*. London, 1970.

Pemble, John. *Venice Rediscovered*. Oxford, 1995.

Perocco, G. and Salvadori, A. *Civiltà di Venezia*. Vol. III. Venice, 1979.

Perosa, Sergio (ed.). *Henry James e Venezia*. Florence, 1987.

Perry, Marilyn. '*Si riconforta d'agi un tempo ignoti*: Nineteenth-century Transformations in Venice'. Extract from the *Bollettino del Centro Internazionale di Studi di Architettura Andrea Palladio*. Vicenza, 1976.

Radnor, Helen, Countess-Dowager of. *From a Great-grandmother's Armchair*. London, 1927.

Reumont, A. *Rawdon Brown. Archivio storico italiano*. Series IV, Vol. 16. Florence, 1885.

Rolfe, F. W. ('Baron Corvo'). *The Desire and Pursuit of the Whole: A Romance of Modern Venice*. London, 1934.

—*The Venice Letters*. London, 1987.

Romanin, S. *Storia Documentata di Venezia*. 2nd edn, 10 vols. Venice, 1912–21.

Ruskin, J. *St Mark's Rest*. Orpington, 1894.

—*The Stones of Venice*. 2 vols. Orpington, 1898.

Russell, J. M. *From Nineveh to New York: the Strange Story of the Assyrian Reliefs in the Metropolitan Museum and the Hidden Masterpiece at Canford School*. New Haven and London, 1997.

—*The Final Sack of Nineveh*. New Haven and London, 1998.

Santalena, A. *Napoleone I a Venezia*. Venice, 1907.

Shand-Tucci, D. *The Art of Scandal: the Life and Times of Isabella Stewart Gardner*. New York, 1997.

Shelley, Frances, Lady. *The Diary of Frances, Lady Shelley*, ed. R. Edgcumbe. 2 vols. London, 1912–13.

van Someren, Ivy. 'Baron Corvo's Quarrels', *Life and Letters*, and the *London Mercury*. Vol. 52, 1947.

Sparrow, W. Shaw. *Memories of Life and Art through Sixty Years*. London, 1925.

Stark, Freya. *Traveller's Prelude*. London, 1950.

Symonds, J. A. *The Letters of John Addington Symonds*, ed. H. M. Schueller and R. L. Peters. 3 vols. Detroit, 1967–9.

—*The Memoirs of John Addington Symonds*, ed. and intr. Phyllis Grosskurth. London, 1984.

Symons, A. J. A. *The Quest for Corvo*. London, 1952.

Tanner, Tony. *Venice Desired*. Oxford, 1992.

Trevelyan, G. M. *Manin and the Venetian Revolution of 1848*. London, 1923.

Wagner, Richard. *My Life*. Anonymous tr. London, 1911.

—*Selected Letters of Richard Wagner*, tr. and ed. Stewart Spencer and Barry Millington. London, 1987.

Waterfield, Gordon. *Layard of Nineveh*. London, 1963.

Waterfield, Lina. *Castle in Italy*. London, 1961.

Weeks, Donald. *Corvo*. London, 1971.

Whitehouse, H. Remsen. *The Life of Lamartine*. 2 vols. London, 1918.

Zorzi, Alvise. *Venezia Scomparsa*. Milan, 1984.

—*Venezia Austriaca*. Rome, 1985.

Zorzi, Rosella Mamoli. 'Henry James in un diario "veneziano"', in Perosa, S., *Henry James e Venezia* (above).

Index

Index

281

Shelley, Mary (*née* Godwin), 41, 50, 69–70

Shelley, Percy Bysshe: first meets Byron, 41; in Milan, 50; accompanies Claire Clairmont to Venice, 52; moves to Este, 53; and Byron's women, 54; drowned, 69–70; in Pisa, 69; grave, 176

Sicily: revolution in (1848), 131; earthquake (1908), 239–40

Sickert, Walter, 219–20

Silsbee, Captain, 168

Silvestrini, Fanny, 56, 68

Smith, Elder (publishers), 188

Smith, George, 190

Smith, Joseph, 3–4, 105

Someren, Dr Ernest von, 242, 244–5, 248–9, 256

Someren, Ivy von, 242–5, 248–9, 256

Soranzo-Cappello, Palazzo, 168

Spiera, Domenico, 104

Spohr, Ludwig, 146

Sposalizio, lo (Marriage with the Sea ceremony), 9

Stephanie, Princess of Austria, 210

Story, William Wetmore, 180

Strachey, Lytton, 123

Stravinsky, Igor, 258

Studio, The (periodical), 228

Symonds, Catherine (*née* North), 117, 122

Symonds, John Addington: influence on Horatio Brown, 114–15, 117–18; at Davos, 115, 121; homosexuality, 117–22; in Venice, 117–18; biographies of, 122–4; *Memoirs*, 119, 122, 124

Symonds, Madge, 124

Symons, A. J. A., 249, 251n, 252n

Talleyrand, Charles de, 17

Tanner, Tony, 84n

Temple, Catherine (Henry James's aunt Kate), 160

Temple, Minny (Henry James's niece), 177

Tennyson, Alfred, first Baron: *The Idylls of the King*, 201

Tennyson, Hallam, 117, 190

Tennyson, Lionel, 117

Tessarin (piano teacher), 145, 150

Thorwaldsen, Bertel, 47

Tiepolo, Bajamonte, 129n

Tiepolo, Domenico, 185, 217n

Tiepolo, Giambattista, 23, 217

Tintoretto, 78, 98

Tomasini, Count, 146

Tommaseo, Niccolò, 130–33, 136, 139

Torcello, 161

Torresella, Ca', 116, 121, 125, 127, 240

Trelawny, Edward John, 176

Trieste, 74, 128, 132

Trollope, Anthony, 163

Tron, Andrea (*il Paron*), 6

Tulard, Jean, 39

Turner, Joseph Mallord William, 76, 84

Twain, Mark, 179

Vendramin-Calergi, Palazzo, 153–4, 157

Veneziano, Lorenzo, 31

Venice: Republic ends (1797), 1–2, 7–10, 76, 143; as pleasure capital, 2–3, 258; decline, 4–7; constitution and government, 5–6, 10–11, 15–16; art works and goods transferred to Paris, 11–12, 14–15; under Austrian occupation and rule, 11, 13–16, 73–5, 130; typhoid epidemic (1802), 17; Curia meets in, 18; French reoccupy and repress (1806), 20–22; Napoleon's alterations to, 27–30, 33, 37;